AUTODESK® INVENTOR® 2012
AND **INVENTOR LT**™ **2012**

ESSENTIALS

AUTODESK OFFICIAL TRAINING GUIDE

Thom Tremblay

WILEY

Wiley Publishing, Inc.

Senior Acquisitions Editor: Willem Knibbe
Development Editor: Jim Compton
Technical Editor: Dan Hunsucker
Production Editor: Liz Britten
Copy Editor: Kim Wimpsett
Editorial Manager: Pete Gaughan
Production Manager: Tim Tate
Vice President and Executive Group Publisher: Richard Swadley
Vice President and Publisher: Neil Edde
Book Designer: Happenstance Type-O-Rama
Compositor: Chris Gillespie, Happenstance Type-O-Rama
Proofreader: WordOne, New York
Indexer: Ted Laux
Project Coordinator, Cover: Katie Crocker
Cover Designer: Ryan Sneed
Cover Image: Thom Tremblay

For general information on our other products and services or to obtain technical support, please contact our Customer Care Department within the U.S. at (877) 762-2974, outside the U.S. at (317) 572-3993 or fax (317) 572-4002.

Wiley also publishes its books in a variety of electronic formats. Some content that appears in print may not be available in electronic books.

Library of Congress Cataloging-in-Publication Data is available from the publisher.

10 9 8 7 6 5 4 3 2 1

Dear Reader,

Thank you for choosing *Autodesk Inventor 2012 and Inventor LT 2012 Essentials*. This book is part of a family of premium-quality Sybex books, all of which are written by outstanding authors who combine practical experience with a gift for teaching.

Sybex was founded in 1976. More than 30 years later, we're still committed to producing consistently exceptional books. With each of our titles, we're working hard to set a new standard for the industry. From the paper we print on, to the authors we work with, our goal is to bring you the best books available.

I hope you see all that reflected in these pages. I'd be very interested to hear your comments and get your feedback on how we're doing. Feel free to let me know what you think about this or any other Sybex book by sending me an email at nedde@wiley.com. If you think you've found a technical error in this book, please visit http://sybex.custhelp.com. Customer feedback is critical to our efforts at Sybex.

Best regards,

NEIL EDDE
Vice President and Publisher
Sybex, an Imprint of Wiley

To you, the men and women inventing the machines. And to the people like my dad, Tom Tremblay, and Mack Kendall, who use those machines to make our lives better. May the wheels keep turning for us all.

ACKNOWLEDGMENTS

I want to thank the tremendous team at Sybex for their patience and professionalism, specifically, Willem Knibbe, Pete Gaughan, Jim Compton, Liz Britten, Kim Wimpsett, and everyone else who worked hard behind the scenes who I didn't get a chance to communicate with directly. Special thanks once again to Dan Hunsucker for being the technical editor. If you're in the Kansas City area and want to learn Inventor from a real expert, you'll be in great hands with Dan. Thanks to Joe Astroth and Nancy Clark-Brown of Autodesk for their support. Of course, many thanks to my family for putting up with my absence on the weekends and nights.

—Thom Tremblay

ABOUT THE AUTHOR

Thom Tremblay is a subject-matter expert on the Autodesk Strategic Universities team and has worked with hundreds of companies to help them understand how Inventor can help them with their designs. He is an Inventor Certified Professional and has been working with Inventor for more than 10 years and with other Autodesk products for more than 25 years. He has used Autodesk software to design everything from cabinets and castings to ships and video monitors. He has close ties to the Inventor community; is a frequent speaker at colleges, universities, and training centers; and presents at Autodesk University annually.

CONTENTS AT A GLANCE

CONTENTS

CHAPTER 2   Creating 2D Drawings from 3D Data   33

CHAPTER 3   Learning the Essentials of Part Modeling   63

CHAPTER 6   **Creating Advanced Drawings and Detailing**   **127**

CHAPTER 14   Working with Non-Inventor Data   297

CHAPTER 15   Automating the Design Process and Table-Driven Design 317

INTRODUCTION

Welcome to Autodesk Inventor and Inventor LT Essentials. This book is intended to be a direct, hands-on guide to learning Inventor by using Inventor. The book includes lessons for absolute beginners, but experienced users can also find exercises to show them how tools they're not familiar with work.

Nearly all of the 200 exercises can be started from an existing file, so you need to do only those exercises that will help you most.

Who Should Read This Book

Autodesk Inventor and Inventor LT Essentials is designed to meet the needs of the following groups of users:

- ▶ Professionals who use 2D or 3D design systems and want to learn Autodesk Inventor at their own pace

- ▶ Professionals attending instructor-led Inventor training at an Autodesk Authorized Training Center

- ▶ Engineering and design students who need to learn Inventor to support their education and career

What You Will Learn

Inventor Essentials covers the most common uses of the tools in Autodesk Inventor and Inventor LT. Not every option is covered, but as you will learn, you will easily understand the options once you learn to use the primary tool.

The first eight chapters cover the core of Inventor in a way that steps the reader through creating drawings, parts, and assemblies in phases so there is a better opportunity to absorb the concepts.

The second portion of the book consists of seven chapters that focus on tools and workflows specific to types of design and on reusing data and automating the design process. I recommend readers complete the work in these chapters to learn alternative workflows that may not be an obvious fit for their design needs but may help them.

What You Need

To perform the exercises in this book, you must have Autodesk Inventor 2012 or Inventor LT 2012. Note that some features are not available in Inventor LT. Inventor LT is focused on translation, part modeling, and drawings and is a robust tool that can be made more effective by understanding its capabilities.

To make sure that your computer is compatible with Autodesk Inventor 2012, check the latest hardware requirements at www.autodesk.com/inventor.

What Is Covered in This Book

Autodesk Inventor and Inventor LT Essentials is organized to provide you with the knowledge needed to master the basics of Inventor.

Chapter 1: Connecting to Inventor's Interface   This chapter presents the interface, the basics of working with Inventor, and how to become productive with Inventor.

Chapter 2: Creating 2D Drawings from 3D Data   Creating 2D documentation of your designs is critical. This chapter presents the basic tools for placing views and dimensions in your drawings.

Chapter 3: Learning the Essentials of Part Modeling   Building parametric solid models is essential to the effective use of Inventor. This chapter will introduce the tools you need to build basic parts in Inventor.

Chapter 4: Putting Things in Place with Assemblies   Most products are made of many parts. Assembly tools help you control the position of the components relative to one another.

Chapter 5: Customizing Styles and Templates   Using standards in manufacturing improves quality and efficiency. The same is true for Inventor. This chapter helps you understand the options that are available for building your own design standard.

Chapter 6: Creating Advanced Drawings and Detailing   This chapter focuses on creating and editing more complex drawing views and adding finishing touches to your drawings.

Chapter 7: Advanced Part Modeling Features   Advanced geometry requires more advanced modeling tools. Learn the use of advanced fillets, lofts, and other tools that create the complex shapes you need.

Chapter 8: Advanced Assembly and Engineering Tools   An assembly is more than a group of parts. Inventor features many engineering-based tools that work in the assembly. This chapter also describes tools to help you control complex assemblies.

Chapter 9: Creating Plastic Parts   Plastics have a number of common features that make them easier to assemble. These features are developed using specialized tools in Inventor.

Chapter 10: Working with Sheet Metal Parts   The process of manufacturing sheet metal parts heavily influences how they are designed in Inventor. Creating material styles makes it easy for you to change the components by changing the style.

Chapter 11: Building with the Frame Generator   Using traditional solid modeling tools to build metal frames is arduous and time-consuming. The Frame Generator tools shortcut the process and make even complex frames easy to design.

Chapter 12: The Weldment Environment   A weldment is a combination of an assembly and a part model. Inventor puts the needs of manufacturing first when defining a weldment, saving you time.

Chapter 13: Creating Images and Animation from Your Design Data   Sharing images and animations made from your designs can help others understand how your designs are created and understand their value. This chapter guides you through tools for sharing your work with others.

Chapter 14: Working with Non-Inventor Data   Inventor has the ability to import and export data to and from nearly any other design system. This chapter helps you understand what options you have in working with that data.

Chapter 15: Automating the Design Process and Table-Driven Design   If you have repeatable design processes and products that share a lot of component families, this chapter can help you see opportunities to greatly increase your efficiency.

Appendix: Inventor Certification   Show the world that you know Autodesk Inventor by becoming an Autodesk Certified User, Associate, or Expert. This appendix will help you find the resources in the book to get certified.

Exercise Data   To complete the exercises in *Autodesk Inventor Essentials*, you must download the data files from www.sybex.com/go/inventor2012essentials.

Please also check the book's website for any updates to this book should the need arise. You can also contact the author directly by email at inventor .essentials@yahoo.com.

The Essentials Series

The Essentials series from Sybex provides outstanding instruction for readers who are just beginning to develop their professional skills. Every Essentials book includes these features:

► Skill-based instruction with chapters organized around projects rather than abstract concepts or subjects

► Suggestions for additional exercises at the end of each chapter, where you can practice and extend your skills

► Digital files (via download) so you can work through the project tutorials yourself. Please check the book's web page at `www.sybex.com/go/inventor2012essentials` for these companion downloads.

Connecting to Inventor's Interface

To access the power of Autodesk Inventor 2012, you have to start with the interface. To some extent, Inventor is an interface between your ideas and the computational abilities of your computer.

The ability to navigate and leverage the nuances of a program's interface can be the difference between struggling and excelling with the application. In this chapter, you will see the components of Inventor's dialogs, ribbons, tabs, and viewing tools that will help you create your designs. You will also learn how to modify the interface to increase your comfort with Inventor.

▶ **Exploring inventor's graphical user interface**

▶ **Setting application options**

▶ **Using visualization tools**

▶ **Working with project files**

Exploring Inventor's Graphical User Interface

When you first see Inventor's interface, you will probably think it is rather bare. With no file open, you just have the absolute basics there. Even when a file is loaded, your design remains the focus of the interface. In Figure 1.1, you can see the primary elements of the interface that will be referred to in this chapter.

Application Menu   Quick Access Toolbar   Ribbon   Title Bar   Help Tools   ViewCube

Browser   Status Bar   Design Window   Navigation Bar

FIGURE 1.1 Elements of the Inventor user interface

Users of other current Autodesk or Microsoft applications will recognize the Ribbon-style interface and the Application icon in the upper left. Inventor's adoption of the Ribbon interface goes beyond most other applications by actively offering you tools when they're most needed. But let's not get ahead of ourselves; let's start by getting more detail on these features of the interface.

Across the top of the Inventor window is the title bar. It will let you know you're using Autodesk Inventor, or it will display the name of the active file when you're editing one.

In the upper-left corner is an icon with a large *I* on it. Clicking it will open the Application menu (Figure 1.2), which displays tools for creating and manipulating files on the left and displays a list of recently opened files on the right. If you want to be able to return to a file frequently, you can select the icon to the right of the filename and "pin" it to the list.

You can also toggle the list between recent documents and the documents that are currently open and change the list from filenames to icons showing the files.

At the bottom of the menu are buttons to exit Inventor and to access the application options, which you will explore later in this chapter.

FIGURE 1.2 The expanded Application menu and Quick Access toolbar

The Quick Access toolbar is embedded in the title bar next to the Application icon and contains common tools to access new file templates, undo and redo edits, and print. The toolbar is dynamic, and different tools will appear depending on the active file. For example, one of those part-time tools is a drop-down menu that allows you to change the color of the active part.

You can customize this toolbar by adding commonly used tools to the toolbar. To do this, select the desired tool from the Ribbon, right-click, and select Add To Quick Access Toolbar from the context menu.

Opening a File

Knowing this much of the interface will allow you to access the Open dialog box and see how the rest of the interface works. In this exercise, you will open a file in Autodesk Inventor:

1. Start Autodesk Inventor if it is not already up and running.

2. Expand the Application menu, and select Open from the options on the left.

3. In the Open dialog, find the Project File drop-down, and set the active project file to iLogic 2012 Samples.ipj, as shown in Figure 1.3.

You can also access the Open tool on the Quick Access toolbar.

FIGURE 1.3 Changing the active project file changes where Inventor looks for files

4. Double-click the Railing Basic folder, shown in the file list in the middle of the dialog.

While you are in the Open dialog, notice the tools at the top. These tools allow you to navigate to other folders as you would in Windows Explorer, to change the way files are displayed (including the option of thumbnail images), and to add new folders.

5. Select the BaseMount.iam file in the file list.

Selecting an Inventor file from the file list window will generate an image in the Preview pane on the left side of the dialog.

6. Double-click that file or click the Open button to bring this file into Inventor's Design window.

7. To see the complete model, move your cursor near the ViewCube in the upper right of the Design window. When the icon that looks like a house appears, click it.

Clicking the Home view icon will restore a point of view for the model that was saved with the model previously. Your screen should now resemble Figure 1.1.

Exploring the Ribbon

You will now see that the Ribbon has more options available. These options take the form of tools are grouped into panels on tabs. Let's look at these in order from the broadest to the most specific:

Tabs   The options shown as Assemble, Design, Model, and so on are referred to as *tabs*. The active tab always contrasts with the others that just appear as names on the background of the Ribbon. The active tabs will change automatically as you transition from one working environment to another.

There are tabs that will appear temporarily when you start using specialized tools or enter a specialized environment such as doing sketching (Figure 1.4) or renderings of your 3D model. These tabs will activate automatically but will also have a special green highlight to help them stand out and remind you that these tools are available.

FIGURE 1.4   The Sketch tab is not normally displayed but gets special highlighting when it is.

Panels   In these tabs are special collections of tools that are sorted into *panels*. For example, in Figure 1.4, you can see Draw, Constrain, Pattern, and other panels on the Sketch tab. You will notice that the most commonly used tools appear with larger icons so they're easier to locate. At times, not all of the tools in a panel can fit, so some of the panels (Draw and Constrain) have arrows pointing down next to their names. This indicates that you can expand the panel to see more tools. It is also possible to permanently select tools that you don't often use to be placed in this expandable portion of the panel. You can even rearrange the order of the panels in a tab.

Tools   The last element of the Ribbon is the icon or tool. Many of the tools will display near the icon. As you become more comfortable with these tools, you can save space on your screen by turning off the display of the names. You can also hide or partially hide the Ribbon if you prefer having a larger Design window.

Any time you see an arrow pointing down next to a word or icon in Inventor, it means there are additional options.

Let's try a few of these options so that you can make yourself more comfortable once you start using Inventor for your regular work:

1. Keep using or reopen the BaseMount.iam file used in the previous exercise.

 To the right of the tab headers is a gray icon with an arrow pointing upward. Clicking this arrow will cycle the various ways of displaying the Ribbon.

2. Click the icon once to change the Ribbon from displaying all the panels within a tab to showing only the first icon with the title of the panel below it, as in Figure 1.5.

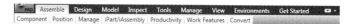

FIGURE 1.5 The Assemble tab showing Panel Buttons mode

By hovering over or clicking the icons that represent a panel (or the panel or tab titles of the next steps), you will cause the full view of the panel to appear under the Ribbon.

3. Click the same icon a second time, and you will reduce the tab to showing only the title of the panel, as in Figure 1.6.

FIGURE 1.6 Another cycling of the Ribbon viewing options shows the Panel Title mode.

4. Now pick again to reduce the menu even further, as you can see in Figure 1.7.

FIGURE 1.7 The Ribbon can be reduced to showing only the titles of the tabs in Tab view.

5. Click the icon one last time to restore the Ribbon to its original size with the default panels displayed.

Depending on your needs and personal preferences, you can use these various modes full-time or just temporarily. Clicking the down arrow to the right of the icon displays a menu that allows you to jump directly to the mode you want.

Rearranging the Panels

Let's do one more exercise displaying the Ribbon tools:

1. Keep using or reopen the BaseMount.iam file used in the previous exercise.

2. Make the Assemble tab active by clicking the name or header.

   The bar that the panel titles are on can be used as a grip.

3. Click and drag in the Manage panel (Figure 1.8) so that it appears between the Component and Position panels.

FIGURE 1.8 Any panel can be relocated to suit your tastes.

4. Right-click in one of the panels, and expand the Ribbon appearance by hovering over the words in the context menu.

5. Select Text Off from the menu.

   This will remove the names of the tools in the panel. This cuts down on the screen area covered but keeps the tools readily available.

6. Right-click again in a panel to open a menu with Ribbon appearance options.

7. Select Reset Ribbon.

8. Click Yes in the warning dialog that appears.

After a few moments, the icon names will reappear, and the panels will revert to their original positions. This is a great safety net for experimenting with interface personalization.

Finally, note that hovering your cursor over a tool in the Ribbon will open a *tooltip* that will give you basic information, the correct name of the tool, and, when applicable, the keyboard shortcut for the tool. If you leave the cursor over that tool a little longer, the tooltip will expand to offer visual information about the use of the tool (Figure 1.9).

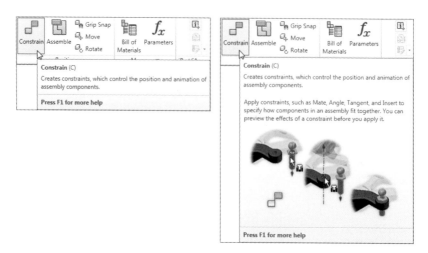

FIGURE 1.9 Continuing to hover expands the tooltip.

Using the Browser

Inventor's process of design is often referred to as *parametric solid modeling*. Although parameters play an important role in using Inventor, what makes its design process powerful and flexible is its ability to maintain a history of how the parts were constructed. This history will also show how they are related to one another in an assembly. The interface to see these actions is the Browser.

On the left side of the screen is a column that contains a hierarchical tree showing the name of the active file at the top, the Representations and Origin folders, and then the components or pattern of components that make up your assembly. Understanding how to read the Browser and how to control it is an important step in understanding how to control and edit your designs.

Let's do some exploration of the Browser to see what it can tell you:

1. Keep using or reopen the BaseMount.iam file used in the previous exercise.

 2. In the Browser, find the Origin folder, and click the plus sign to the left of the folder to expand the folder's contents.

3. Pass your mouse over the planes and axes displayed in the Browser, and see how those entities preview in the Design window to the right.

4. Right-click the XY Plane icon, and select Visibility from the context menu that appears.

5. In the Browser, locate the CollarBottomPlate_1 component.

6. Double-click the icon that looks like a cube to activate this part for editing.

7. This will activate the part to make it editable.

The Browser now displays the features that make up the active part (see Figure 1.10). Since it is a part file, the Ribbon has also changed, making the Model tab active for adding features to the part.

You can also acti-vate components by double-clicking the geometry in the Design window. Selecting a compo-nent and then right-clicking will allow you to open the part.

FIGURE 1.10 The Browser will reflect the status of the part or assembly and its history.

It's also important to know how to return to the assembly view. On the right end of the Model tab is the Return panel. Click the icon for the Return tool. This tool will appear at the end of a number of Ribbons when editing parts and assemblies.

There are additional options in the Return tool that you will use later in the book. Return's primary function is to take you up a step in the hierarchy of the model you're in.

Inventor is not only capable of creating and editing parts while in the assem-bly, but it prefers to work that way. There is no need for Inventor's sake to open a part in a separate window to edit it, though at times you may find it easier to navigate. Once a part is activated, the inactive components in the assembly are grayed out in the Browser and fade in the Design window to make it easier to focus on the part you're editing.

Let's open one of the parts to see what other changes occur when opening a separate window to use for editing. In the Browser, right-click the Collar_1 part, and select Open from the context menu. This will open the part in another window and add file tabs on the bottom of the Design window.

Exploring the File Tabs

Once you've opened at least two files in Inventor, the File tabs appear to make it easier to navigate between the files as well as to find the file that you want to switch to.

In Figure 1.11, you can see the file tabs at the bottom of the design window. These tabs display the names of the files.

FIGURE 1.11 File tabs let you quickly switch between open files and even preview the file before you select it.

The first two buttons on the left will arrange your open files by cascading them or by displaying them as tiles side by side.

Let's try using the tools to see what happens:

1. Click the Arrange button on the file tabs bar.

2. The files will stack on top of each other, as shown in Figure 1.12.

3. Look at the Browser, and then click back and forth between the tabs for the BaseMount.iam and Collar.ipt files to see the effect on the Browser.

4. Select the Collar.ipt tab, and pin the small X icon in the upper right of the tab.

   This will close the Collar part and the file tabs but leave the assembly as a floating window.

5. Double-click the top of the floating window frame, or click the Maximize button near the upper-right corner of the window.

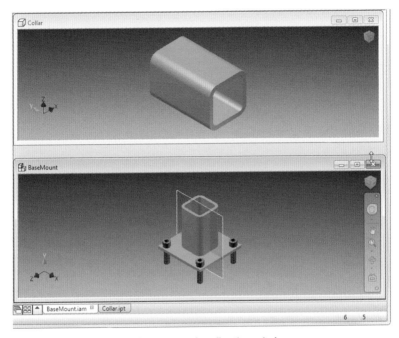

FIGURE 1.12 The files arranged as floating windows

This will restore the assembly to filling the Design window. The Design window has many different tools and enables many different options. I'll cover some of them in future chapters, but let's look at some of the most important ones now.

Highlighting and Enabled Components

Moving your cursor over the components of the assembly in the Design window, you will notice that the parts highlight. Highlighting allows you to see when components stand alone or, as in the case of bolts in this assembly, as a group. When a component is highlighted in the Design window, it will also highlight in the Browser, and vice versa.

Sometimes, you want to visually reference a component but do not want to be able to select that component or activate it. To do this, you can select the part in the Browser or the Design window and deselect Enabled from the context menu. This will fade the part and make it unselectable and disable highlighting of the disabled part.

Working in the Design Window

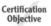
The part of the interface where most of your attention will be focused is the Design window. Not only are your design and its documentation shown there, but with each release of Inventor, more tools can be started from the Design window. Viewing and visualization tools will affect this area and allow you to view and share your designs in exciting ways.

Let's go through some of the tools that exist in and for the Design window and begin to see just how important it is:

Origin 3D Indicator   In the lower-left corner of the Design window, you see a 3D direction indicator. This is a reference for the orientation of the model in relationship to the standard axes of the file.

 Pan   To slide the model or drawing around the Design window, you will use the Pan tool. You can access Pan in several ways. You can find the Pan tool by going to the Navigate panel on the View tab, by going to the Navigation bar in the Design window, by pressing the F2 key, or by clicking and holding the middle mouse button.

 Zoom   The Zoom tool has several optional modes. The basic Zoom tool smoothly makes the model appear larger or smaller depending on the input you give it. You can find the Zoom tool by going to the drop-down under the Navigate panel on the View tab, by locating the same icon on the Navigation bar, by pressing the F3 key and clicking and dragging your mouse button, or by rotating a mouse wheel.

 Free Orbit   When you start Free Orbit by going to the Navigate panel, by going to Navigation bar, or by pressing F4, a reticle will appear on the screen. Moving your cursor around the reticle will display different tools. Figure 1.13 shows icons inside, outside, and near the x- and y-axes of the reticle. Clicking inside the reticle will orbit the model in a tumbling manner. Clicking and dragging near the x- or y-axis or just outside of the reticle will isolate the orbit around an axis.

View History   You can return to a previous view or views by pressing the F5 key until a view that you had before is restored on the screen.

The ViewCube   It's very likely the current view of our assembly isn't the only useful view that you may need to develop the design. The ViewCube allows you to rotate your design and position it based on standard views aligned with the faces, edges, and corners of the cube. Rotating the model using the ViewCube works in a way similar to using the Free Orbit tool.

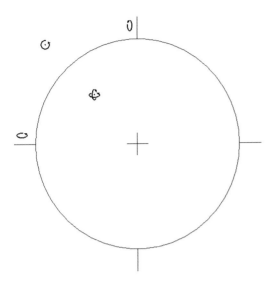

FIGURE 1.13 It is important to be able to easily reposition your view of the model for editing.

The ViewCube is probably the most important tool in the Design window, so it's the one you'll try in the following exercise:

1. Keep using or reopen the BaseMount.iam file used in the previous exercise.

2. Move your cursor to the ViewCube and over the face labeled Front.

3. When the face highlights, click it to rotate your model.

4. Now click the arrow on the right side of the cube that is pointing at the side of the cube. This will rotate your view to the Right side.

5. Move your cursor to the upper-right corner of the ViewCube, and select it.

6. Now click the ViewCube, but continue to hold your mouse button down and move your mouse around to orbit the view.

7. After you've rotated your part, press the F6 key to return to the Home view of the assembly.

    Now, your screen should look as it did at the beginning of the exercise.

8. Click the face labeled Right.

9. After the view updates, right-click the ViewCube, hover over Set Current View As, and select Front from the menu that appears (see Figure 1.14).

FIGURE 1.14 Faces on the ViewCube can be redefined as the Front or Top.

10. Now orbit the view to something you think offers a better view than the current Home view.

11. Right-click the ViewCube, and use the Set Current View As Home with the Fit To View option.

The other option for defining a new Home view is Fixed Distance. This option will maintain the zoom scale and position even if additions to the model go outside the Design window.

The ability to define the orientation of the ViewCube and the Home view will prove useful as you gain experience.

Checking Out the Status Bar

On the bottom edge of the Inventor window is a bar that will give you information about expected inputs for tools. The status bar will also give you feedback on information needed by Inventor as well as the number of files that are being accessed and parts that are being displayed when working in an assembly.

Using Marking Menus

As you create drawing views, parts, and assemblies and as you use other tools, you will see dialog boxes for these tools.

Inventor 2011 also incorporates several "Heads Up" interface tools that put common commands at the mouse cursor. *Marking menus* work in two modes: Menu and Marking.

Menu Mode   When you are editing a file and right-click in the Design window, a "rose" or "compass" (see Figure 1.15) of tools will appear. As you move toward the tool, a shadow or ray will highlight it, and clicking the mouse with this highlighting active will select the tool.

FIGURE 1.15 Marking menus place common tools where they are needed most.

Marking Mode   Once you're experienced with the tools offered in the marking menu, you can begin using Marking mode. To do this, you click and drag your right mouse button in the direction of the tool and release the button to activate the tool. The tool will flash to confirm that you've selected it rather than showing all the options.

Setting Application Options

Many settings allow you to tailor Inventor to your needs. Changing the tools in the Ribbon is just the beginning. To really affect the way Inventor behaves, you will need to make changes to the application options.

To access the Application Options dialog, you can go to the Application menu and click the Options button at the bottom; or, go to the Tools tab and select the Application Options tool. This will open a large dialog box with 14 tabs and an enormous number of options. I will focus on a few of these options, but I strongly recommend that you explore the others.

Using the Import/Export Buttons

At the bottom of the Application Options dialog are buttons that allow you to export your settings for backup or to share with others. You can also import one of these backups or import the settings another user has.

Exploring the General Tab

Once you're comfortable with how you typically use Inventor, you may want to make changes to some of the basic settings. On the General tab, you can change how Inventor will start up, how long you have to hover over an icon before the tooltip will appear, and even how much room on your hard disk can be used by the Undo tool.

Exploring the Colors Tab

Certification
Objective

This tab has the favorite tools for exploration for most Inventor users. You can change the color and look of your Design window background, control the color of the sketch objects and dimensions, and change the color scheme of the Ribbon icons.

Follow these steps to save your current settings and experiment with some changes:

1. Keep using or reopen the BaseMount.iam file used in previous exercises.

2. Expand the Application menu, and click the Options icon.

Export...

3. At the bottom of the dialog, select and click the Export button.

   A dialog will appear showing a couple of default settings backups. You can save your settings in this folder after you've made some changes.

4. Click Cancel in the dialog box.

5. Now select the Colors tab.

6. Select Presentation from the Color Scheme list, and notice the change in the preview window above.

7. Drag the title bar of the dialog to the left so you can see part of the Design window of Inventor behind.

8. Click the Apply button at the bottom of the dialog. See Figure 1.16 for reference.

FIGURE 1.16 The Design window with the Presentation color scheme

9. Now use the Background drop-down list, and change the setting to
1 Color.

10. Click Apply to see the effect.

Now try experimenting with different Color Scheme values as well as changing the color theme and background until you find something that is pleasing
to you. You can also use an image file for the background of your screen to give
additional realism or a special effect.

For this book, I will use Presentation with 1-Color to keep the components in
the Design window easy to see for the printed graphics. This is a quick way to
generate images for your technical documents as well.

Exploring the Display Tab

This tab controls a number of display effects you've already encountered. For
example, when you disabled the Collar_1 part in the assembly, it faded from
view. On the Display tab, you can use the Inactive Component Appearance section to disable that fading.

Certification
Objective

Similarly, when you selected the Home view, the model had an animated transition into position. The speed of that transition is controlled with the slider bar under Display.

Changing the Minimum Frame Rate (Hz) value to a higher number will cause Inventor to make parts of an assembly invisible while zooming, panning, or orbiting in order to maintain the chosen frame rate. The real use of this value is to allow you change the view quickly while still being able to see what position the model is in.

Other settings allow you to reposition the ViewCube on the screen and control the visibility of the Origin 3D indicator or its axis labels.

Exploring the Hardware Tab

Most of the settings for hardware are fairly self-explanatory. A very important item is the Software Graphics check box. If you experience frequent crashing in Inventor, you should select this check box (see Figure 1.17), restart, and see whether the crashing stops.

FIGURE 1.17 Selecting the Software Graphics option can help overcome stability issues.

The majority of crashes in Inventor begin as a conflict between the graphics driver, Windows, and Inventor. Selecting Software Graphics disconnects Inventor from communicating directly with the graphics driver. If the crashing stops, you should verify that your video card is supported and make sure you have the certified driver for the card. The Additional Resources section under Help has a link to look up the certified driver for approved video cards.

The Diagnostics tool at the bottom can help test whether the graphic drivers are WHQL-certified for Windows and whether your graphics card is capable of offering acceleration.

Inventor's Help system uses multiple resources to locate information for you. The Help tools are on the right end of the title bar.

Exploring the Assembly Tab

This tab's settings are primarily at-large assembly needs and specialized options. You can control whether the inactive components of the assembly remain opaque when a component is activated for editing; you can also change this option on the View tab by extending the Appearance panel.

Exploring the Drawing Tab

This tab has some settings that should be very interesting to AutoCAD users. The Default Drawing File Type setting can be selected, allowing the legacy Inventor IDW files, and you can select whether AutoCAD DWG files that are opened will be imported to Inventor or opened for viewing, printing, and measurement. You can even set which AutoCAD release format the DWG will be created in.

You can set some overall dimension preferences, and you can control whether line weights are displayed. For users with limited graphics power, you can change the View Preview Display setting to see views with a full preview, with a partial view, or with a bounding box.

If you choose to create drawings in DWG format, they can be created in 2000, 2004, 2007, or 2010 format.

Exploring the Sketch Tab

In Chapter 3, you will begin exploring part modeling. When you first begin to use sketching tools, a grid will be displayed. For clarity, the graphics in this book will not display this grid. If you prefer not to see it, you can disable parts or all of it in the Display section of the Sketch tab.

In the Heads-Up Display settings, you can control how dimensions are displayed on entities as you sketch them. Another preference that many people have is to disable the tools that automatically project edges during sketch or curve creation. These tools typically include Autoproject in the description. Many users will also choose not to use the setting to look at the sketch plane when sketches are created.

Exploring the Part Tab

A common change made on the Part tab is to change the default plane that a sketch is created on when parts are created. You can also choose not to have a sketch created automatically when you start a new part.

Using Visualization Tools

The ability to communicate a design visually is a great asset of Autodesk Inventor. Changing the color of the Design window or setting the background to be an image can give an interesting effect.

Increasingly, designers will use a rendering to present new concepts rather than creating detail drawings that may not be understood by people setting budgets. Regardless of the reason, the visualization capabilities that reside within the modeling environment can be just plain fun.

Understanding the Visual Styles

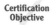

You can find the tools covered in this section on the View tab in the Appearance panel. I will review many of them, but I'm sure you will find yourself experimenting with them for a long time to come.

Realistic This visual style works at two levels. First, it uses the common color library that is shared among most Autodesk design products, giving you a different appearance than the other modes. Realistic also lets you very quickly create a ray-traced rendering that is more than suitable for communicating a design concept. Although this option is in the modeling environment, it really isn't intended to be the setting used while doing modeling or assembly functions. Not all graphics cards are capable of working with the ray-tracing capabilities.

Shaded This mode has been available throughout Inventor's history and is the environment that most users work in.

Shaded With Hidden Edges This mode highlights the visible edges of the components and generates hidden edges that show through the components to make it easier to find faces that are otherwise obscured.

See Figure 1.18 for an illustration of these three modes.

FIGURE 1.18 The Realistic, Shaded, and Shaded With Hidden Edges visual styles

Wireframe With Hidden Edges   Working in wireframe is comfortable for users who have experienced older 3D systems. The addition of displaying the hidden edges makes it easier to sort out what is in the foreground and in the background.

Monochrome   This will make your model look like Shaded mode but with gray-scale shades replacing the colors of the components.

Illustration   This mode is in some ways a mirror to Realistic. It makes the model appear more like a line drawing by adding edges and varying line weights to the display.

See Figure 1.19 for the last three modes described.

FIGURE 1.19 Wireframe with Hidden Edges, Monochrome, and Illustration Visual Styles

Using Shadows

Shadows can assist in understanding the contours of a part, in particular when a part is prismatic and faces can be obscured in Shaded mode. These shadows can be displayed all at once, in any combination, or individually.

Ground Shadows   A very easy way to add a visual appeal to your model is to have it cast a shadow on the ground. The position of the ground is controlled by the location of the Top face on the ViewCube. The effect is of light shining down on the top of the model.

Object Shadows   Having this option on causes components and features to cast shadows on one another based on the direction of the lighting.

Ambient Shadows   This mode gives a somewhat more subtle but very effective change to the model but adds the effect of ambient occlusion, causing areas where sharp edges meet to be darkened. See Figure 1.20.

FIGURE 1.20 With the model in Shaded mode, turning on Ambient Shadows gives it a little more realism.

At the end of the Shadows flyout menu is a Setting button. When selected, it brings up a dialog where you can establish the direction from which the shadows will be cast. You can also control their density and softness, and the intensity of ambient shadows. You can also turn on image-based lighting here; you will look at that effect a little later in the chapter.

Using Ground Reflections

 Ground reflections are based on a calculated "ground" that lies beneath the lowest component feature or visible sketch point. The ground establishes its location based on the position of the Top face of the ViewCube. The Ground Reflections option is either on or off, but the fun doesn't have to stop there.

Like the Shadows tool, Ground Reflections provides settings in a flyout menu next to the icon. In the settings, you can control the level of reflection, how much it is blurred, and how quickly that blur will fall off. This dialog also controls the settings for the Ground Plane tool, which will be described next.

Using the Ground Plane

This option is really just a switch that controls whether a grid will be displayed on the ground that the reflections and shadows are cast on. As mentioned, its settings are shared with Ground Reflections but can be accessed from its own flyout menu.

Putting Visual Styles to Work

In this exercise, you will get a chance to explore a couple of the options just reviewed:

1. Keep using or reopen the BaseMount.iam file used in previous exercises.

2. Switch your Ribbon to the View tab.

3. In the Appearance panel, click the icon for Shadows, and observe the change to the screen.

4. Right below the Shadows tool, click the Ground Reflections icon.

5. Next locate the Ground Plane tool, and turn it on.

   You will now use some of the tools that were discussed earlier.

6. Use the Visual Style drop-down menu to set your style to Realistic.

7. Now change your Visual Style setting to Watercolor. Note that the reflections and ground shadows disappear but ambient shadows are still generated.

8. Set Visual Style to Shaded when you're done admiring the Watercolor style, and keep this file open.

With a nice basic view, let's make a couple of simple changes to see what the effects are before looking at a few more visualization options:

1. Open the Shadows settings dialog by using the flyout menu next to the Shadows icon.

   If possible, reposition the dialog to see the screen as you make the following changes (because the screen will update while you are making them).

2. At the bottom of the dialog, use the drop-down menu to change Shadow Direction to 45-Degrees Right.

3. Use the slider bar below to change the Density value to 40.

4. Change the Softness value to 15.

5. Reduce Ambient Shadows to 20.

6. Click the Save button and then Done to close the dialog box. See Figure 1.21, and keep the file open for the next exercise.

FIGURE 1.21 Small changes can create a dramatic effect with visualization settings.

With your shadows updated, you can do a little experiment with the reflections:

1. Open the Ground Reflections settings dialog using the flyout menu next to the Ground Reflections icon.

If possible, reposition the dialog to see the screen as you make the following changes (because the screen will update while you are making them).

2. Set the Reflection level to 50%.

3. Set the Blur level to 50%.

4. Now change the value in the Minor text box under Appearance to .3.

5. Remove the check mark from Plane Color.

6. Set the Height Offset value at the top of the dialog to **10mm**. You must enter **mm** to input the metric value into an English units assembly.

7. Click OK to save the changes and close the dialog box.

8. In the Appearance panel, find the drop-down menu for orthographic and perspective projections, and set the view to Perspective.

Another option, **Perspective With Ortho Faces**, can be turned on by right-clicking the ViewCube and selecting it.

9. Press the F6 key to restore the Home view, and compare your screen to Figure 1.22. Keep the file open for the next exercise.

FIGURE 1.22 Some changes may decrease realism but can add energy to the view.

Remember, these changes aren't just for a printed document; you're still in a working assembly file, and you are able to make edits with these view characteristics.

Setting the Lighting Style

This is a very understated name for a setting. Lighting styles do in fact change how lights are positioned (and therefore shadows) in your model, but several of them also come with an environment that offers the effect of putting the model into a different world.

Through settings, you can make the same changes to the lighting style that you were able to make to shadows, but you will be limited in the built-in selections of image lighting sources. This tool's effect is easier seen than described, so let's use it.

You will do only a couple of changes, or you may not get any further in the book. Some of these next changes may not work with all graphics cards.

1. Continue working in the open file.

2. In the Appearance panel, the Lighting Style drop-down currently shows the Two Lights style. Change its value to Old Warehouse.

3. Use the ViewCube or Orbit tool to rotate your part around and see the environment that is shown. Using Pan and Zoom can help with finding some interesting points of view too.

4. Change your lighting style to Empty Lab.

Setting a lighting style can really change a lot of things about how you look at and work with your model. It's also a lot of fun.

Using Color Override

When you begin to create 3D part models, you will use specific materials so that you can monitor and predict the weight and inertial properties of the components you are building. Materials have their own colors. However, you are not limited to having steel look like steel, for example. Using the Color Override option, you can change its color to make it look like anything you want.

Changing a component's color is straightforward, but keep in mind that changing a component's color in the assembly does not change it in the source file. If you want to change the color of something everywhere, you need to do it in the part file.

How easy is it? Let's find out:

1. Continue working in the open file.

2. Holding the Ctrl key, click the Collar_1 part and the CollarBottomPlate _1 components either in the Browser or in the Design window.

3. Find the Color Override drop-down, which will likely show As Material, and select Blue Chrome.

4. As a nice finishing touch, change your visual style to Realistic. See my results in Figure 1.23.

FIGURE 1.23 There is nothing some form of Chrome can't improve.

You can close the BaseMount.iam file by clicking in the X icon in the upper-right corner of the Design window or through the Application menu.

One of the fundamental steps in learning the tools of Inventor is to know where your files are. For that, you need a project file.

WARNING At this time, it is critical that you go to www.sybex .com/go/inventor2012essentials, download the Inventor 2012 Essentials Data.zip file, and expand it to the root of your C drive. This will create a new folder, C:\Inventor 2012 Essentials. The files needed to complete the exercises for this book will be contained in this folder.

Working with Project Files

Certification
Objective
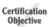

To work with Inventor effectively, you must have an understanding of the role and configuration of the *project file*. The project file is a configuration file that tells Inventor where to look for and store data about a project. Among other things, the project file can also be used to create shortcuts for locating files, change where Inventor looks for templates, and control the user's ability to modify standards.

It's also important if you work with others to have a consensus on how you will work with this data and consistency in your project files. Working from the same file can save a lot of frustration. This can easily be done by simply copying the file among several users.

By now, you should've extracted the data for the files you will use in the book. Now, you will tell Inventor where to find that data.

Creating a Project File

You can create a project file at any time, but you can make it the active file only when all data is closed in Inventor.

1. Make sure that all files are closed in Inventor but Inventor is still running.

2. On the Get Started tab, click the Projects icon in the Launch panel.

   This will open the Projects dialog, where you can control the active project file or edit existing ones.

3. Click the New button at the bottom of the dialog.

   This will launch the Inventor Project Wizard, which will walk you through the process the next time you want to create a new project file.

4. Click the New Single User Project option, and then click the Next button at the bottom of the dialog.

5. Enter 2012 Essentials in the Name field.

6. Enter C:\Inventor 2012 Essentials in the Project (Workspace) Folder field.

7. Compare your settings to Figure 1.24, and click Finish when you're sure everything matches to create your new project file.

FIGURE 1.24 Defining the name and location
of the new project file

Now you have a 2012 Essentials.IPJ file in the folder that you specified.
(The .ipj extension stands for Inventor Project File.) You need to add some
detail to make sure everything will be controlled as needed.

Modifying the Project File

In this exercise, you will add shortcut paths to folders that you will frequently
access and make sure that the standard parts you use are kept where you
need them.

1. In the top window of the Projects dialog, double-click the 2012
   Essentials project file to make it active.

2. In the bottom window, right-click Use Style Library, and switch it to
   Read-Write in the context menu.

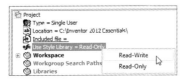

3. Click the Frequently Used Subfolders icon to highlight the row.

4. On the right, click the Add New Path icon.

5. A new row will be added under the row. In the field on the left, type **Assemblies**. On the right, browse to set your path to C:\Inventor 2012 Essentials\Assemblies. See Figure 1.25.

FIGURE 1.25 Creating an easy-to-understand alias representing a file path

6. Click OK to set the path for the shortcut to the assembly files.

   When the new shortcut is created, you will see that the path is different from what it was in the dialog. Instead of showing the full name, it will say *Workspace\Assemblies*. This helps avoid problems if the files need to be moved to another drive.

7. Now add a shortcut for parts pointing toward the Parts folder and for drawings pointing to the Drawings folder.

8. Expand the Folder Options section.

9. Click the Content Center Files icon, and click the Edit icon on the right.

10. Set the path for the Content Center files to C:\Inventor 2012\ Content Center Files, as shown in Figure 1.26, and click OK to complete the edit.

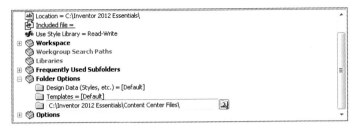

FIGURE 1.26 Setting the path for saving standard components used in an assembly

As mentioned, the project file is critical for working with other users on the same data. The Content Center files path can be set to a common network location so that everyone can find the correct information when editing each other's work.

THE ESSENTIALS AND BEYOND

As you get more experience with the Inventor interface, you will see that it assists you in understanding which environment you are in and what is available to you. Changing colors and setting options that you like is a great way to get more comfortable, and that will lead to you being more productive.

ADDITIONAL EXERCISES

▶ Add the tools that you think you will find useful to your Quick Access toolbar.

▶ Challenge yourself to access tools from different locations to become familiar with other tools around them.

▶ Use different application options especially for sketching and part modeling to see the effect they have on your productivity.

▶ Experiment with color schemes and lighting styles to find ways of maximizing the impression you make on people who see your work.

Creating 2D Drawings from 3D Data

When you've never used Autodesk Inventor, it is very easy to focus entirely on the three-dimensional (3D) design tools, but many people still need to produce two-dimensional (2D) production drawings.

Chances are, if you're reading this book, you have created detail drawings and will likely need to create them in the future. Creating detail drawings from the solid (or surface) model is so easy it can often be thought of as fun.

To create a new drawing in Inventor, it is not necessary to have any 3D file open. In fact, if your system resources are limited, it is best not to have the file open.

▶ **Drawing views of a part**

▶ **Editing views**

▶ **Adding detail to drawing views**

▶ **Dimensioning**

Drawing Views of a Part

When you've created a drawing view, it must accurately reflect the model geometry, and if there is a change to the geometry, it needs to be reflected in all drawing views. This is just standard drafting practice, and the way Inventor works as well, but you may notice things happen a bit more quickly than on the drawing board.

This section introduces the types of drawing views and then proceeds through a series of exercises creating and working with views.

Types of Drawing Views

Certification
Objective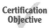

Any type of drawing view that you've ever created on the drafting board or in a 2D CAD system can be created with Inventor. It's just a lot faster in Inventor because you're generating views of the object(s) rather than generating a lot of separate pieces of geometry to represent the same edge or feature.

The Base View   If you think about how you currently do drawing layouts, you are already working with a hierarchy, whether it's conscious or not. You have a view that others are positioned around. In Inventor, this is referred to as the *base view*, and there can be as many as you need or as many components as you like, all on one page.

Projected Views   Once a base view is placed, you can immediately place standard orthographic projections and isometric views from that base view. Any change that is made to the scale, position, or contents of the base view will be reflected in the projected view by default.

Section Views   These are placed much like projected views but with a section line defining what geometry will be generated. The section line can be multisegmented or include arcs.

Auxiliary View   A specialized view requires the selection of an existing drawing view edge to project around to display the true shape of a face.

> A section view can be made to any depth or even defined outside a part to create a custom view.

Detail View   This is another type of view that is hard to make in a 2D system, especially if the geometry may change. For this view, you can use round or rectangular boundaries with smooth or rough edges for the view. The detail view can also be created with any scale.

Starting a New Drawing

To have a view, you must first have a drawing. Beginning a new drawing is just like creating any other file in Inventor; click a template and get to work.

1. On the Quick Access toolbar, click the New icon.

2. Make sure that 2012 Essentials.ipj is listed as the active project file in the dialog box.

3. In the New File dialog box, select the Metric tab (see Figure 2.1).

4. Locate and double-click the ANSI (mm).idw template file.

FIGURE 2.1 Templates are organized by model units.

This will open a new drawing page in the Design window and update the Ribbon to present the Place Views tab and its tools.

Placing the Base and Projected Views

Now you will begin the process of creating your drawing. For this exercise, you will use the marking menu tools.

1. Right-click in the Design window, and move up to select the Base View tool; or, right-click and drag up quickly to activate the tool.

2. In the dialog, click the icon to select an existing file at the end of the File drop-down.

3. Using the same Open dialog you used in Chapter 1, use the parts shortcut in the upper left; then open the Parts\Chapter 2 folder, and select the 30 Degree Adapter part file.

   If you move your cursor over the drawing page, a preview will appear, showing how the component will be sized and positioned on the page.

4. In the upper right, click a few different options in the Orientation field and see the effect each one has on the preview. Make sure you end up back at the Front view.

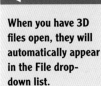

When you have 3D files open, they will automatically appear in the File drop-down list.

5. In the lower left of the dialog, set the view scale to .7 and see the effect on the preview.

   At the bottom of many dialogs is an arrow icon. Clicking this will cause the dialog to roll up to just its title bar. If a dialog is in your way, use this option to make it easier to see your screen. Moving your cursor near the dialog will expand it to its full size, and reselecting the arrow will hold the dialog open.

6. Position the view similar to Figure 2.2, and click the mouse to place the drawing view.

FIGURE 2.2 Placing the base view of the adapter

7. Now move your cursor down and to the right and to the upper-right corner, and click the mouse to place the views that are shown in Figure 2.3. You must right-click and select Create from the context menu to generate the views.

The ability to quickly place the base view and the projected views in one step is a great way to quickly see how the drawing will lay out.

FIGURE 2.3 Locating the bottom, side, and isometric views

Placing a Section View

Section views are very important for detailing machine parts and assemblies. In this exercise, you will see how easy they are to create:

1. Open c2-02.idw from the Drawings\Chapter 2 folder, making certain that the 2012 Essentials project file is active.

2. Start the Section tool from the Create panel on the Place Views tab.

3. Click the projected view to the right of the base view to choose it as the parent of the section view.

4. As you move over and around the parent view, you will see dotted lines that show alignment to view geometry. When an inference line appears from the center of the top face (see Figure 2.4), click to start creating a section line.

FIGURE 2.4 Inference lines will allow the section to be connected to view geometry.

5. Drag the line down through the part to define the section line, and click a second point to start creating the section view. See Figure 2.5. Right-click and select Continue from the context menu to finish defining the section line.

FIGURE 2.5 Include some overlap of the view in the section line length.

6. The Section View dialog will appear, allowing you to change the scale and view identifier. Move your mouse to the right to see a preview of the view. See Figure 2.6.

FIGURE 2.6 Placing the section view

7. Click the location for the view to generate the view. Figure 2.7 shows the result.

It is possible to define a section view of nearly any existing drawing view. Auxiliary views are very similar to section views but are defined by model geometry.

FIGURE 2.7 The finished section view

Creating an Auxiliary View

Auxiliary views can be a challenge to define accurately with a 2D CAD system. In this case, you want to more easily detail the round face of the part, which does not align with a standard orthographic projection.

1. Open c2-03.idw from the Drawings\Chapter 2 folder, making certain that the 2012 Essentials project file is active.

2. Move your cursor near the base view, and when it highlights, right-click to bring up the marking menu and context menu with other tools.

3. Select Create View ➤ Auxiliary View from the context menu.

4. After the Auxiliary View dialog appears, click the angled edge on the top of the base view, as shown in Figure 2.8.

FIGURE 2.8 Selecting an edge for the projection reference

5. Click to place your view, as shown in Figure 2.9.

FIGURE 2.9 An easy auxiliary view

Creating a Detail View

The auxiliary view offers more clarity, but the section view offers an opportunity to see things otherwise obscured in an orthographic view. To do so, you'll create a detail view to add clarity:

1. Open c2-04.idw from the Drawings\Chapter 2 folder, making certain that the 2012 Essentials project file is active.

2. Start the Detail tool from the Ribbon or from the context menu.

3. Click the section view as the parent, which will open the Detail View dialog.

4. Set Scale to 2 and Fence Shape to Rectangular; then click near the O-ring groove, and drag the fence, as shown in Figure 2.10.

5. Drag the new view to any open spot on the page, and click to place it.

Now that you have a collection of views, you should make the drawing look better as a whole. By moving, rotating, or even changing the appearance of the views, you can make a big difference.

FIGURE 2.10 Setting up the focus of the detail view

Editing Views

The detail drawing is an important communication tool, so it is equally important to make it as clear as possible. In this section, you will focus on tools that will help you put the finishing touches on your drawings.

View Alignment

When views are created from other views, they inherit the appearance and scale of the parent view. Projected, auxiliary, and section views also inherit alignment from the parent view. Using this alignment and sometimes breaking the alignment make it simple to reorganize the drawing.

The simplest way to add clarity to a drawing is to shuffle the position of the drawing views. Doing this is a simple drag-and-drop operation.

1. Open c2-05.idw from the Drawings\Chapter 2 folder, making certain that the 2012 Essentials project file is active.

2. Click and drag the base view up and to the left. In Figure 2.11, you can see how the views projected from it and their children keep the alignment of orthographic projection.

You can even move drawing views to the opposite side from where they were created.

F I G U R E 2 . 1 1 Moving a view does not break its proper alignment with others.

3. Move the right side view and the section views to give more space to them. Notice that they remain in alignment with the base view but do not change its position.

4. Move the detail view to the left of the title block, as shown in Figure 2.12.

F I G U R E 2 . 1 2 The detail view is free to be moved anywhere.

Moving views goes a long way toward making things look better. Sometimes, you may not want to maintain view alignment, or there may be times where it impedes the detailing of geometry.

Changing Alignment

It is possible to edit a view and break its alignment to a parent view using simple right-click options or using the tools in the Modify panel. You can also add alignment between views using tools from the same menus.

For example, to change the location of the auxiliary view, you need to break its alignment with the base view. To make it easier to dimension, you may want to rotate it as well. The Rotate tool will do both steps for you.

1. Open c2-06.idw from the Drawings\Chapter 2 folder, making certain that the 2012 Essentials project file is active.

2. Click the auxiliary view, right-click, and select Rotate from the context menu.

3. In the Rotate View dialog, keep the rotation method By Edge, but set the alignment to Vertical and check that the direction is set to clockwise.

4. Click the straight edge on the right side of the view per Figure 2.13.

FIGURE 2.13 Rotating the drawing view can make detailing easier.

5. Click OK after the part has been rotated.

Now that the view has been rotated, you can detail it. But you may also want to reestablish an alignment with the base view to help others understand the geometry.

This exercise shows an uncommon and specialized drawing practice. It is built around the classic drafting idea of making it easier for people to recognize the geometry.

1. Open c2-07.idw from the Drawings\Chapter 2 folder, making certain that the 2012 Essentials project file is active.

2. In the Modify panel, expand the options under Break Alignment, and select Vertical.

3. Click the rotated auxiliary view and then the base view. See Figure 2.14 for the results.

FIGURE 2.14 Views can be aligned to other views that were not originally their parent.

Now that you think you have enough room between the views and they are aligned, you will make some of them easier to interpret.

View Appearance

Changing how a view looks or is scaled can have a dramatic effect on how easy it is to understand.

You can use a number of techniques, including removing hidden lines, adding shading, changing scale, or turning the visibility of selected entities off altogether. Any or a combination of these can be done without changing the accuracy of the view.

A quick way to add clarity is to remove hidden lines when they're not needed to understand the geometry of the component. In this exercise, you'll also add shading.

1. Open c2-08.idw from the Drawings\Chapter 2 folder, making certain that the 2012 Essentials project file is active.

2. Double-click in the auxiliary view (upper left) to open the Drawing View dialog.

3. Deselect the Style From Base check box.

4. To the left of the Style From Base icon, click the Hidden Line Removed icon, and click OK to close the dialog and apply the change.

5. Double-click the isometric view to edit it.

6. Click the Shaded icon.

7. Select the Display Options tab in the dialog, and then remove the check mark from Tangent Edges.

8. Change the scale of the view to .5.

9. Click OK to update the drawing. See Figure 2.15.

FIGURE 2.15 Updated drawing views

Removing unneeded hidden lines and adding shading can make the drawing easier to understand without adding more views. You could continue to make adjustments to the views for hours. Let's instead turn our attention to detailing the views you have.

Adding Detail to Drawing Views

There are many things that you add to a drawing to make it complete. Much of the work is tedious but necessary. Reducing the time it takes to add all of the detail is one of the unsung strengths of Inventor. In the next several pages, you will see some great examples of the productivity tools for detailing and dimensioning.

Most of the tools you will be using are located on the Annotate tab. This is one time where Inventor doesn't automatically change the active tab, because everyone uses the detailing tools differently.

Center Marks and Centerlines

You often need to add geometry to the drawing views to assist in locating dimensions. The next several exercises will walk you through the most commonly used tools for this purpose, center marks and centerlines.

Center marks make it easy to locate the center of a hole or radius.

1. Open c2-09.idw from the Drawings\Chapter 2 folder, making certain that the 2012 Essentials project file is active.

2. Click the Annotate tab in the Ribbon to change your active tab and see the Annotation tools.

3. Zoom in on the bottom view in the lower left of the drawing.

4. Click the Center Mark tool on the Symbols panel of the Annotate tab.

5. Move your cursor near the edge of one of the holes. When it highlights, click your mouse to place a center mark.

6. Repeat to place center marks on all four holes, as shown in Figure 2.16.

FIGURE 2.16 Placing center marks on holes by simply picking them

7. To connect the center marks, drag the center mark extensions toward each other.

Now that you've added and edited center marks for a basic rectangular hole pattern, you can now move on to bolt circles.

Center marks and centerlines have many uses in Inventor. The ability to easily make them and drag-edit the extents of these marks helps the user to save time cleaning up the drawing. They can also be used to show linear alignments between holes or even bolt circles.

1. Open c2-10.idw from the Drawings\Chapter 2 folder, making certain that the 2012 Essentials project file is active.

2. Zoom in on the rotated auxiliary view in the upper-left corner.

3. Select the Centerline tool from the Symbols panel of the Annotation tab.

You can also easily create a series of centerlines in an arc based on a center.

4. Begin by selecting the hole at 12 o'clock of the round face; then click the holes at 3 o'clock, 6 o'clock, and 9 o'clock, as shown in Figure 2.17.

FIGURE 2.17 As you place the center marks for the bolt circle, the centerline previews.

5. Finish the Bolt circle by clicking the 12 o'clock hole again; then right-click and select Create from the context menu. See Figure 2.18.

FIGURE 2.18 Generating a bolt circle with the Centerline tool

6. Press the Esc key to leave the Centerline tool.

You can use the Centerline Bisector tool on straight or curved segments to find the midline between them. Straight segments do not need to be parallel.

1. Open c2–11.idw from the Drawings\Chapter 2 folder, making certain that the 2012 Essentials project file is active.

2. Zoom in on the section view on the right side of the drawing.

3. Select the Centerline Bisector tool on the Symbols panel of the Annotation tab.

4. Click the Orange lines in the lower left and lower right of the open portion of the part to place a straight segment.

5. Click the green arcs on the left and right to place a curved segment.

6. Place another straight segment by picking the blue angled line at the top left and top right.

7. You can also extend the straight segments beyond their original size for clarity. See Figure 2.19.

FIGURE 2.19 Placing a complex centerline bisector

While you are looking at the section view, you should improve its appearance.

Editing a Detail View Placement and Callout

Previously, you moved views around to improve the layout of the drawing. Callouts, section lines, and detail boundaries can also be edited to improve their clarity.

1. Open c2–12.idw from the Drawings\Chapter 2 folder, making certain that the 2012 Essentials project file is active.

2. Zoom in on the section view.

3. Select the letter *C* in the detail view boundary, and drag it to where the upper-right corner is now.

   In addition to relocating the callout, you can change the letter by editing the text to read whatever you like.

4. Click the boundary. When the corners and center highlight, drag the center upward and to the right a short distance.

5. Select the *SECTION A-A* text, and drag it below the view so it is legible. Figure 2.20 shows the result.

SECTION A-A
SCALE .7

FIGURE 2.20 Relocate the section view label for a better drawing view.

Now that the views have been updated with new or repositioned elements, you should turn your attention to dimensioning.

Dimensioning

If you've used traditional 2D CAD tools in the past for drafting, then the tools Inventor uses to apply dimensions should seem familiar but different at the same time. Rather than offer the user a broad array of dimensioning tools, Inventor uses intelligence that changes the type of dimension based on the selected geometry. Add the ability to change many options while you are placing the dimension, and you are sure to appreciate the power available to you.

The General Dimension Tool

To place individual dimensions in the drawing, the General Dimension tool will give you most anything you will need. For horizontal, vertical, aligned, radial, and diameter dimensions, you can just use this tool.

1. Open c2–13.idw from the Drawings\Chapter 2 folder, making certain that the 2012 Essentials project file is active.

2. Zoom in on the bottom view in the lower left of the drawing.

Dimension

3. From the Dimension panel of the Annotate tab, select the Dimension tool.

4. Click the center marks in the lower- and upper-right corners (Figure 2.21).

FIGURE 2.21 Click the center marks or other geometry to place dimensions.

5. Move your cursor to the right. You will see the dimension change to dotted lines when you have good spacing away from the geometry.

6. Click to place the dimension.

7. When the Edit Dimension dialog appears, deselect the Edit Dimension When Created check box, and click OK to close the dialog.

8. The General Dimension tool is still running. Click the radius in the lower-right corner, and notice that you are now creating a radial dimension. This dimension will snap at common angles.

9. Click to place the new dimension (Figure 2.22).

FIGURE 2.22 Adding a radial dimension

10. Pan up to the base view.

11. Click the upper edge of the base of the part and then the lower edge of the angle face. Notice that the dimension now turns to an angular dimension.

12. Place the new dimension to the side, as shown in Figure 2.23.

13. Now select the top edge of the angle portion.

14. Place the linear diameter above the drawing view (Figure 2.24).

As you see, the General Dimension tool is incredibly flexible.

FIGURE 2.23 Even angular dimensions can be placed with the General Dimension tool.

FIGURE 2.24 The geometry selected determines the type of dimension placed.

The Baseline and Baseline Set Dimension Tools

When you need to place several dimensions from the same datum, you can use the baseline dimensioning tools, Baseline and Baseline Set. The difference between the two is that Baseline Set keeps the placed dimensions' styles and precision linked along with other variables.

1. Open c2-14.idw from the Drawings\Chapter 2 folder, making certain that the 2012 Essentials project file is active.

2. Zoom in on the bottom view in the lower left of the drawing.

3. From the Dimension panel of the Annotate tab, expand the Baseline tool, and select Baseline Set.

   The tool will start immediately and wait for you to select the geometry.

4. Click the left edge of the square face, the top-left hole, the top-right hole, and the right edge.

5. Right-click and select Continue from the context menu to stop selecting geometry and begin placing dimensions.

6. The preview of the dimensions will appear. Move them above the view.

7. Click to place the dimensions, and then right-click and select Create from the context menu to finish. See Figure 2.25.

FIGURE 2.25 Placing multiple dimensions with the Baseline Dimension tool

The Chain and Chain Set Dimension Tools

Used commonly in architecture and when part cost is more important than high precision, the Chain dimensioning tools work very much like the Baseline tools but place dimensions in a series rather than from a common datum.

1. Open c2-15.idw from the Drawings\Chapter 2 folder, making certain that the 2012 Essentials project file is active.

2. Zoom in on the bottom view in the lower left of the drawing.

3. From the Dimension panel of the Annotate tab, select the Chain Dimension tool.

   The tool will start immediately and wait for you to select the geometry.

4. Click the top edge of the square face, the top-left hole, the bottom-left hole, and the bottom edge.

5. Right-click and select Continue from the context menu to stop selecting geometry and begin placing dimensions.

6. The preview of the dimensions will appear. Move them to the left of the view.

7. Click to place the dimensions; then right-click and select Create from the context menu to finish. See Figure 2.26.

FIGURE 2.26 Chain dimensioning is much easier with a specific tool.

The Ordinate and Ordinate Set Dimension Tools

The Ordinate dimensioning tools work much like the Baseline tools but place the dimension value at the end of the extension line, as shown in Figure 2.27.

The difference between the two is that the Ordinate Dimension tool prompts for the placement of a datum point in the view. The Ordinate Set dimension tool does not, and it therefore has a workflow that is essentially the same as that of the Baseline Dimension tool.

FIGURE 2.27 Ordinate dimensions work with the same workflow as chain dimensions.

Editing Dimensions

When you placed the baseline dimension set, it was placed almost as a unit. The dimensions share many properties. You can still change these properties, and if need be, you can make a dimension independent.

1. Open c2-16.idw from the Drawings\Chapter 2 folder, making certain that the 2012 Essentials project file is active.

2. Zoom in on the bottom view in the lower left of the drawing.

3. Click the 72.00 dimension on the left.

   Once you've selected the dimension, two drop-downs will become active in the Format panel on the Annotate tab.

4. On the lower drop-down, change the Dimension style to Default—mm [in] (ANSI).

5. Right-click the 14.00 dimension, and select Detach Member from the context menu.

6. Double-click the 14.00 dimension.

7. When the Edit Dimension dialog opens, select the Precision And Tolerance tab.

8. In the Precision field on the right, use the Primary Unit drop-down, and change the value to 1.1. Click OK. See Figure 2.28.

You can also delete a member and use the Arrange tool to bring the dimensions back in order.

FIGURE 2.28 The dimensions can still be edited after being placed.

The Edit Dimension dialog offers a lot of options that I didn't cover in the exercise, including tolerancing, fits, and even the ability to define an inspection dimension.

The Hole and Thread Notes Tool

Inventor's part modeling tools give you the ability to define holes by thread and their clearances for fasteners based on standards. To document these features, use the Hole and Thread Notes tool, which extracts the information directly from the feature.

1. Open c2-17.idw from the Drawings\Chapter 2 folder, making certain that the 2012 Essentials project file is active.

2. Zoom in on the rotated auxiliary view in the upper left of the drawing.

3. Find and start the Hole and Thread tool in the Feature Notes panel of the Annotation tab.

4. Click the hole at 3 o'clock, and place the dimension above and to the right of the hole.

5. Press the Esc key to end the tool.

Now, you will edit the annotation to add detail.

6. Double-click the Hole note.

7. In the Edit Hole Note window that appears (Figure 2.29), press the Home key or click the cursor before the text <THDCD>.

FIGURE 2.29 The Edit Hole Note window

8. Click the Quantity Note icon to add the ability to display the number of like holes in the hole note. Then click OK. See Figure 2.30.

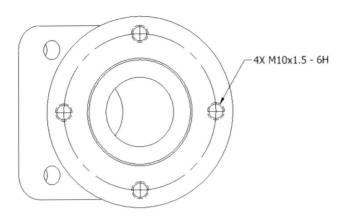

4X M10x1.5 - 6H

FIGURE 2.30 The Hole note can also display the number of holes.

Retrieving Model Dimensions

The parametric dimensions that are used in sketches to construct the parts can also be used to detail the part.

1. Open c2–18.idw from the Drawings\Chapter 2 folder, making certain that the 2012 Essentials project file is active.

2. Zoom in on the rotated auxiliary view in the upper left of the drawing.

3. Right-click in the drawing view, and select Retrieve Dimensions from the context menu; or, select the Retrieve tool from the Dimension panel of the Annotate tab.

4. Once the Retrieve Dimensions dialog is open, select one of the tapped holes in the drawing view.

   The drill diameter of the holes and the diameter of the bolt circle will be displayed. When Inventor needs more information from the user, an icon will appear in the dialog with a red arrow. Often, the button will be depressed, and selection can be made immediately. Sometimes, you will need to select the button to begin picking entities.

5. Click the icon to select dimensions, and click the 90mm diameter of the bolt circle.

6. Click OK to close the dialog and include the dimension in the drawing view, as shown in Figure 2.31.

FIGURE 2.31 Reusing model dimensions in the drawing view

Associativity

The ability to create drawing views and annotate them should be clear by this point. What I haven't done is demonstrated the advantage of creating 2D parts from 3D geometry. When you edit a 3D part, any change is reflected in the 2D drawing.

This capability is key for productivity and really demonstrates the final value of creating 2D drawings from 3D parts. The technique used in this exercise is not the most common way of making the changes, but it does show a technique that is available.

1. Open c2-19.idw from the Drawings\Chapter 2 folder, making certain that the 2012 Essentials project file is active.

2. Zoom in on the rotated auxiliary view in the upper left of the drawing.

3. Right-click the 90mm diameter dimension. Because it is a model dimension, it will offer a special option.

4. Select Edit Model Dimension from the context menu.

5. In the Edit Dimension dialog, change the value to **85mm**, and click the green check mark to make the change; close the dialog. See Figure 2.32 for the results.

FIGURE 2.32 Any change to the geometry of the model is reflected in the drawing views.

The drawing view that you were focused on is not the only view that was changed. All views of this part on all pages in any drawing file will be updated based on this change.

THE ESSENTIALS AND BEYOND

There are countless ways to approach creating your detail drawings, and Inventor maintains Autodesk's legacy of flexibility but adds a level of simplicity that's not possible when creating 2D drawings from scratch.

ADDITIONAL EXERCISES

▶ Experiment with all the tools on the Place Views tab.

▶ Use DWG templates to create drawings that can be read using AutoCAD.

▶ Work with individual dimensions and dimension sets to see what method you might typically want to use.

▶ Try breaking the alignment of the section view to see that it still maintains its definition.

Learning the Essentials of Part Modeling

Part modeling is typically the primary focus when beginning to learn Autodesk Inventor 2012. The tools involved are the ones you will spend a majority of your time using, but they are pretty straightforward.

In this chapter, you will look at the most commonly used tools and understand how to construct one of the most challenging things you can do with Inventor, the parametric sketch. It is challenging because, unlike most features, there aren't many limitations. You will have to use your judgment about what to include and exclude from the sketch. As you gain experience with your designs, this will become second nature.

Here is the process of beginning a new part, in shorthand: create a sketch that defines the most important elements of the part's geometry, and then make that sketch into a 3D shape. Along the way, you'll add features that complete the part. That really is how simple the process is.

▶ **Defining a parametric sketch**

▶ **Creating 3D geometry: The parametric solid model**

Defining a Parametric Sketch

The term *parametric* refers to the process of using values (parameters of the object being designed) to define the size, location, and other properties of the object's features. In the sketch, this is most easily recognized in the dimensions that you add, but there are other types of constraints that add control to the geometry.

In this chapter, you will create the part shown in Figure 3.1. Let's begin by constructing your first sketch. You will control the sketch by placing dimensional constraints (size values) as well as geometric constraints (vertical, parallel, and so on).

FIGURE 3.1 The 30-degree adapter you will build

Creating a Sketch

When Inventor begins a new part file, it will start in the sketching environment by default.

1. Open the New File dialog from the Application menu, the Quick Access toolbar, or the Launch panel of the Get Started tab.

2. In the Metric tab, double-click the Standard (mm).ipt template.

    Notice that the new file already has a Sketch tab active and that Sketch1 is active in the Browser.

3. Right-click, and start the Line tool in the marking menu or find it in the Draw panel.

4. Begin the line segment by clicking below and to the left of the projected center point (the green dot) of the part.

5. Begin moving your cursor to the right. You will see a dimension appear for the length of the line and the angles as you move around.

6. Position your cursor to the right of the part center with the line horizontal.

    As you are sketching, icons will appear that look like the constraint icons in the Constrain panel. In this case, the Horizontal constraint icon will appear when the line is horizontal.

For clarity, I have disabled the Grid, Axes, and Minor Axes options in the Application Options dialog's Sketch tab.

7. The dimension value is highlighted, so type **60** to specify the length value for the line (Figure 3.2).

FIGURE 3.2 Entering a dimension value will lock in that size.

8. Press the Tab key to set that length value. When your line is horizontal, click the mouse to create the segment. Note that the Line tool is ready to create another segment.

9. Enter a value of **30** for the next segment, and use the Tab key to set the angle to **100**.

10. Click in the Design window to place the new segment, and notice the new dimensions that appear, as shown in Figure 3.3.

FIGURE 3.3 Adding values to dimensions creates the parametric dimensions on the fly.

11. Move your cursor to the left. Look for an icon that shows the new segment is parallel to the first. Move to the left until you also see a dotted "inference" line that aligns you with the starting point of the first segment.

12. Click the mouse when your line is parallel with an aligned endpoint, as shown in Figure 3.4.

FIGURE 3.4 If you don't specify a dimension value, no dimension is added to the sketch.

13. Now move your cursor down to the original start point. The point will highlight, and a glyph will appear, showing that there will be a connection called *coincidence* between the points, which means the endpoints of the line segments are attached to one another and will move together.

14. Click the mouse to connect the lines. See Figure 3.5.

FIGURE 3.5 The initial shape is done.

15. Press the Esc key to finish the Line tool. You can also select Finish Sketch from the marking menu.

Now that you have your initial shape, you can modify it to be the correct shape and size. Getting your sketch close to correct is good, but as long as you have the elements you need, you can modify it to be correct.

Adding and Editing Geometric Constraints

Creating the sketch added sizes and created relationships between sketch elements. At this point, you could easily make this into a solid model.

What you really need, though, is a square centered on the center point of the part. Now, you will make modifications to fix this and see some other options along the way:

1. Continue using the drawing from the previous exercise or open c3-01.ipt from the Parts\Chapter 3 folder, making certain that the *2012 Essentials* project file is active.

2. Right-click in the Design window, and select Show All Constraints. You can also press the F8 key to do this. Figure 3.6 shows the result.

F I G U R E 3 . 6 You can display the geometric constraints of the sketch as well as the dimensional.

This will display the relationships between the elements. The yellow blocks at the corners represent coincidence.

3. Hover over the Perpendicularity icon in the lower-left corner, and it will highlight the segments that are constrained.

4. Hover over the other icons to see what constraints exist beyond the dimension values. Be sure to include the icons in the corners, which will expand.

5. Press F9, or right-click and select Hide All Constraints to turn them off.

6. Select the angular dimension.

7. Once it is highlighted, press the Delete key to remove it.

8. Right-click in the Design window and select See All Degrees Of Freedom to see the display shown in Figure 3.7.

FIGURE 3.7 Showing the degrees of freedom of the sketch can help you understand where to add constraints.

This will display bold, red arrows showing how elements of the sketch can still be moved with a simple click and drag. As you apply constraints, these degrees of freedom will disappear. You can also see how many constraints need to be added to have a fully constrained part on the right end of the status bar.

9. Click the upper-right corner of the sketch, and drag it to the left. Notice how the length still remains 30mm. You can move other elements as well.

10. In the Constrain panel, find the Perpendicular Constraint tool and start it.

11. Click the top and right lines to apply the constraint.

The curved arrow will disappear, showing that the angle of the right line can no longer change.

12. Find and start the Horizontal constraint.

13. Click the center point of the sketch, and then move to the middle of one of the vertical lines.

14. When its midpoint highlights (turns to a green dot), click it, and the two points will align to one another.

You will also see a dramatic effect on the degrees of freedom of the sketch. A more subtle change will be a difference in the color of the lines that are now constrained.

15. Find and start the Vertical constraint.

16. Select the center point and the midpoint of one of the horizontal lines.

All the degrees of freedom of the sketch will disappear, and the status bar will report that the sketch is fully constrained, as shown in Figure 3.8.

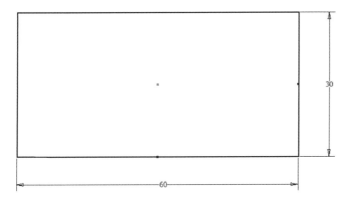

FIGURE 3.8 The fully constrained sketch

17. Press the Esc key to end the Vertical constraint tool.

When you're creating sketches for your own geometry, you won't create them as loosely as this exercise. It is also important that you create your sketches to be the approximate size of the finished shape. This will save you additional editing when you begin editing the dimensions.

Editing Dimensions

This is the step where you will begin to see the value of parametrics. Creating things to be the right size today doesn't mean you won't need to change that size tomorrow. That is why approximating the geometry and adding precise dimensions that change it is a great workflow.

Certification
Objective

1. Double-click the 30 dimension to edit its value.

2. When the Edit Dimension dialog appears, change the value to 40, and click the green check mark to make the change.

3. Edit the same dimension, and instead of entering a value, click the 60 dimension to link the two together.

4. Click the check mark to accept the new value.

Note that the value has been set to d0, and an *fx* now appears in front of its value in the sketch. The d0 value refers to the name of the dimension it is linked to, and fx denotes that this dimension is based on another parameter.

5. Double-click the bottom dimension to edit it.

6. Enter the value of **Width=100**, and accept it.

This will change the name of that dimension from d0 to Width and update the sketch to show the new size. You may have to zoom out to see the sketch now.

7. Double-click the vertical dimension to see that it now refers to a value of Width since it must remain associated to the other dimension regardless of what changed.

8. Close the Edit Dimension dialog without changing anything.

9. Select the vertical dimension again, and delete it.

10. Locate the Equal constraint or press the = key, and select first a horizontal and then a vertical line to link their sizes.

11. After the sketch updates, use the marking menu to select Finish Sketch or select it from the Exit panel on the Sketch tab.

Once the sketch is finished, the Ribbon will update to show the Model tab, and the sketch will move to the Home view. This doesn't happen if you've orbited the sketch while you were editing it.

Creating a Pattern in a Sketch

Using a pattern to replicate sketch geometry is much faster than creating and dimensioning separate instances of the geometry.

Certification
Objective

1. Open the c03-02.ipt file from the Parts\Chapter 3 folder, making certain that the *2012 Essentials* Project File is active.

2. Double-click the icon next to Sketch1 in the Browser.

3. Click the Rectangular Pattern tool in the Pattern panel of the Sketch tab.

4. When the Rectangular Pattern dialog opens, pick the circle in the sketch for the geometry which will be duplicated.

5. Pick the selection icon for Direction 1 and then pick the bottom horizontal line in the sketch to set the direction.

6. Set the count for Direction 1 to 5 and the Spacing to **20 mm**.

7. Pick the selection icon for Direction 2 and pick the vertical line on the left.

8. Click the Flip icon to change the direction of the second pattern direction.

9. Set the count for Direction 2 to **5** and the Spacing to **20 mm** as shown in Figure 3.9.

FIGURE 3.9 Building a pattern of holes

10. Click OK to create the pattern.

The two directions in the Rectangular pattern do not need to be perpendicular to each other. They can even be collinear going in opposite directions.

Using Sketches for Concept Layout

Certification
Objective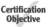

Using 2D to test a concept is not new. Using a combination of parametric dimensions and sketch constraints can bring this idea up to date and offer quick changes to test an idea.

1. Open the c03-03.ipt from the Parts\Chapter 3 folder, making certain that the *2012 Essentials* Project File is active.

2. Double click the sketch icon in the browser to activate the Linkage sketch.

   Under the sketch in the browser you will see three instances of Sketch Block named Link 1 and two circles and a line that also reside in the sketch.

   ⌨ Create Block **3.** In the Layout panel of the Sketch tab click the Create Block tool.

   Adding entities to a Sketch Block allows you to group the sketch elements together without creating a series of sketches.

4. Click the pink circles and line

5. Pick the Insert Point select tool and then pick the center of the right circle.

6. Enter **Link 2** for the Block Name and click OK to create a new Sketch Block.

7. Click the center point of the circle on the right of the new block and drag it to the center point at the top of the vertical red bar on the right (see Figure 3.10) and release when it shows it is creating a constraint between centers.

FIGURE 3.10 Dragging sketch constraints between sketch blocks

8. Click and drag the center of the new block on the left to the center point of the vertical bar on the left.

9. Now click and drag one of those endpoints to see how the linkage moves.

10. Double-click one of the instances of Link 1 in the Design window.

11. When the sketch geometry appears, click the **50 mm** dimension and change it to **80 mm**.

Finish Edit Block

12. Click the Finish Edit Block icon on the Exit panel of the Sketch tab.

13. Move the links using the new part length.

Sketch blocks can be simple or complex as needed to help you predict how a mechanism will work. Sketch blocks are quick and the sketch can be used to build 3D data and help to speed the development of an assembly.

Understanding Sketch Alerts

Occasionally a sketch may be missing constraints that will affect your ability to create geometry. Inventor includes tools that will help you to locate and correct these missing constraints.

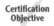
Certification
Objective

1. Open c03-04.ipt from the Parts\Chapter 3 folder, making certain that the *2012 Essentials* Project File is active.

Extrude

2. Click the Extrude tool on the Model tab in the Create panel.

A preview of a surface model will appear. Inventor will extrude a surface when there is no closed profile. Even though the dimensions create an intact perimeter, Inventor needs line and arc endpoints to be coincident to form a completely closed sketch.

Instead of stopping the command the user can force the issue by telling Inventor that you want to create a solid.

3. In the Extrude tool click the Solid option in the Output group.

This will cause an error to be presented in the dialog. It will also activate an icon at the bottom of the dialog with a red cross. This is called the Sketch Doctor.

4. Click the Examining Profile Problems tool.

The message in the Sketch Doctor - Examine dialog will tell you about the open loop in the profile.

5. Click Next to continue.

6. In the Sketch Doctor - Treat dialog (Figure 3.11) click the Close Loop treatment option and the click Finish.

FIGURE 3.11 Selecting the treatment option for sketch problems

A new Redundant Points dialog (Figure 3.12) will appear and in the Design window these points will be highlighted.

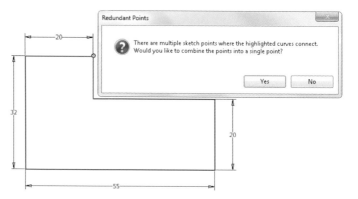

FIGURE 3.12 The problem points are highlighted in the Design window

7. Click Yes to combine the points and make a closed sketch.

8. Click OK to close the dialog informing you that the sketch is now closed.

9. Start the Dimension tool and pick the green line in the sketch.

10. Pick a place to position the new dimension.

This will launch the dialog shown in Figure 3.13, warning you that adding the dimension will over constrain the sketch. This means that this new dimension is redundant. The dialog will give you the option of just canceling the placement of the dimension or placing it as an associative dimension.

FIGURE 3.13 A dialog will warn you if you are placing dimensions that cannot be used in the sketch

11. Click Accept to place the driven dimension in the sketch.

The power of placing geometric and dimensional constraints can quickly turn against you if you're unable to overcome mistakes. The Sketch Doctor and warnings regarding an over-constrained state help you keep working by fixing the problems and moving on.

Now, it's time to start making some 3D geometry.

Creating 3D Geometry: The Parametric Solid Model

In Chapter 2, you created 2D drawings from an existing solid model. You also made a change to that model that updated all of the drawing views by accessing the value of a dimension. That dimension was part of a sketch that defined the placement of features also based on parameters.

These parameters can be as simple as a fillet radius, or they can be based on the clearance hole standards for a particular type of fastener. Either way, when you work with a parametric model, you open up a new world of control over your designs.

Now, you have a sketch that represents the geometry from which you'd like to make your first feature. When you start a part, the first feature you create will be a sketched feature, most commonly an extrusion or a revolved feature.

 N O T E   The following modeling exercises will describe the procedures using the mini-toolbar and in-window tools. All the tools and options are also available in the Ribbon or in dialog boxes.

Extruding the Base Feature

Certification
Objective 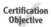 The first feature in a part is referred to as the *base feature.* It is usually beneficial to define as much geometry as possible with the base feature.

1. Continue using the drawing from the previous exercise, or open
   c3-05.ipt from the Parts\Chapter 3 folder, making certain that
   the *2012 Essentials* project file is active.

2. In the Design window, click one of the sketch lines. As you do so,
   commonly used tools will appear.

 3. Click the Create Extrude tool on the left.

4. An initial preview of the extrusion will appear with a mini-toolbar
   appearing in the middle of the screen and a full dialog. Both show
   the current value for the extrusion distance.

> If you want to
> reduce the size of
> the dialog, you can
> click the arrow icon
> at the bottom of
> the dialog. Moving
> near the dialog will
> expand it temporar-
> ily, or you can click
> the down arrow
> while the dialog is
> expanded to lock it
> into full size again.

5. Click and drag the arrow at the end of the extrusion until the value in
   the mini-toolbar reads 15; or, highlight the value in the mini-toolbar,
   and enter 15. See Figure 3.14.

FIGURE 3.14 The option in the dialog updates while
you drag the direction arrow.

6. Moving near the mini-toolbar will also display additional options. Click
   the green check mark, which represents OK to create the feature.

The extrusion is generated on the screen, and a feature named Extrusion1 appears in the Browser.

Setting the Material and Color

You can also do things such as establish the material your part is made from to monitor its weight or inertial properties. You can even pick a specific color if you like.

 1. In the Browser, right-click the part icon at the top, and select iProperties from the context menu.

2. In the dialog, go to the Physical tab, and use the Material drop-down to select Cast Iron as the material. Notice that it updates the mass; make note of what that value is.

3. Click OK to accept this change.

4. In the Quick Access toolbar, locate the drop-down that shows As Material for the part's color. Select a color you like, and feel free to change it whenever you want.

Setting the material from which the parts will be made from is very important for estimating costs, weight, and so on. Color changes can help highlight components or make them appear more realistic.

At various times while working in this and other chapters, you should go back to the Physical tab and update the properties to see how changes are affecting these values.

Adding an Edge Fillet

One of the best practices for modeling is not to include incidental fillets in the sketch. It is better and easier to place fillet features to the model instead.

1. Continue using the drawing from the previous exercise, or open c3-06.ipt from the Parts\Chapter 3 folder, making certain that the *2012 Essentials* project file is active.

2. Click one of the short, vertical edges.

3. When the icons appear for the most common options, select the Create Fillet tool.

4. Click the remaining three short edges.

▶

It is possible to click faces and edges through a part by hovering over their location. You can also orbit while in a command without interrupting it.

5. An arrow icon will follow your selections. Drag it to create a 14mm radius on the four corners, as shown in Figure 3.15.

FIGURE 3.15 The fillets will develop as you drag them.

6. A quick right-click and drag to the right will give you the same effect as clicking OK.

Fillets are very common, and in Chapter 7, I cover additional techniques for placing them. It is also possible to place fillets with several different values at the same time.

Reusing Sketch Geometry

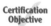
Certification
Objective

On a complex part where there are many features created from the same base plane, you can sometimes use a single sketch to define more than one feature.

1. Continue using the drawing from the previous exercise, or open c3-07.ipt from the Parts\Chapter 3 folder, making certain that the *2012 Essentials* project file is active.

2. Click the small + icon in the browser next to Extrusion1. This will expose the sketch that was consumed by that feature.

3. Right-click the sketch, and select Share Sketch from the context menu.

The sketch will now appear both under and above the extrusion feature. It will also become visible in the Design window so other features can use it. In this case, you need to add to it first.

4. Click the top face of the extrusion. When you do, icons will appear for Edit Extrude, Edit Sketch, and Create Sketch.

5. Click Edit Sketch.

6. The Center Point Circle tool is on the marking menu and in the Draw panel. Start it, and draw a circle based on the part center point with a diameter of 40.

7. Draw a larger circle using the same center with no diameter dimension; then press the Esc key to stop the Circle tool. See Figure 3.16.

Your sketch may rotate so that you're looking directly at it. I have disabled this feature in the application options to show that sketches can be edited in this way as well.

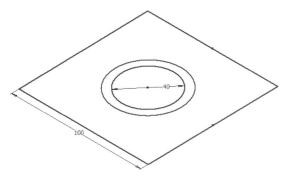

FIGURE 3.16 Adding new geometry to an existing sketch

8. Now start the Dimension tool, and click the two circles. This will create a dimension showing the distance between the perimeters. Set it to 8, and finish the Dimension tool.

9. Finish editing the sketch.

Now, you will create more sketch geometry that is based on the center of the part. This is why it can be very useful to think about centering a part on the origin planes.

1. Continue using the drawing from the previous exercise, or open c3-08.ipt from the Parts\Chapter 3 folder, making certain that the *2012 Essentials* project file is active.

2. Expand the Origin folder in the browser.

3. Click the XZ plane. This will highlight the plane in the Browser and present you with the Create Sketch icon.

4. Click the icon to start a new sketch on that plane.

5. The center point of the part will automatically project into the new sketch, but it will be difficult to see it from the top.

6. Right-click in the Design window, and select Slice Graphics or press the F7 key to remove some of the part to expose the new sketch.

7. Start a new line at the part center point, going straight up roughly 30mm.

8. Move your mouse to the endpoint of the new line just created, click, and drag an arc tangent to the last line, as shown in Figure 3.17.

FIGURE 3.17 A tangent arc can be created using the Line tool.

9. Now add a straight line that is tangent to the arc. A glyph will appear that shows when the line is tangent. Press the Esc key to finish the Line tool.

10. Select Create Dimension from the marking menu.

11. Click the arc, and set the radius to **100**.

12. Click the second straight line, right-click, and click Aligned to dimension the overall length of the line to 30.

13. Now click the first line and then the second line. Because they are not parallel, an angular dimension will appear. Position it as shown in Figure 3.18, and set its value to **30**.

14. Finish the sketch.

Getting feedback on constraint conditions like tangency during the sketching process helps you know you're getting the control you need from the beginning.

FIGURE 3.18 Adding new geometry to an existing sketch

Connecting to Other Sketch Data

Linking to geometry in other sketches helps keep things in line.

1. Continue using the drawing from the previous exercise, or open c3-09.ipt from the Parts\Chapter 3 folder, making certain that the *2012 Essentials* project file is active.

2. Start a new sketch on the XZ plane.

3. Use the Project Geometry tool on the marking menu or from the Draw panel, and click the top 30mm line to link it into the current sketch.

4. In the Draw panel, expand the Rectangle tool, and start the Three Point Rectangle tool.

5. Start the rectangle at the top end of the projected line. Drag to the right so it is perpendicular to the projected line, and click.

6. Drag the third point down approximately 10mm, as shown in Figure 3.19.

FIGURE 3.19 A three-point rectangle can be placed at any initial angle.

7. Stop the Rectangle tool by pressing the Esc key or by selecting Done from the marking menu.

The new rectangle will eventually be revolved so that even though you are looking only at the side, it would be best to dimension it as its final diameter. Using the Centerline override, you can get the dimension tool to recognize this.

8. Click the short line that is collinear with the 30mm line.

If the long line highlights instead of the new, short one, wait two seconds, and a pop-up will appear, allowing you to click the overlapping edge you want to use. Select the short one.

9. In the Format panel, click the Centerline override.

10. Start the Dimension tool and click first the centerline and then the opposite end of the rectangle.

11. Place the dimension, and set its value to 110mm. See Figure 3.20.

12. Place a 10mm dimension for the thickness by picking long lines at the top and bottom of the rectangle.

FIGURE 3.20 A linear diameter can be placed in the sketch.

13. Finish the Dimension tool and editing the sketch.

Let's keep building on your part. Moving forward, you will be switching files because some of the basics will be prepared for you so you can focus on new things.

Creating a Revolve Feature

For many users, revolving is the second most commonly used sketching feature after extruding. If you make turned components, it may be your number-one tool.

Certification Objective

1. Open c3-10.ipt from the Parts\Chapter 3 folder, making certain that the *2012 Essentials* project file is active.

2. Click an element of the rectangle in Sketch3, and choose the Create Revolve icon.

3. Because there are multiple visible sketches with more than one complete profile, you will need to click the shape of the rectangle.

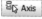 **4.** Now click the Axis icon on the mini-toolbar to let Inventor know you're done selecting profiles.

5. Select the centerline that is in line with the 30mm dimension.

This will immediately produce a preview of the new feature (Figure 3.21). Note that an arrow allowing for the changing of the angle is available.

6. Finish the Revolve tool by pressing the Esc key.

Now, you can complete the main features of the part.

FIGURE 3.21 A preview of the Revolve tool

Creating Sweep Features

In this exercise you'll create two features. The first will establish the outer portion and will be hollow. The second will cut through the top and bottom plates.

1. Open c3-11.ipt from the Parts\Chapter 3 folder, making certain that the *2012 Essentials* project file is active.

2. Start the Sweep tool from the Create panel on the Model tab.

Because there is more than one option, the button for profile selection in the dialog will have a red arrow. This means Inventor needs you to make a selection.

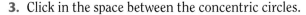

3. Click in the space between the concentric circles.

4. Because Optimize For Single Selection is selected, Inventor now wants you to click the path. Select the part of the lines and arc going to the disk on top, as shown in Figure 3.22.

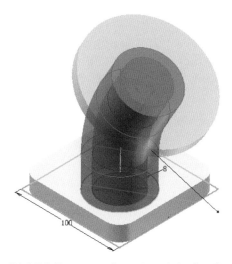

FIGURE 3.22 A preview of the first Sweep tool

5. Click OK in the dialog box to finish the tool.

This consumed the sketch that you used for the sweep path.

6. Expand the Sweep feature in the Browser.

7. Right-click, and make Sketch2 Visible.

8. Start the Sweep tool, and use the inner circle for your profile.

9. Select the same path sketch.

10. Set your option in the dialog to Cut.

11. Click OK to create the feature.

12. Turn off the visibility of the two sketches. Figure 3.23 shows the part at this point.

FIGURE 3.23 Most of the part is finished.

By sharing a sketch that defines more than one feature, you can control the relationships between the various sketches. Now, you will focus on adding a few placed features to complete the part.

Placing Concentric Holes

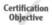
Certification
Objective

Hole features are critical geometry, and having the standards included in Inventor makes it easier to add them.

1. Open c3-12.ipt from the Parts\Chapter 3 folder, making certain that the *2012 Essentials* project file is active.

2. Start the Hole tool from the marking menu or the Modify panel of the Model tab.

3. In the Hole dialog, set the placement to Concentric.

4. Select the top face of the bottom extrusion as the plane for the hole to begin.

5. Click the nearest fillet face for the concentric reference.

6. Set the hole type to Clearance for an ISO 24017 Hex Head Cap Screw with an M10 thread and Normal fit. See Figure 3.24.

FIGURE 3.24 A clearance hole can size itself based on standards.

7. Make sure the Termination setting is Through All.

8. Click OK to place the hole feature.

There are several ways to make the bolt pattern across the bottom plate. You could repeat the Hold command for each corner or do a rectangular pattern. Since the first feature is centered on the z-axis of the part, you can use a circular pattern.

Creating a Circular Pattern

Now, you will make three more holes the easy way, and they will be associative to any change to the original hole:

1. Open the c3-13.ipt file making certain that the *2012 Essentials* project file is active..

2. Select the Circular Pattern tool from the Pattern panel of the Model tab.

3. In this case, you only need to select the Hole1 feature for the features selection.

4. In the dialog, click the Rotation Axis button.

5. Expand the Origin folder in the Browser if needed, and select Z Axis.

6. Set the value in the Placement field to 4, and check the preview.

7. When the preview shows new holes added to the other corners, click OK to create them. Figure 3.25 shows the adapter at this point.

FIGURE 3.25 Using pattern saves on repetition and helps prevent mistakes.

Now, you can place the final holes on the part.

Placing Sketched Holes

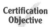
Certification
Objective

To create complex patterns of holes, you can develop a sketch that includes a number of hole centers or naturally occurring points. By selecting them, you can place many holes in a single feature.

1. Open c3-14.ipt from the Parts\Chapter 3 folder, making certain that the *2012 Essentials* project file is active.

The dotted lines and circle that appear in the sketch have an override applied to them: Construction. This prevents them from being recognized as profiles by the 3D features but allows them to be used to construct other things. In this case, you'll use them for the location of the center points for holes. The corners of the square have an override applied as well. This will make the Hole tool find them automatically.

2. Start the Hole tool. As mentioned, four locations will be selected.

3. Set the type to Tapped Hole, the thread type to ISO Metric profile, and the size to 10. Select the Full Depth check box for the threads.

4. Change the termination to To, and click the lower side of the cylindrical face so the holes stop there. See Figure 3.26.

5. Select OK to complete the hole.

Now that you have your holes, you need to add some fillets to the model.

FIGURE 3.26 Hovering over an obscured object will eventually cause a drop-down to appear, allowing you to select it.

Adding an Edge Fillet

Fillets are another critical feature in machine parts. There are many options, but for this chapter, you will focus on the edge fillet and placing fillets of more than one radius using a single feature.

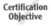
Certification
Objective

1. Open c3-15.ipt from the Parts\Chapter 3 folder, making certain that the *2012 Essentials* project file is active.

2. Click the round edge where the sweep meets the extrude. This will present a choice of the Fillet or Chamfer tool.

3. Select the Create Fillet tool.

4. Add the edge where the sweep feature meets the revolved feature.

5. Drag or enter a radius value of **6**.

6. In the Fillet dialog, click where the words *Click to add* appear.

7. This will add a new row for using another radius size. Click the radius value of the new row, and change it from 6 to 2.

8. Click the outer edges of the extrusion and revolved features near the first set of fillets. See Figure 3.27.

9. Click OK to finish applying the fillets.

FIGURE 3.27 You can place fillets with different radii in one fillet feature.

The option of placing a fillet or a chamfer on a sharp edge makes perfect sense, so it is great that you have access to the option by simply picking a sharp edge.

Applying a Chamfer

Chamfers and fillets have similar locations, but their options are quite different. For this exercise, you will use two of the three options.

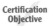

1. Open c3-16.ipt from the Parts\Chapter 3 folder, making certain that the *2012 Essentials* project file is active.

2. Click the sharp edge on the interior of the revolved feature.

 3. Select the Create Chamfer tool. The default is 45 degrees. Drag the Chamfer value to 2mm, as shown in Figure 3.28.

F I G U R E 3 . 2 8 Applying a chamfer to the model edge

4. Finish the chamfer.

5. Rotate the part so you can see the bottom.

6. Select the sharp inside edge, and select the Chamfer tool.

7. Set the option to Two Distances (you may have to reselect the edge).

8. Set the first value to 2 and the second distance to 4.

9. Finish the chamfer. See Figure 3.29 for the finished adapter.

FIGURE 3.29 Adding the second chamfer with two different sizes

THE ESSENTIALS AND BEYOND

There are many more options in part modeling that will be covered in Chapter 7. In this chapter, you worked with the basic tools that will allow many people to do most of the things they need to do. You may also have noticed that the tools do a good job of prompting you for the things they need to help you.

ADDITIONAL EXERCISES

▶ Try modeling the base with the Polygon tool.

▶ Explore whether using an extruded circle is more appealing to you than using the Revolve tool.

▶ Try modifying the angular dimension on the sweep path sketch to see the effect.

▶ Experiment with different types of holes to see how they change with different fasteners.

Putting Things in Place with Assemblies

Not many people need to work on parts that exist on their own. Working with assemblies is not only necessary; in many ways, Inventor prefers to work with assemblies.

To become really proficient with Inventor's assembly environment, you must understand how to use assembly constraints and when to use which ones. Once you're familiar with the tools, it is best to think about how things fit together from a more elemental standpoint.

▶ **Creating an assembly**

▶ **Understanding grounded components**

▶ **Applying assembly constraints**

▶ **Working with the content center**

▶ **Using the bolted connection generator**

▶ **Saving time with the assemble tool**

Creating an Assembly

To create an assembly, you follow the same basic process as beginning any other type of file in Inventor. Starting a new assembly file will change the Ribbon to display tools that you need for the assembly process.

1. Open the New dialog in Inventor, navigate to the Metric template tab, and start a new assembly using the Standard (mm).iam template.

2. Select Place Component from the marking menu or the Component panel of the Assemble tab.

3. Go to the Parts folder and then to Chapter 4; double-click the c4-01.ipt file and click OK.

The component will appear in the assembly immediately, and as you move your cursor, you will see that part follow, though it is faded. This is Inventor allowing you to place multiple instances of the component in your assembly.

4. Press the Esc key to finish placing components.

5. Orbit your assembly so that you can see the Top, Front, and Right faces of the ViewCube.

6. Begin placing another component in the assembly, this time selecting the c4-02.ipt file from the same folder.

7. After placing one instance, end the command (see Figure 4.1 for reference).

FIGURE 4.1 Placing components into a new assembly

8. Set this point of view to be your new Home view.

Take a moment to look at your Browser. The components you placed appear just as if you'd placed views in a drawing or features in a part. You will see the name of the part displayed, followed by a colon and an additional number. This number denotes which instance of the component you are looking at.

Understanding Grounded Components

The first component placed in an assembly is referred to as the *base component* and, as in the real world, should be the component that the largest number of other components are attached to or rely upon for their foundation.

In the Browser, notice a thumbtack icon overlaying the cube icon that represents the part. This thumbtack means the component is *grounded*, which means you don't need to constrain the base part to the coordinate system of the assembly file. Any or all components can be grounded, and the base component can be "ungrounded" if you want to be able to reorient it in the assembly.

Applying Assembly Constraints

The purpose of constraining components together in an assembly is to mimic the behavior of components in the real world. The constraints you apply do this by removing degrees of freedom from the components. Although it is not necessary to remove all the degrees of freedom, you will need to remove as many as needed to properly position the part. Inventor has relatively few constraint tools, but some of them can be used in many ways.

There are four tabs in the Place Constraint dialog: Assembly, Motion, Transitional, and Constraint Set. Each accesses tools that offer different ways to solve your assembly. The selections area on each tab and with each type will offer buttons with different colors that are reflected in the assembly as you select the entities. In this section, you'll use exercises to better understand the most commonly used constraint tools.

The Assembly tab (Figure 4.2) offers four types of assembly constraint: Mate, Insert, Angular, and Tangent. Each offers at least two solutions. In addition, the Transitional tab offers its own constraint. For the most part, you will be able to see the options each constraint offers by looking at the icons for its solutions.

Certification Objective

◄

If you know you need three instances of a component, you can also drag an instance from the Browser into the Design window to place another.

Certification Objective

FIGURE 4.2 The Assembly tab of the Place Constraint dialog

The Mate Constraint

This tool has two primary options: a Mate solution and a Flush solution. Each will reposition components based on the selected geometry with the ability to apply an Offset value in the dialog that will create a gap or an interference between the component depending on whether the value is positive or negative and how the parts are aligned.

The Mate solution works on planes, axes, and points, and it behaves as though it puts these entities in opposition to one another. If you put a box on top of another box in the real world, you could say that the top of the lower box was pushing against the bottom of the upper one. In Inventor, this would be a Mate/Mate constraint.

First, you will use the Mate solution in your assembly:

1. Open the c4-01.iam from the Assemblies\Chapter 4 folder making certain that the *2012 Essentials* project file is active.

2. Launch the Constrain tool from the Position panel or from the marking menu.

3. Set Constraint Type to Mate, and leave Solution at its default (Mate).

4. In the Selection group, the button for 1 will be depressed. Click the blue face on the red part for the first selection.

5. Once the first object is clicked, the second one will be enabled. Click the blue face on the purple part.

 The two parts will automatically snap together (see Figure 4.3). You can turn this off by deselecting the Preview icon in the dialog.

FIGURE 4.3 The components will move into position as you apply constraints.

6. Click Apply in the dialog or right-click and select Apply from the context menu to create the first constraint and prepare for another.

7. Orbit your assembly, and select the yellow face of the red part and the yellow face of the purple part.

8. Click OK to place the constraint and close the tool.

9. Drag the purple part in the assembly. You can see that it is still able to slide from side to side.

The Flush solution works only on planes and controls the alignment of faces to one another.

1. Open the c4-02.iam from the Assemblies\Chapter 4 folder, making certain that the *2012 Essentials* project file is active.

2. Launch the Constrain tool from the Position panel or the marking menu.

3. Set Constraint Type to Mate, and set Solution to Flush.

4. Select the sides of the two components, as shown in Figure 4.4.

FIGURE 4.4 The Flush constraint aligns faces.

5. With Preview on, the components will align. Click OK to create the constraint.

The simple Mate constraint and its solutions cover the needs of many Inventor users. To better understand what constraints are missing in an assembly, you can use the Degrees of Freedom (DOF) tool.

Certification
Objective

DEGREES OF FREEDOM

As mentioned earlier in this chapter, Inventor uses the concept of degrees of freedom to describe what movement can be realized by a component. Unless a component is grounded or constrained, it has six degrees of freedom—three rotational and three translational around and along the x-, y-, and z-axes. As you apply constraints, the ability to move in particular directions will be removed.

The Insert Constraint

The Insert constraint is a hybrid, combining a Mate constraint on the axis and between the adjacent faces of curved edges. It has many uses, but it is most commonly used to put round parts in round holes.

1. Open the `c4-03.iam` from the `Assemblies\Chapter 4` folder, making certain that the *2012 Essentials* project file is active.

2. Switch the Ribbon to the View tab.

Degrees of Freedom

3. Click the Degrees Of Freedom tool in the Visibility panel.

   An icon will appear on the purple part, showing that it has all six degrees of freedom.

4. Launch the Constrain tool from the Assemble tab in the Position panel or the marking menu.

5. Set Constraint Type to Insert, and leave Solution set to Opposed.

6. Select the circular edge of the hole on the purple part's flat face, and then select the circular edge of the hole on the red part, as shown in Figure 4.5.

7. When the parts are aligned, click OK.

   The DOF icon has now changed to show one remaining rotation of freedom.

8. Drag the purple part to see how it moves.

Being able to exercise the remaining degrees of freedom is not limited to a single component. You can use this to show how a mechanism works.

F I G U R E 4 . 5 Applying constraints does not automatically restrict all movement.

The Angular Constraint

There are three solutions for the Angular constraint, allowing the flexibility to, for example, set the axis of rotation apart from the components, along with other options that give less control. For this exercise, you will use the most precise solution, the Explicit Reference Vector tool:

1. Open the c4-04.iam from the Assemblies\Chapter 4 folder, making certain that the *2012 Essentials* project file is active.

2. Launch the Constrain tool from the Assemble tab in the Position panel or the marking menu.

3. Set Constraint Type to Angle, and make sure the solution type is set to Explicit Reference Vector.

4. For the first selection, click the narrow face on the side of the purple part.

5. For the second, click the face on the red part, as shown in Figure 4.6.

6. For the third, click the circular edge of the hole in the purple part.

FIGURE 4.6 Complexity in a constraint also adds reliability and stability.

7. Click OK to complete constraining of the purple part. The purple part can no longer rotate freely around the axis of the hole. This constraint is a great option for aligning faces that aren't flush on all sides.

The Tangent Constraint

When rounded faces need to stay in contact with other rounded faces, the Tangent constraint is often the only tool you will need. The constraint can have Inside or Outside solutions.

A good use for an Inside solution could be a pin following a curved face. An Outside could be rollers in contact with each other.

1. Open the c4-05.iam file from the Assemblies>Chapter 4 folder, making certain that the *2012 Essentials* project file is active.

2. Launch the Constrain tool from the Assemble tab in the Position panel or the marking menu.

3. Set Constraint Type to Tangent, and make sure the solution type is set to Outside.

4. Make your first selection, the blue, curved face on the orange part.

5. Make the second selection, the blue face on the fray part.

6. Click OK to bring the parts together.

7. Drag the orange part to see that the selected faces stay in contact.

The tangency added will follow the entire cylindrical face. If the face isn't a full cylinder, components constrained to it will follow the curvature of the face even if it moves off the end of it.

The Transitional Constraint

A fifth type of constraint is available on its own tab. Where the Assembly tab's Tangent constraint works well for simple curved faces, the Transitional constraint works best with changing faces such as cams.

1. Open the c4-06.iam file from the Assemblies\Chapter 4 folder, making certain that the *2012 Essentials* project file is active.

2. Launch the Constrain tool from the Assemble tab in the Position panel or the marking menu.

3. In the Place Constraint dialog, switch the tab to Transitional.

4. Click the yellow face on the orange part for the first selection.

5. Click the yellow face on the gray part for the second.

6. Click OK to accept the constraint. See Figure 4.7.

7. Drag the orange part to see how the Transitional and Tangent constraints work together to position the two components.

FIGURE 4.7 Different types of constraints can be combined to create useful models.

Adding a Transitional constraint offers more flexibility on the type of faces to which you can constrain than the Tangent constraint. Now, you will take a look at working with other data sources in the assembly.

Working with the Content Center

Place from Content Center

Many companies choose to limit the number of components by copying the ones they use to a custom library and limiting access to others.

During installation, you have the option of installing various types of standard components. Depending on the options you choose, you will have tens or hundreds of thousands of standard components available to you. Rather than creating part files for bolts, nuts, and so on, you can select them from a library.

1. Open the c4-07.iam from the Assemblies\Chapter 4 folder, making certain that the *2012 Essentials* project file is active.

2. Locate the Place From Content Center tool under the Place tool in the Component panel of the Assemble tab.

   This will launch the Place From Content Center (Figure 4.8) dialog, where you can locate many kinds of standard components.

FIGURE 4.8 Hundreds of thousands of standard components are built into Inventor.

3. Expand the categories by selecting Fasteners ➤ Bolts ➤ Hex Head.

4. Double-click ISO 4017.

   When the dialog disappears, a small preview of the fastener will appear. This preview is one of the available sizes for the bolt.

5. Hover over the edge of the hole in the purple part until the fastener resizes based on the hole's size.

6. After the bolt resizes, click when the edge of the hole highlights in red (Figure 4.9).

FIGURE 4.9 The fastener will resize based on an existing hole.

This will temporarily place a detailed preview the bolt in the hole.

7. Without ending the Constraint tool, change the Ribbon to the View tab, and change Visual Style to Shaded With Hidden Edges.

8. Click the Front face of the ViewCube to change the view.

9. Click and drag the red arrow at the tip of the bolt until it shows that the fastener size is at M10 × 35, and then release to set the length (Figure 4.10).

FIGURE 4.10 Fastener lengths can be changed in standard sizes.

10. Click the check mark in the AutoDrop mini-dialog to place the fastener in the assembly.

11. The tool will place the fastener and then offer to place another bolt. Press Esc to finish the command.

12. Switch to the Home view, and move the fastener to see that it is constrained to the hole.

The remaining degree of freedom on the fastener does not need to be removed. As long as the fastener is seated and aligned with the hole, it is effective in the assembly.

Using the Bolted Connection Generator

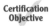
Certification Objective

The process of applying holes to components and then positioning fasteners is not difficult, but it does put the focus on the features of the software rather than the needs of the design.

The Bolted Connection Generator tool will allow you to put standard components into an assembly and use engineering calculations to be sure you are using the correct component.

1. Open the c4-08.iam from the Assemblies\Chapter 4 folder, making certain that the *2012 Essentials* project file is active.

2. Activate the Design tab on the Ribbon.

Bolted Connection

3. Start the Bolted Connection tool.

   The Bolted Connection Component Generator dialog (Figure 4.11) has a number of options, but it works very much like the Hole feature in a part model.

FIGURE 4.11 The Bolted Connection Component Generator dialog

4. In the Type group, set the hole type to Blind Connection Type.

5. For the start plane, use the yellow face of the purple part.

6. For Linear Edge 1, click the left edge of the yellow face. Refer to step 9 if you are prompted for a value for this dimension.

7. Click the bottom edge for Linear Edge 2.

8. You will be able to click Blind Start Plane where the two parts are in contact through the purple part.

9. Set the first dimension to 50mm by clicking the dimension, entering the value, and clicking the green check mark to close the dialog.

10. Set the second dimension to 15mm (Figure 4.12).

FIGURE 4.12 The dimensions locate the placement of the bolted connection.

11. In the Thread group, set the Thread class to ISO Metric Profile.

12. Set the diameter to 10mm.

13. Click where it says *Click to add a fastener* in the column on the right.

    After a short time, a list of bolts that will fit the hole as currently defined will appear. You can filter the list to see only those bolts of a single standard.

14. In the component selection pop-up, change Standard to ISO to filter the options. See Figure 4.13.

FIGURE 4.13 Filtering fasteners based on standards makes selection easier.

15. Click ISO 4017.

16. Change the view in the Design window to the Front view of the assembly.

17. Drag the red arrow at the end of the bolt until it shows you are placing an M10 × 35 bolt (Figure 4.14).

FIGURE 4.14 In a bolted connection, you can drag the hole depth and bolt length.

18. Click OK to finish the tool and OK again to approve the creation of a file.

19. Double-click the red part to see that a tapped hole has been added to it.

20. Click the Return tool at the end of the Ribbon to return to the assembly.

Placing fasteners using this tool saves time over placing holes in advance and using the Content Center. If the assembly changes, you may have to edit the bolted connection and click OK to update it. There are more Design Accelerator tools that I will review in Chapter 8.

Saving Time with the Assemble Tool

The Assemble tool works as a shell for many of the constraint tools. Based on the geometry you select, it will preview a constraint and allow you to select a different option or enter an offset or angle value using a mini-toolbar near the cursor.

Assemble

1. Open c4-09.iam from the Assemblies\Chapter 4 folder.

2. Start the Assemble tool from the Position panel of the Assemble tab.

3. Click the blue face of the purple part and then the blue face of the red part.

4. Click the Apply icon in the mini-toolbar to add this Mate/Mate constraint, and move to the next constraint.

5. Now select the yellow face on the purple part and the yellow face on the red part. Apply the constraint.

6. Now click the faces on the left of each part, and notice that the mini-toolbar shows that it will add a Mate/Flush constraint.

7. Click the OK button on the mini-toolbar to finish using the Assemble tool on the purple part.

8. Press the Enter key or the spacebar to start the Assemble tool again.

9. Click the underside of the bolt where the shaft meets the head.

10. Click the hole in the purple part, and click OK to place an Insert constraint between the bolt and the hole feature (Figure 4.15).

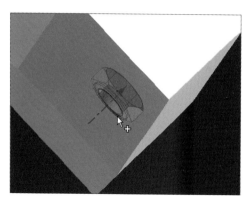

FIGURE 4.15 Clicking the second edge
will preview how the component will be repositioned.

The Assemble tool works well, and some experienced users are beginning to prefer it to using the traditional Place Constraint dialog. A couple of things to keep in mind are that you should not select a grounded component and you must restart the Assemble tool when you want to apply constraints to different parts.

The Essentials and Beyond

This chapter was designed to cover the basics of the assembly process of Inventor. Because of the simplicity of assemblies in Inventor, I covered the most commonly used tools and even some more advanced options.

Additional Exercises

▶ Review the components in the Content Center to see the extent of the options.

▶ Experiment with the Assemble tool for doing all of the exercises.

▶ Work with different fasteners and standards in the Bolted Connection Component Generator dialog.

Customizing Styles and Templates

Consistent standards improve communication and quality. Inventor comes with several standards from around the world that can be used as a foundation for constructing a company-specific standard. In Inventor, these standards are based on a collection of styles. In this chapter, you will see how to modify a few of these styles to understand the process.

Another easy way to create consistency among several users is to use templates with these styles preconfigured. These templates can even be configured to shortcut the process of defining a part, assembly, or drawing.

▶ **Working with styles**

▶ **Defining a new material**

▶ **Defining a title block**

▶ **Saving a new template**

▶ **Creating a quick-start template**

Working with Styles

A good strategy for making changes to styles is to start small and work your way up. Some style elements are shared as a resource for others. By establishing the properties of these resources, you can simplify configuring others above them.

Creating a Standard

You'll begin the process by creating a new standard, the specific settings of which will be defined in following exercises:

1. Open the file c5-01.idw from the Drawings\Chapter 5 folder. Make certain that the *2012 Essentials* project file is active.

2. Switch the Ribbon to the Manage tab, and from the Styles And Standards panel, launch the Style And Standard Editordialog (Figure 5.1).

FIGURE 5.1 The Style And Standard Editor controls all aspects of element display in a drawing.

3. In the top right of the dialog, set the drop-down to Local Styles.

   The column on the left of the dialog has the various categories of styles.

4. At the top of that column, right-click the Default Standard (ANSI-mm) standard, and select New Style from the context menu.

5. In the dialog, enter **Essentials (in)** as the name, and leave ANSI as the standard it is based on.

6. Click OK to create the standard.

7. In the dialog, double-click the new standard to make it active.

It is good practice to create your own style as you've begun doing, rather than just modifying an existing standard or style. That way, you can maintain the original, and it will allow more flexibility for developing templates without generating error messages.

Creating a New Object Default Set

Instead of lines, arcs, and circles, Inventor drawings consist of objects. A visible line is a different type of object than a hidden line, and therefore, it can be controlled independently. A standard refers to the Object Default Set to know how to display the elements of the drawing.

1. Continue using the open file or open c5-02.idw from the Drawings\ Chapter 5 folder, making certain that the *2012 Essentials* project file is active.

2. Start the Style and Standard Editor from the Styles and Standards panel of the Manage tab.

3. Expand the Object Defaults category in the column on the left.

4. Right-click the Object Defaults (ANSI-mm) style, and create a new style from the context menu.

5. Name the new style **Essentials (in)**, and click OK to create it.

Creating a new Object Default Set is optional when creating a new standard but makes it easier to keep standards unique. If you share an Object Default Set between standards, a change to it is reflected in all of them. The same will be true for many of the modifications made in this chapter, which are also essential stages in building a standard.

Defining a Text Style for Dimensions and Notes

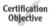

Certification
Objective

The text style is a perfect example of a style you create once that is used by more than one object type.

1. Continue using the open file, or open c5-03.idw from the Drawings\ Chapter 5 folder, making certain that the *2012 Essentials* project file is active.

2. Start the Styles and Standards Editor from the Styles And Standards panel of the Manage tab.

3. Expand the text styles, right-click the Note Text (ANSI) style, and select New Style from the context menu.

4. Set the new text style name to **Essentials Text**, and click OK to add it to the standard.

5. On the right side of the dialog, select Arial from the Font drop-down menu.

6. In the Paragraph Settings area, click the Color (By Layer) icon to open the Color dialog.

   Black is already selected in the dialog, but in the upper left of the dialog, the By Layer override is selected. This will change the color of the text to match whatever layer it is set to.

7. In the Color dialog, deselect the By Layer override, and click OK to set the color of the text to black. See Figure 5.2.

8. Click the Save icon at the top of the dialog to save the new standard in the drawing.

Now that you have a new text style, let's put it to work.

FIGURE 5.2 Changing the properties of the text used in dimensions and notes

Defining a New Dimension Style

There are many opinions on the proper way to display dimensions even in relatively well-defined standards like ISO. Now that you have your text style, you can practice creating a simple change to define a new dimension style.

1. Continue using the open file, or open c5-04.idw from the Drawings\ Chapter 5 folder, making certain that the *2012 Essentials* project file is active.

2. Start the Style and StandardsEditor from the Styles And Standards panel of the Manage tab.

3. Expand the dimension styles, right-click the Default (ANSI) style, and select New Style from the context menu.

4. Set the new dimension style name to **Essentials (in)**, and click OK to add it to the standard.

5. With the Essentials (in) standard highlighted, click the Text tab on the right side of the dialog.

6. Change Primary Text Style to the Essentials Text style using the drop-down menu.

7. In the Orientation group of the Text tab, change the first Linear option to display the text over the dimension line.

8. Change the Diameter and Radius options to display the dimension value in line with the leaders, as shown in Figure 5.3.

FIGURE 5.3 Changes to style options are represented in the icons.

9. Click the Save icon at the top of the dialog to save the new standard in the drawing.

Now, you can change some of the appearance settings that will have an effect on the other changes you've made.

Setting Layer Properties

Layer properties can be set from the Annotation tab in the drawing, but establishing them in the Style and Standards dialog is a good place, too.

1. Continue using the open file, or open the c5-05.idw from the Drawings\Chapter 5 folder, making certain that the *2012 Essentials* project file is active.

2. Start the Style and Standards Editor from the Styles And Standards panel of the Manage tab.

3. Expand the layers styles, and click the Dimension (ANSI) layer to see its properties and the properties of the other layers in the dialog window on the right.

You can change the layer properties displayed by clicking their current value and using a drop-down or a dialog box to change them. You can also click the light bulb icon to change the visibility of the layer.

4. Click the black rectangle in the Dimension (ANSI) row to open the Color dialog.

5. Click the dark blue swatch in the top row of the Color dialog, and click OK to set the color of the Dimension layer.

6. Now change the color of the Hatch (ANSI) layer to the lightest gray on the bottom row.

7. Finally, change the color of the Hidden (ANSI) layer to the light red on the top row.

You can also define custom colors in the dialog.

8. Click the Save icon at the top of the dialog to save the changes to the layers in the drawing.

Note that the changes to the layer styles have updated the drawing appearance.

Setting the Object Defaults

As mentioned earlier in the chapter, the Object Default Set controls the elements that determine the appearance of the elements in the drawing. The preceding exercise changed the colors of the layers that objects were on, but the Object Default Set determines the default layer and other styles that the objects use in the first place.

1. Continue using the open file, or open c5-06.idw from the Drawings\ Chapter 5 folder, making certain that the *2012 Essentials* project file is active.

2. Start the Style and Standards Editor from the Styles And Standards panel of the Manage tab.

3. Return to the Object Defaults style, and select the Essentials (in) style to display its setting on the right.

4. Click the Object Style column header twice to sort the styles alphabetically.

5. Scroll down using your wheel button or the slider bar on the right until you see the various dimension types that use the Default—mm (ANSI) dimension style.

   Clicking an object style or layer on the right will display a drop-down list of options.

To speed things up, you can click a drop-down and press the key of the first letter to jump to that value. In this case, you can press E.

6. Change all of the objects using the Default—mm (ANSI) style to the Essentials (in) style using the drop-down menu.

7. Save the changes by clicking the Save icon at the top of the dialog.

8. Change the Filter drop-down above the Object Type column to Model/View Objects.

9. Locate the objects using the Hidden Narrow (ANSI) layer, and change them to the Hidden (ANSI) layer.

10. Click the Save icon at the top of the dialog to save the changes to the Object Default Set.

11. Click Done to close the dialog box.

Now, you have control over the object that will be added to your drawing going forward. You can update the existing objects or even publish these changes to be used in other drawings or templates in the future.

Saving the Standard

The standard as you've defined it so far is ready to use as a starting point for further style definitions. Later, there may be elements that you change in a drawing that you may not want to reuse in others, or you may want to change certain properties in individual templates rather than globally changing the standard. So, this is a good time to save the standard in its current form.

1. Continue using the open file, or open c5-07.idw from the Drawings\ Chapter 5 folder, making certain that the *2012 Essentials* project file is active.

2. Click the Save tool in the Styles And Standards panel of the Manage tab.

3. In the Save Styles To Style Library dialog, set the value in the Save To Library? column to Yes only for the items you created. See Figure 5.4.

FIGURE 5.4 Saving the unique styles so that they can be reused

4. Click the Cancel button in the dialog.

The previous exercise shows you that you can still choose what changes get saved to the standard. Some of the changes will affect objects that are used in standard templates, and saving the changes made to the layers at this point may cause conflicts with the default templates. It is best for you to make these changes to your templates with your own preferences when the time comes.

Changing a Color Style

Styles exist in other file types as well. In part and assembly files, there are styles for the colors and materials and even lighting. Making changes to these styles is easy and a little more direct than changing the styles in a drawing.

1. Open c5-02.ipt from the Parts\Chapter 5 folder.

2. Start the Style and Standards Editor from the Styles And Standards panel of the Manage tab.

3. Expand the Color category in the column on the left.

Looking at the list, you will see that the active color will be in bold. This color may be displayed in the Quick Access toolbar if it is set to something other than As Material.

If you choose to reuse the same layer names as stock templates, you can edit the layer properties of the individual templates without editing the standard.

4. Right-click the current color, Blue Pastel, and select New Style from the context menu.

5. Set the new style name to Essentials Blue, and click OK to save it in the current file.

6. Double-click the new style to make it the active style for the part.

   On the Basic tab of the dialog, you can change the color properties to affect the appearance of the part. The Texture tab allows you to select an image file that will add a visual texture to the part. The Bump Map tab will allow you to apply a texture that will appear to alter the surface of the part.

7. In the Colors group on the Basic tab, click the Ambient icon to open the Color dialog.

8. Near the bottom of the Color dialog, click the Define Custom Colors icon to expand the color selection options:

   Define Custom Colors >>

9. Below the words *Custom colors* is a series of empty color fields. Click one to begin editing it.

10. In the lower right of the dialog, enter the following values for your new color:

   Red: 60

   Green: 80

   Blue: 140

11. Click the Add to Custom Colors button to make the changes to the selected color.

12. Click OK to change the ambient color of the part. See Figure 5.5.

▶

The Realistic Color section allows you to select a color that will be the same in several Autodesk applications.

FIGURE 5.5 Defining a custom color for parts

13. Back on the Basic tab, set the Shininess level to 60%.

14. Click Save at the top of the dialog and then Done at the bottom to close it.

The results may not be earth-shattering, but the ability to customize the colors can really add a nice touch for visualizing your designs.

Defining a New Material

In the iProperties section of the Physical tab, when you change the material of a part, it may change color as well, simply because a color is associated with a particular material. The two are, in fact, completely separate ideas.

The Material value is what the mass and inertial properties of the part are based upon, and although Inventor has many materials built in, it is common for users to want to add a specific one for their needs.

1. Continue using the open file, or open c5-03.ipt from the Parts\ Chapter 5 folder.

2. Start the Style and Standards Editor from the Styles And Standards panel of the Manage tab.

3. Expand the Material category in the column on the left.

4. Double-click Aluminum-6061.

5. Review the Material properties on the right, changing the Default Units drop-down to see the updated values.

6. Close the dialog by clicking the Done button at the bottom.

You can right-click a material similar to one that you want to add to the library and select New Style to get a head start. After you've adjusted the appropriate material properties, you can save the material in the part, save it into the standard, or export it to be used by others.

Saving changes made to the choice of materials to your standard is a good way to ensure accuracy and quality and is highly recommended.

> In addition to existing corporate and vendor material specifications, there are many online resources for getting information about materials.

Defining a Title Block

A common need for new users of Autodesk Inventor is to modify the title blocks of their drawing templates to match their existing drawings. The process is relatively simple but not obvious. You will make a simple change, but the workflow is the same regardless of complexity.

1. Open c5-08.idw from the Drawings\Chapter 5 folder, making certain that the *2012 Essentials* project file is active.

2. In the Browser, locate and expand the Drawing Resources folder, and then expand the Title Blocks folder.

3. Right-click the ANSI-Large title block, and select Edit from the context menu.

   Opening a title block for editing will show you something that looks like a disaster (see Figure 5.6). As you look closer, you will see that all the dimensions are there to control the location of lines, text, and properties that automatically populate as you begin to place views of components in the drawing.

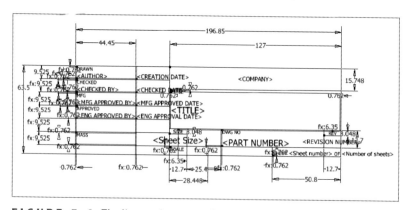

FIGURE 5.6 The line work, text, and properties behind a title block

4. Zoom in on the lower-left corner of the title block. Make sure you can clearly see the space with the word *Mass* in the upper-left corner.

5. Select the property text *<ENG APPROVED BY>* above the Mass cell.

6. Press Ctrl+C to copy the property to the Windows Clipboard.

7. Press Ctrl+V to paste a copy back into the title block.

   The copied property will usually be duplicated just above the original text.

8. Click and drag the new text down to the open cell below the word *Mass*.

9. Use a Coincident constraint to connect the origin point of the text to the point at the intersection of the title block, as shown in Figure 5.7.

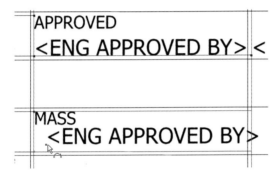

FIGURE 5.7 Sketch constraints work to control the location of text in the title block.

10. Once the text moves, use the Esc key to stop the constraint.

11. Right-click the property and select Edit Text from the context menu.

12. Remove the existing text from the bottom window of the dialog.

13. In the Format Text dialog, change the Type drop-down to Physical Properties—Model and the Property drop-down to Mass.

14. Click the Add Text Parameter button to update the property below.

15. The new property will appear in the Text window. See Figure 5.8.

16. Click OK to update the title block.

17. Select Finish Sketch from the marking menu.

18. Click Save As from the dialog that appears to create a new title block using your changes.

FIGURE 5.8 The line work, text, and properties behind a title block

Another dialog will appear for the name of the new title block.

19. Give the new title block the name **Essentials**, and click Save.

20. Under Drawing Resources ➤ Title Blocks in the Browser, double-click the Essentials title block to place it in the drawing.

You've now added a new resource to the drawing that can be shared with others or used to define a new personalized template for future drawings.

Saving a New Template

Now, you can create a template based on the existing drawing. It is really a very easy thing to do.

1. Open the c5-09.idw from the Drawings\Chapter 5 folder, making certain that the *2012 Essentials* project file is active.

2. Under the Application menu, expand the Save As options, and select Save Copy As Template, as shown in Figure 5.9.

 3. In the Save Copy As Template dialog, click the Create New Folder icon.

4. Name the new folder **Essentials**, and double-click to open it.

5. Give your new template the filename of **Essentials 1**, and click the Save button.

FIGURE 5.9 The Save Copy As Template tool shortcuts navigating to the Templates folder

6. Start the New File tool from the Quick Access toolbar, and note that there is now a tab in the dialog named Essentials.

7. Select the tab to see your new template ready to be used. See Figure 5.10.

FIGURE 5.10 If users share a common template source, it is easy to rebuild existing templates.

Now, you've created a new drawing template, and you can create as many different templates as you like. You can even open existing AutoCAD templates and make them Inventor templates.

Creating a Quick-Start Template

If you create components of similar sizes on a regular basis and have a consistent format for your drawings, you can configure a template to shortcut the drawing view placement process.

1. Open c5-10.idw from the Drawings\Chapter 5 folder, making certain that the *2012 Essentials* project file is active.

2. Under the Application menu, expand the Save As options, and select Save Copy As Template.

3. Navigate to the Essentials folder if you did the previous exercise. If you did not, please review steps 3 through 5.

4. Save the new drawing template as Essentials Six View.

5. When you have returned to the Inventor Design window, start the New File tool.

6. Double-click the Essentials Six View template to create a new drawing.

   This will open the Select Component dialog, where you will select the file from which you want to create drawings.

7. Click the c5-04.ipt from the Parts\Chapter 5 folder, and then click OK to close the dialog.

This will generate a new drawing with the same scale, spacing, and positions as the drawing from which you built the template. Comparing the new drawing to the c5-10.idw file will allow you to see the difference more clearly.

THE ESSENTIALS AND BEYOND

Changes that you make to the standards and their various styles will be limited only by you or your company's existing guidelines. Careful consideration of strategies for templates can save many hours if done correctly.

ADDITIONAL EXERCISES

▶ Open an existing DWG-based template only, and set up the Object Defaults Set to use its layering and other features.

▶ Try taking a part and creating a template from it that you could use as a "starter part."

▶ Seek out a specialized material that you use and add it to the Style library.

▶ See what other types of view will work in a preconfigured, multiple-view template.

Creating Advanced Drawings and Detailing

In Chapter 2, you learned how to create the basic drawing views and what some might consider advanced drawing views of a part file. Placing views of assemblies is not any different from an individual part file.

In this chapter, I will expand on those lessons, and you will begin to work with very advanced drawing creation and editing tools. You will also explore additional dimensioning and annotation tools.

▶ **Creating advanced drawing views**

▶ **Using advanced drawing annotation tools**

Creating Advanced Drawing Views

The part modeling process normally combines the uses of sketched and placed features. In Chapter 2, you created a section view that is based on a sketch. Projected views are placed by projecting from a parent view.

Advanced drawing views often use sketches for their definition and can even use more than one sketch. Even a projected view utilizes advanced technologies to help make decisions on your behalf.

Projecting Views from a Section View

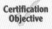
Certification
Objective

The section view in the drawing you will edit has the best orientation for creating other views, but you may not want all of them to have sectioned parts.

1. Open the c6-01.idw file from the Drawings\Chapter 6 folder, making certain that the 2012 Essentials project file is active.

Projected

2. Right-click the section view, select Projected View from the marking menu, and drag the new view above and to the right of it.

3. Click the page to place the view; then right-click and select Create from the context menu to generate the view, as shown in Figure 6.1.

FIGURE 6.1 Placing an isometric view of a section view

4. Select the Projected View tool from the marking menu, and click the section view as the parent.

5. Place the view to the right of the section view, and create the new view. Figure 6.2 shows the result.

FIGURE 6.2 A complete view can be projected from a section view.

The new view is not a partial view; it is a full view. Inventor recognizes that the projected view should be the full visible geometry.

Creating a Sketch in the Drawing View

There are many uses for creating sketches in a drawing view. In this case, you need to create geometry to modify the drawing view:

1. Open c6-02.idw from the Drawings\Chapter 6 folder, making certain that the 2012 Essentials project file is active.

2. When you hover over the view, the boundary will highlight. When the view highlights, click the view, and then select Create Sketch from the Sketch panel on the Place Views tab.

3. When the Sketch tab appears, draw a spline in the view similar to the one in Figure 6.3.

F I G U R E   6 . 3 Define a sketch in the drawing view to make changes to the view.

4. After the loop of the spline is closed, you can right-click and select Finish Sketch on the marking menu to finish the sketch.

   It is important to verify that the sketch is associated with the drawing view.

5. To verify association, drag the drawing view, and make sure the sketch moves with it.

If the sketch is not attached to the drawing view, delete the sketch you made, and go through the steps again to make sure that the view is highlighted when you start the Create Sketch tool.

The Break Out View

The sketch you created will be used as a boundary to remove part of the components of the assembly so you can see the interior.

1. Open c6-03.idw from the Drawings\Chapter 6 folder, making certain that the 2012 Essentials project file is active.

Break Out

2. Click the Break Out tool in the Modify panel of the Place Views tab.

3. Select the left view, and when the Break Out dialog opens, you will notice it has already selected the spline since it was the only closed profile.

    You will then need to select the depth to which you cut through the parts.

4. Hover over a curved edge. When the green dot appears, click it, as shown in Figure 6.4.

There are several options for selecting what components will be cut using the Break Out tool.

FIGURE 6.4 After you select the profile, you determine the depth of the cut.

5. Click OK to generate the view.

This generates and cuts any and all parts down to the selected point, but the traditional line view drawing still makes it difficult to distinguish the components.

Changing Part Drawing Behavior

In this exercise, you will modify how Inventor processes generating the drawing view of certain parts in the assembly:

1. Open c6-04.idw from the Drawings\Chapter 6 folder, making certain that the 2012 Essentials project file is active.

2. Double-click the break out view to edit it.

3. Deselect the Style From Base check box.

4. Then select the checkbox just to the left of the Shaded icon, and click OK to update the view.

In Figure 6.5, you can see there are a couple of errors. The first is that the screw and washer appear to be floating in the middle of the view. The second is a gear that is sectioned because of the way it was created. The third item flagged is not a mistake, but I want to show the seal on the shaft sectioned.

FIGURE 6.5 You can control whether parts are sectioned or even visible in a drawing view.

When you move your cursor over the view, all the edges highlight as you pass over them. By default, Inventor uses an Edge priority for selecting geometry in a drawing. You want Inventor to highlight the parts as you pass over them instead. This will make selecting them much easier.

5. Find the Selection drop-down on the Quick Access toolbar, and change the current selection priority to Part Priority by selecting it from the list.

6. Hold the Ctrl key to select the screw and the washer. Right-click the edge of one of the parts, and then select Section Participation from the context menu.

7. This will extend to another context menu. Select Section from this menu.

   The view will regenerate with the screw and washer affected by the break out section, and therefore, they will disappear.

8. Select the gear, and choose None from the Section Participation options.

9. Select the seal, and then choose Section.

This will again update the view to show the seal sectioned around the shaft. These changes will each update the view to appear like Figure 6.6.

F I G U R E 6 . 6 The updated view with the updated part visibility options

Part Visibility

If the screw and washer in the previous exercise weren't in a section or break out view, it would be possible to just remove the visibility. To do this, you must break the association between the drawing view and the design view of the assembly using the view edit dialog. This has been done for you in the file referenced in the next exercise.

1. Open c6-05.idw from the Drawings\Chapter 6 folder, making certain that the 2012 Essentials project file is active.

2. From the Quick Access toolbar, set the Selection filter to Part Priority.

3. Hover over the shroud. When it highlights, right-click and deselect Visibility.

The drawing view will regenerate the previously hidden edges that are now visible (Figure 6.7).

FIGURE 6.7 Selecting a part and turning it off in the view

View Suppression

A drawing view can be a stepping-stone to generate another, more important view. Being able to remove the clutter of the parent view can be useful.

1. Open c6-06.idw from the Drawings\Chapter 6 folder, making certain that the 2012 Essentials project file is active.

2. View1 is the *base view* in the drawing. It is in the upper-left corner. Hover over it, and when the view highlights, right-click.

3. Select Suppress from the context menu.

Even though View1 is the base view for all the other views, you removed it without disruption to the rest of the drawing.

Drawing Element Suppression

You can suppress individual lines and other elements of the drawing view:

1. Open c6-07.idw from the Drawings\Chapter 6 folder, making certain that the 2012 Essentials project file is active.

2. Zoom in on the isometric view in the upper-right corner.

3. Click and drag a window from left to right around the entire view.

4. When the lines in the drawing highlight, right-click and deselect Visibility from the context menu. Figure 6.8 shows the result.

FIGURE 6.8 A view can have visible edges removed for a more pictorial look.

Once an edge has been suppressed, it will remain that way even if the geometry changes size. New geometry added to the components will appear in the drawing view, so it is good practice to monitor suppressed edges.

Break View

When a part is long or has a large portion that consists of the same geometry, a *break* view can remove a portion of the drawing to make it easier to detail the dissimilar portions.

1. Open c6-08.idw from the Drawings\Chapter 6 folder, making certain that the 2012 Essentials project file is active.

2. Zoom out until you can see the entire drawing view as it extends beyond the border of the drawing.

3. On the Place Views tab, locate and start the Break tool in the Modify panel.

4. Click the Drawing view to open the Break dialog.

5. Set the Gap value to .5.

6. Click the first point of the break just to the right of the red part and the second just to the left of the threaded end, as shown in Figure 6.9.

FIGURE 6.9 Defining the points for the break view

7. Add a dimension to the length of the gray shaft (Figure 6.10).

FIGURE 6.10 Adding a dimension to the break view

The dimension will show the true length of the visible portion of the bar.

Slice View

A *slice* view is different from a section view in that only the geometry of the cut portion is visible. It can be used for something like a rotated section or to modify another view at cutting planes using a sketch.

1. Open c6-09.idw from the Drawings\Chapter 6 folder, making certain that the 2012 Essentials project file is active.

Slice

2. Start the Slice tool from the Modify panel on the Place Views tab.

3. Click the isometric view as the view to be modified.

   Once the target view has been selected, you need to select a sketch that will be used to cut the view.

4. Select the vertical lines in the side view of the part, and click OK. Figure 6.11 shows the result.

FIGURE 6.11 A slice view can show how the shape of a component is structured.

This will update the isometric view to show the portions of the part where the lines pass through it.

Custom View

The ViewCube in parts and assemblies aligns with the standard view options for placing drawing views. At times, these views just can't properly describe the geometry. For these times, you can create a *custom* view.

1. If you created a new template in Chapter 5, use `Essentials 1.idw` to start a new drawing. If not, start a new drawing using the `Standard (mm).idw` template available on the Metric tab.

Base

2. Start the Base View tool, which is in the Create panel of the Place Views tab and on the marking menu.

3. When the Drawing View dialog opens, use the Browse tool to locate the files. Find `c6-01.ipn` in the `Assemblies\Chapter 6` folder.

   The `.ipn` extension is for Inventor presentation files. A presentation file is used to create an exploded view of an assembly.

Certification
Objective

4. Once the exploded assembly is selected, its preview will appear. Below the list of standard view orientations is the Change View Orientation button. Click it.

   This will open the presentation file in a specialized Custom View tab with file-viewing tools.

5. Position the exploded view similar to Figure 6.12.

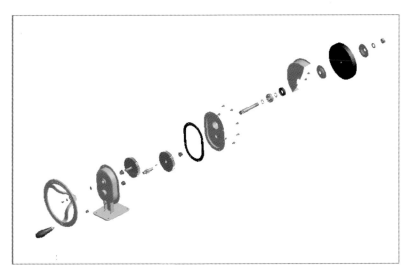

FIGURE 6.12 Positioning the parts for a drawing view

6. Once the view is positioned, click the Finish Custom View tool at the end of the Custom View tab.

7. The new preview will be of the view you established. Set the scale so that it fits across the page, as shown in Figure 6.13, and make it a shaded view.

FIGURE 6.13   The exploded view placed in the drawing

8. Click to place the view, and then right-click and select Done to finish the command.

The presentation file can also create animated assembly instructions, and you will do that in Chapter 13.

Using Advanced Drawing Annotation Tools

In Chapter 2, I covered the elements of dimensioning that will make up the bulk of typical detailing. Many other tools are necessary to make a complete drawing. The next group of exercises will focus on these tools.

Automated Text

In Chapter 5, you augmented a title block to include the values of the part's Mass properties. You can add these values to annotation text as well.

1. Open c6-10.idw from the Drawings\Chapter 6 folder, making certain that the 2012 Essentials project file is active.

2. Just above the title block is a line of text. Double-click the text to open the Format Text dialog.

3. In the Format Text dialog, change the Type drop-down to Physical Properties—Model and the Property drop-down to Mass.

 4. Click the Add Text Parameters button to update the property below.

5. Click OK to update the text.

   The value of the mass will appear, but it will likely be listed as N/A because the part's Mass properties are out of date. To update them, you will need to open the part file and update it.

6. Right-click one of the drawing views, and select Open from the context menu.

7. When the part file opens, right-click the Part icon at the top of the Browser, and select iProperties. This will open the c6–09.ipt iProperties dialog.

8. Click the Physical tab, and click the Update button.

9. Return to the drawing to see the results.

   THE APPROXIMATE WEIGHT OF THE FINISHED PART IS 0.237 lbmass

10. Close both the drawing and the part file without saving the changes.

Leader Text

You can use the Text tool to place text in a rectangular space on the drawing. The Leader Text tool automatically places the text at the end of a leader.

1. Open c6-11.idw from the Drawings\Chapter 6 folder, making certain that the 2012 Essentials project file is active.

Leader
Text

2. You can find the Leader Text tool on the marking menu. You can also find it in the Text panel on the Annotate tab. Start the Leader Text tool.

3. Click the top machined surface of the part, and then click a second point to locate where the text will be generated.

You can continue to click points to string the leader through.

4. Right-click and click Continue from the context menu to open the Format Text dialog.

5. Type in anything you like, and then click OK to generate the text. See Figure 6.14 for an example.

FIGURE 6.14 Text attached to the leader

Notice in this example that you can create multiple rows of text in the leader.

Special Symbols

Many types of symbols are needed for drawings. Inventor includes a wide selection of symbols and the ability to define your own. These symbols can be placed directly or attached to a leader.

1. Open c6-12.idw from the Drawings\Chapter 6 folder, making certain that the 2012 Essentials project file is active.

Surface

2. In the Symbols panel of the Annotate tab, locate and start the Surface tool.

3. Click the top surface that the Leader Text is attached to.

4. Right-click and click Continue from the context menu to open the Surface Texture dialog (Figure 6.15).

FIGURE 6.15 The Surface Texture dialog is very thorough.

5. Make any changes in the dialog, and click OK to place the symbol.

6. The Symbol tool will continue to work. Click the face on the far right, drag a leader away from the part, and click a second point for the leader.

7. Right-click and click Continue to launch the dialog again, and place a Surface symbol on the leader. See Figure 6.16.

FIGURE 6.16 Symbols can be attached to leaders as well.

8. Right-click and choose Done, or press the Esc key to stop the Surface symbol tool.

Although this exercise covers only one type of symbol, nearly all of them work in the same way.

Balloon

The exploded presentation view is a great way to display the physical makeup of an assembly, but you also need to be able to document what the components are. Calling out the parts using *balloons* and generating a list of the parts can help create a more complete document.

1. Open c6-13.idw from the Drawings\Chapter 6 folder, making certain that the 2012 Essentials project file is active.

Balloon

2. The Balloon tool is on the marking menu (in an open part of the Design window) and on the Annotate tab in the Table panel. Start the tool.

3. The Balloon tool will go directly into component-selection mode. Click the wheel on the left end.

   This will launch the BOM Properties dialog to define the source of the balloon information based on the bill of materials (BOM) structure.

4. Leave the BOM View value as Structured, and click OK.

5. Click a second point to set the length of the leader.

6. Right-click and click Continue to place the balloon. Then press the Esc key to end the Balloon tool. See Figure 6.17.

FIGURE 6.17   Placing a balloon in the drawing view

7. Click the leader of the balloon, and the grip points will highlight. Click the point at the tip of the arrow, and drag it to the housing to the right.

8. When the edge of the part highlights, release the mouse to attach the balloon to the other part.

The balloon number will update to correspond with the value gathered from the bill of materials contained in the assembly.

Auto Balloon

The Balloon tool is effective, but a faster alternative is Auto Balloon.

1. Open c6-14.idw from the Drawings\Chapter 6 folder, making certain that the 2012 Essentials project file is active.

Auto Balloon

2. The Auto Balloon tool is on the Annotate tab in the Table panel. You will have to expand the flyout of the Balloon tool to access it. Start the Auto Balloon tool.

This tool works a little differently because it will open a dialog box (see Figure 6.18) immediately. This dialog has a lot of options for determining how to prioritize what information is entered into the balloons.

FIGURE 6.18 The Auto Balloon dialog

3. Click the drawing view if the Select View Set button is depressed (see Figure 6.18). This will activate the Add or Remove Components tool.

4. Drag a window around several components toward the right end of the exploded view. See Figure 6.19.

FIGURE 6.19 Select the components to be ballooned

If you right-click a balloon, you can attach other balloons by clicking another part.

5. In the Placement group of the dialog, set Offset Spacing to 10. Then click the Select Placement icon, and move your cursor over the screen to see a preview of the balloons.

6. Click to place the balloons on the screen, and then click OK.

Creating a Parts List

Certification Objective

The *parts list* is a way of documenting the bill of materials of the assembly. You do not have to present the entire BOM or be limited to what is contained in it.

1. Open c6-15.idw from the Drawings\Chapter 6 folder, making certain that the 2012 Essentials project file is active.

2. Find the Table panel on the Annotate tab, and start the Parts List tool.

3. The Parts List dialog that opens (Figure 6.20) has a number of options similar to those in the Auto Balloon dialog.

FIGURE 6.20 The Parts List dialog has many options.

4. For simplicity, you can leave the options alone. Click the drawing view, and then click OK.

5. Place the parts list in the drawing.

6. Drag the left edge of the column to resize the various columns (Figure 6.21).

ITEM	QTY	PART NU
1	1	Grinder Base
2	1	Grinder Face
3	1	Spur Gear2
4	1	Gasket
5	1	Flywheel Handle

FIGURE 6.21 Drag the separation lines to resize the parts list's columns.

7. Moving over portions of the text will present a cursor that will allow you to click and drag the location of the parts list.

8. Locate the parts list above the title block and against the right border of the drawing. The parts list will snap into place. See Figure 6.22.

FIGURE 6.22 The parts list added to the drawing

The initial size of the columns and other properties of the parts list are controlled by the style and standards. This is another element that will likely be set once within a company and left alone.

Editing Dimension Values

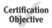
Certification Objective

When you set the dimension styles, the purpose was to make as many dimensions as possible appropriate for your needs. That doesn't mean you won't need to make changes to some.

1. Open c6-16.idw from the Drawings\Chapter 6 folder, making certain that the 2012 Essentials project file is active.

2. Double-click the 66.00 dimension. This will open the Edit Dimension dialog.

3. Choose the Precision And Tolerance tab, and set Tolerance Method to Symmetric and the Upper value to 0.01, as shown in Figure 6.23.

4. Click OK to update the dimension, as shown in Figure 6.24.

FIGURE 6.23 The Edit Dimension dialog

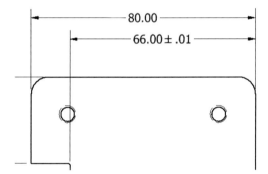

FIGURE 6.24 The dimension updated with the tolerance

There are also other ways to dimension the part.

Placing Ordinate Dimensions and Automated Centerlines

Ordinate dimensions (like baseline dimensions) can be placed either as individuals or as a set. The Ordinate Set option will keep the members styled as a set and also automatically does some spacing of the dimensions.

1. Open c6–17.idw from the Drawings\Chapter 6 folder, making certain that the 2012 Essentials project file is active.

2. Right-click within the boundary of the view, and select Automated Centerlines from the context menu.

The Automated Centerlines dialog (Figure 6.25) will allow you to select whether to include cylindrical extrusions or faces that have a radius, and you can also choose whether to select objects with an axis that is normal or parallel to the view.

FIGURE 6.25 The Automated Centerlines dialog

3. Keep the defaults, and click OK to place the centerlines.

4. Locate the Ordinate dimension tool in the Dimension panel on the Annotate tab, expand it, and select the Ordinate Set tool.

5. In the status bar, Inventor will ask you to click an origin point. Click the center mark of the large hole in the lower-right corner of the part.

6. Then click the vertical edges of the part shown in red in Figure 6.26 and the center marks highlighted with green dots.

FIGURE 6.26 Selecting elements of the drawing view on which to place ordinate dimensions

7. When you've selected all the elements, right-click and select Continue from the context menu.

8. Drag the location of the dimensions above the model geometry, and click to place the dimensions.

9. Right-click and select Create to complete the dimensions. Figure 6.27 shows the result.

FIGURE 6.27 The ordinate dimensions placed in the drawing

> You can drag ordinate dimensions to change their spacing, and grips allow you to change the location of jogs in the dimension line.

Ordinate dimensions can be placed in more than one direction on the view.

Hole Tables

Certification Objective

When you have a large number of holes, it is more efficient to use a hole table than to dimension the location of each one.

1. Open c6-18.idw from the Drawings\Chapter 6 folder, making certain that the 2012 Essentials project file is active.

2. The Hole Table flyout is located in the Table panel on the Annotate tab. Expand the list, and click the Hole View option.

3. Select the drawing view of the part.

4. Set the origin location to be the center of the large hole in the lower right of the part.

5. A preview of the table will appear. Drag it near the top of the title block against the left edge of the border, and click to place it.

Closer inspection of the drawing will show that it has labeled each of the holes with an alphabetical hole class and then a number that counts how many holes of that size are in the view. The table shows those hole names alone with the dimensional information for placing the holes as well as the description of each hole. To simplify the table, you can group the descriptions together.

6. Double-click the hole table to bring up the Edit Hole Table: View Type dialog. Select the Combine Notes radio button (Figure 6.28) in the Row Merge Options group.

FIGURE 6.28 Merging hole descriptions can make the table less confusing.

7. Click OK to update the table. Figure 6.29 shows the result.

HOLE TABLE			
HOLE	XDIM	YDIM	DESCRIPTION
A1	-196.00	-12.50	
A2	-149.33	-12.50	
A3	-102.67	-12.50	
A4	-56.00	-12.50	Ø6.60 THRU
A5	-196.00	32.50	
A6	-149.33	32.50	
A7	-102.67	32.50	
A8	-56.00	32.50	
B1	-27.00	32.00	
B2	27.00	32.00	
B3	27.00	67.00	M6x1 - 6H
B4	-27.00	102.00	
B5	27.00	102.00	
C1	.00	.00	Ø13.49 THRU ⌴ Ø22.23

FIGURE 6.29 The revised hole table showing the combined notes

There are still more types of annotation that are more specialized, and I will cover them along with the design techniques they document in later chapters.

THE ESSENTIALS AND BEYOND

For many CAD users, creating detail drawings isn't just a final step; it is the most critical. Many companies use these drawings not only to produce their products but as the legal documentation of their products. It takes a strong tool set to produce them accurately and efficiently. Inventor has these tools.

ADDITIONAL EXERCISES

▶ Combine learning from Chapters 5 and 6 to develop an appropriate Parts List style.

▶ Work with the Text tool to see how easy it is to build stand-alone notes.

▶ Explore and compare the behavior of the Ordinate and Ordinate Set tools.

▶ Test the various Tolerance and Fit callouts available in the Edit Dimension tool.

Advanced Part Modeling Features

Now that you've developed the basic skills for part modeling and sketching, it is a good time to let you know that you've already learned some of the most challenging concepts in Inventor. Advanced features in Inventor are as easy to define and often easier to construct than the basic features.

In this chapter, you will create or complete a handful of parts that include complex contours or large numbers of features. As you move beyond basic, prismatic parts, you need to work with more developed sketched and placed features. You will find that the basics learned with extrusions and revolved features will apply directly to the dialogs and workflows of these more advanced tools.

In addition, by completing this chapter and Chapter 3, you will have used the majority of solid modeling tools available in Inventor.

▶ **Projecting sketches and lofting**

▶ **Building a hole pattern**

▶ **Exploring advanced efficiency features**

Projecting Sketches and Lofting

For your first challenge, you will construct a spoke for a hand wheel that will change shape as it passes along a path. To do this, you will use a loft feature, but first, you need to develop some of the elements required to form the feature.

For the second example, you will use a 3D sketch to add a twist to the Sweep tool used in Chapter 3 and see how to easily hollow a part.

Projecting a 3D Sketch

You can use a 3D sketch to create complex geometry for sketched features. It can be created with a stand-alone tool or as an option to a 2D sketch that defines part of it.

To define the second profile, you need to build a plane on a curved face:

1. Open the c7-01.ipt file from the Parts\Chapter 7 folder. Make certain that the 2012 Essentials project file is active.

2. Double-click Loft Sketch 2 in the Browser to edit the sketch.

3. Locate the Project Geometry tool in the Draw panel of the Sketch tab. Expand it, and start the Project to 3D Sketch tool.

4. In the dialog, select the Project check box (Figure 7.1), click the curved face, and click OK.

FIGURE 7.1 Projecting a 2D sketch onto a 3D face

This will create a new 3D sketch, applying the circle to the cylindrical face.

5. Click Finish Sketch in the ribbon or use the marking menu.

Creating the 3D sketch has given you a second profile for your loft. Now, you need a path for the two profiles to transition along.

A 3D sketch can also be created on its own without the use of a 2D sketch.

Defining a Loft Path Between Points

To define a loft along a path, you must create a minimum of three sketches. You need a beginning profile and an end profile, and another sketch to define the path along which the shapes will transition from one to the other.

The path will be built between existing points, ensuring alignment of the profiles you will loft between.

1. Open c7-02.ipt from the Parts\Chapter 7 folder, making certain that the 2012 Essentials project file is active.

2. Create a new sketch by selecting the XZ plane in the Origin folder of the Browser and clicking the Create Sketch icon that appears in the Design window.

Project
Geometry

Now, you will need to use the Project Geometry tool, which is on the Sketch tab in the Drawing panel and on the marking menu.

3. Use the Project Geometry tool to project the center point of the 3D sketch and then to project the point at the center of the red sketch on the wheel into the current sketch.

4. Create a sketch using the parameters and constraints shown in Figure 7.2.

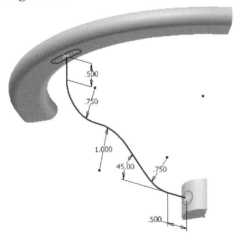

FIGURE 7.2 The sketch of the loft path

The sketch consists of three arcs and three lines. Remember that you can create a tangent arc by clicking the endpoint of a line and dragging the arc.

5. Be sure to finish the sketch. When you are modeling, you cannot save a file while a sketch is active.

Now, you have the pieces in place, so you can create your loft features.

Creating Loft Features

Loft features are created using the Loft tool, which offers several options. For example, you can define whether sketches or model faces are used for profiles (sections) and whether the paths will connect to the geometry. You will now use this tool to create the wheel spoke.

1. Open c7-03.ipt from the Parts\Chapter 7 folder, making certain that the 2012 Essentials project file is active.

2. Start the Loft tool from the Create panel of the Model tab.

   The dialog that opens (Figure 7.3) displays two primary areas for sections and rails or centerlines. As you click geometry, the selected parts will appear in these windows.

FIGURE 7.3 The Loft dialog showing the Center Line path option

   When you start the tool, it will look to select sections first.

3. For the first profile, click the red sketch on the rim of the wheel segment. It is labeled as Loft Sketch 1 in the Browser, or you can select it from the Design window.

4. Click the 3D sketch (Loft Sketch 2) for the second profile.

5. Between the Sections and Rails groups are the Rail options. Set the option for Center Line. This will also change the Loft tab displayed in the dialog to a Curves tab.

6. On the Curves tab, click where it says *Select a sketch* in the Center Line group. Select the sketched path.

   As you've seen with other sketched features in Inventor, a preview will appear when all of the elements needed to define it are satisfied.

7. Once a preview appears like Figure 7.4, click OK to create the feature.

FIGURE 7.4 A preview of the loft feature will appear after the sketches are selected.

8. Drag the end-of-part marker to the bottom of the Browser. The model will generate the pattern of the full solid model. See Figure 7.5.

FIGURE 7.5 Patterning the entire solid allows you to edit a smaller feature set.

The loft has created a connection between the hub and rim of the wheel. The minimum of two profiles were used, but you can add as many profiles as you need to accurately develop the shape you want.

Creating a Sweep

To create a sweep, you define a profile, a path, and optionally, a *guide rail* or *guide surface*. For this exercise, you will use the optional guide rail, which will steer the profile as it sweeps along a path.

1. Open c7-04.ipt from the Parts\Chapter 7 folder, making certain that the 2012 Essentials project file is active.

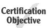 Sweep 2. Start the Sweep tool from the Create panel of the Model tab.

   Since there is only one closed profile in the model, it will automatically be selected for the profile.

3. Select the dashed line as the path. This preview will appear like an extrusion.

4. Change Type From Path to Path & Guide Rail.

   When you change the option, an icon appears with a red arrow, which indicates that Inventor needs input from the user. You must satisfy all of these red arrows to complete the feature.

5. Select the curved line that is part of a 3D sketch as the guide rail.

6. Click OK to create the new feature, as shown in Figure 7.6.

FIGURE 7.6 Using the guide rail allows the feature to be more complex.

The use of the 3D sketch's Helical curve allows the profile to twist around the path.

Creating a Shell

When parts are hollowed with a consistent wall thickness along a face, using the Shell tool is much more efficient than building the walls separately.

Certification
Objective

1. Open c7-05.ipt from the Parts\Chapter 7 folder, making certain that the 2012 Essentials project file is active.

 2. Start the Shell tool from the Modify panel of the Model tab.

The Shell dialog (Figure 7.7) opens and you will be prompted to click the faces you want removed to create the hollowed shape and to name a thickness for the remaining walls.

FIGURE 7.7 Expanding the Shell dialog gives access to additional wall thicknesses.

3. Select the yellow face to be removed, and set the Thickness value to 5mm.

 4. Expand the dialog by clicking the icon on the bottom of the dialog.

5. Click where the dialog says *Click To Add*; then click the green face on the part, and set the value to 15mm.

6. Click OK to create the shell feature, as shown in Figure 7.8.

FIGURE 7.8 The resulting shell shows the difference in wall thickness.

You can also create a shell feature without a removed face to create a hollow part, and you can select multiple faces to open up the part as much as needed.

Building a Hole Pattern

In Chapter 3, there were exercises for placing holes on a sketch and concentric to a curved face or edge. In this section, you'll explore an additional technique for placing holes, namely a *linear hole,* and then, you will use the *rectangular pattern* to replicate it. This is a common need on things such as mounting plates that need to attach to several components.

Using a Linear Hole Placement

Linear hole placement requires selecting a face on which to place the hole. Once you've done that, you can simply click OK to generate the feature. You can also click one or two edges to locate the hole relative to them using parametric dimensions placed for you.

1. Open c7-06.ipt from the Parts\Chapter 7 folder, making certain that the 2012 Essentials project file is active.

2. Start the Hole tool by selecting it from the Modify panel on the Model tab. It is also on the marking menu.

Hole

3. Set the hole class to Counterbore. Set the hole type to Clearance Hole, and then set the standard to be ANSI Metric M Profile. Set the fastener type to Socked Head Cap Screw, and set the size to M4 and the termination to Through All.

4. Click the top face of the plate near the notch.

5. Click the edges shown in Figure 7.9, and set their offset values to 14mm.

F I G U R E 7 . 9 Placing the hole based on the edges of the part

6. Click OK to place the hole.

The diameter and depth of the counterbore and the size of the hole were all determined by selecting the fastener that will go through it. With the hole in place, you can replicate it using the Rectangular Pattern tool.

Creating a Rectangular Hole Pattern

Let's create a series of these holes. In your plate, they will be spread perpendicularly, but the pattern can go in any two directions.

Certification Objective

1. Open c7-07.ipt from the Parts\Chapter 7 folder, making certain that the 2012 Essentials project file is active.

2. Go to the top icon of the Pattern panel on the Model tab, and click the Rectangular Pattern tool.

 Rectangular

3. The dialog will need you to select a feature, so click the counterbore hole created in the previous exercise.

4. Click the button with the red arrow in the Direction 1 group, and then click the short edge from which the counterbore hole was positioned.

5. Set the number of instances to 3 and the distance between them to 34.

6. Click the icon for Direction 2, and select the longer edge from which the hole was positioned.

7. To set the proper direction of the new instances, click the Flip button.

8. Set the number of instances to 2 and the distance to 52 per Figure 7.10.

FIGURE 7.10 Creating a pattern of holes

9. Click OK to place the pattern on the part.

   One of the occurrences in the pattern is not needed. It interferes with other features of the part.

10. Locate the Rectangular Pattern1 feature in the Browser, and expand it.

11. Hover over the Occurrence icons until the hole that overlaps the notch in the part highlights, as shown in Figure 7.11.

12. Right-click and click Suppress on the context menu. The completed feature will look like Figure 7.12.

FIGURE 7.11 Individual instances in a pattern can be suppressed.

FIGURE 7.12 The hole pattern with one occurrence suppressed

It is possible to suppress any number of members and to change whether they're suppressed at any time.

Exploring Advanced Efficiency Features

Among Inventor's advanced features are editing tools that enable you to increase efficiency by replicating features, editing features after their creation, and even replacing a portion of an existing feature to give it a new contour.

In the next group of exercises, you will convert a simple block into a complex bottle using simple tools. You will see how a good workflow allows the complex problem to be broken down into a few simple steps.

Combining Fillet Types

Certification
Objective Placing individual types of fillets is an easy process, but sometimes, combining types of fillets can allow you to build. That's how you'll begin to add some nice shape to your bottle.

1. Open c7-08.ipt from the Parts\Chapter 7 folder, making certain that the 2012 Essentials project file is active.

2. Orbit the part so that you can see the right and top face.

   For this exercise, you will use the names of the ViewCube faces to identify the faces on the part and the edges where they intersect.

3. Start the Fillet tool, which is in the Modify panel of the Model tab or in the marking menu.

   When the tool starts, a dialog and a mini-toolbar will appear. For the exercise, you will focus on the mini-toolbar.

 4. In the mini-toolbar, use the drop-down to change the fillet type to Full Round Fillet.

5. Click the Right, Top, and Left faces of the part. As soon as you click the third, the preview of the fillet will appear.

 6. Move back toward the mini-toolbar, and it will expand. Click the Apply button (green plus sign) to add the fillet, and continue selecting other options.

 7. On the mini-toolbar, change the fillet type to Edge Fillet.

8. Return to the Home view, click the edges shown in Figure 7.13, and set the radius to 3. Do not click OK or Apply.

FIGURE 7.13 Place a constant radius on the model edges.

9. In the mini-toolbar, change the type of edge fillet to Add Variable Set, and click the edge shown in Figure 7.14.

10. Click near the middle of the curved edge to place an additional radius reference point.

11. Set the radius to **6** and the edge position to **.5**, as shown in Figure 7.14, but do not click OK or Apply yet.

> The standard fillet type will resolve the edges with tangency. There is also an option with edge fillets to apply G2 continuity for smooth transitions.

FIGURE 7.14 Add a point along the edge to add another radius.

The final step, adding a setback, can also be done with the mini-toolbar, but you will use the dialog instead.

12. Click the Setbacks tab in the dialog; click Vertex 1 at the intersection of the Bottom, Front, and Left faces; and set the Setback values for the three edges to 8.

13. Pick Click To Add below Vertex 1 to add another vertex at the intersection of the Bottom, Front, and Right faces. Set their values to 8 as well, as shown in the dialog in Figure 7.15, and click OK.

FIGURE 7.15 The Setbacks tab of the Fillet dialog doesn't offer more options than the mini-toolbar but can present them better.

Setbacks add a softer corner and are popular on items such as consumer products. By building the constant and variable radius features at once, setbacks can be included.

Adding a Draft Angle

When creating an extrusion, sweep, and a few other features, you can include a draft angle, referred to in their dialog boxes as a Taper value. Sometimes it is best to add draft after the fact. With the bottle, for example, you need to include draft on a face that couldn't be added at the time the main feature was created. For that purpose, you can use the Draft tool.

1. Open c7-09.ipt from the Parts\Chapter 7 folder, making certain that the 2012 Essentials project file is active.

2. Be sure that you can orbit the part to see the green face on the bottom.

3. Start the Draft tool on the Modify panel of the Model tab.

   The Face Draft dialog will prompt you with an icon to select the pull direction. The pull direction is a face or plane around which the draft angle pivots.

4. Select the green face on the part to use it for the pull direction.

5. Then select the side face of the recessed extrusion, and set the angle to 15 degrees, as shown in Figure 7.16.

FIGURE 7.16 Like some other features, draft provides an arrow you can drag to change its angle.

6. Click OK to add the draft to the part.

You can also place draft based on a plane or a sketch. The plane can even be set away from the faces to be drafted.

Replacing One Face with Another

In cases where a complex shape makes up only a portion of a part, you can replace a planar face with a contoured one. To continue building the bottle, you'll use that technique to build a curved face that couldn't readily be created with the original feature.

1. Open c7-10.ipt from the Parts\Chapter 7 folder, making certain that the 2012 Essentials project file is active.

    At the bottom of the feature tree is a surface feature created by extruding an open profile. It is also possible to revolve and loft a surface by selecting the option.

2. Click the surface that passes through the part.

 3. Select the Edit Sketch tool from the screen.

4. The model will reposition so the view is normal to the sketch.

5. Press F7, or right-click and select Slice Graphics to remove the solid model down to the sketch, as shown in Figure 7.17.

FIGURE 7.17 The Slice Graphics function can expose sketches within the model.

You will notice that there is sketch geometry that makes up the perimeter of the portion of the part that the sketch intersects. This geometry cannot be created using the normal Project Geometry tool. It has to be created using Project Cut Edges.

6. Use Finish Sketch to return to the 3D model.

7. Expand the Surface panel on the Model tab, and select the Replace Face tool.

    Replace Face

8. Click the large recessed face on the front of the part.

9. In the dialog, click the New Faces selection button, and then click the surface.

10. Click OK to update the model.

11. In the Browser, right-click the ExtrusionSrf1 feature, and then deselect Visibility.

Another tool that can be used for this is Sculpt, which you'll use in Chapter 9. Replace Face is more basic and works well for substituting geometry.

Mirroring

Pattern tools reduce the tedium of creating repeated features. Creating a mirror feature can save work when there is symmetry in the part.

1. Open c7-11.ipt from the Parts\Chapter 7 folder, making certain that the 2012 Essentials project file is active.

 Mirror   The Mirror tool is located in the Pattern panel of the Model tab.

2. Start the Mirror tool.

3. In the dialog, select the Mirror A Solid option.

Choosing this option will limit your selection option to clicking the mirror plane.

4. Click the XY Plane under the Origin folder, and click OK to create the full body shown in Figure 7.18.

FIGURE 7.18 Use the Mirror tool instead of modeling both sides.

This part could've been modeled as a quarter of the body, mirroring it around the YZ plane and then the XY plane. Once the symmetrical portions are mirrored, you can add unique features to the different areas of the part.

Creating an Offset Work Plane

Work planes are needed when faces don't exist on which to create sketches or to use to develop other features. These can be developed by selecting edges, points, or other planes.

1. Open c7-12.ipt from the Parts\Chapter 7 folder, making certain that the 2012 Essentials project file is active.

   The Work Plane tool is available on the marking menu. More options are available in the Work Features panel on the Model tab (Figure 7.19).

FIGURE 7.19 Filters make creating work planes easier.

2. Expand the Origin folder in the Browser.

3. Start the Offset From Plane option from the Work Planes drop-down, and click the XZ plane in the Browser.

4. Click and drag the new plane until its value reads 80 or type in the value.

5. Click the OK icon to create the plane.

Similar filters can also be found for work axis and work point features.

The work plane you created will be used to build a sketch. It is also possible to start a new sketch, click a face or plane, and drag as you did in this exercise and simultaneously create a new plane and sketch on it.

Using a Fillet to Close a Gap

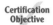

If you look closely at the model you are about to open, you will see a gap between the cylinder on the top and the main body. In these situations, applying an edge fillet is not possible because the faces do not intersect. In these cases, a face fillet will bridge a fillet across gaps.

1. Open c7-13.ipt from the Parts\Chapter 7 folder, making certain that the 2012 Essentials project file is active.

2. Start the Fillet tool from the marking menu or the ribbon.

 3. Change the option in the mini-toolbar (or dialog) to the Face Fillet option.

4. Click the cylindrical face of the Top Boss feature and one of the large curved faces just below it.

   With the default options, you need to click only two faces.

5. Selecting the faces will cause the tool to preview a fillet that can solve between the faces.

6. Set the radius to 3, and click OK from the mini-toolbar (Figure 7.20) to generate the fillet.

FIGURE 7.20 Creating a fillet between faces can close a gap.

You can use this option to close large gaps or problematic edges.

Adding a Coil

Threaded hole features do not generate physical threads, but if you need threads or to represent a coil of any type, there is a specific feature for it. In this case, you'll use a coil to create threads for the mouth of the bottle.

1. Open c7-14.ipt from the Parts\Chapter 7 folder, making certain that the 2012 Essentials project file is active.

Coil 2. Start the Coil tool from the Create panel on the Model tab.

3. The profile will be automatically selected. Click the y-axis from the Origin folder for the axis of the coil. It may be necessary to use the direction button in the dialog to make sure the coil is going toward the body of the part.

   This will open the Coil dialog. This dialog has three tabs for selecting geometry, specifying the coil, and controlling the ends of the coil.

4. Switch to the Coil Size tab and set the type to Revolution And Height, set the Height value to 7, and set the Revolution count to 2, as shown in Figure 7.21.

FIGURE 7.21 Using the Coil tool to generate threads

5. Click OK to generate the coil feature.

This feature can be created using pretty much any profile as long as it doesn't intersect itself. This makes it flexible for many things.

Using Open Profiles

All of the sketched features you've created have used closed profiles to generate solid features and open sketches to create a surface feature. An open profile is capable of creating a solid when it can intersect with existing solid geometry. You'll take advantage of that to create a stop on the neck of the bottle.

1. Open c7-15.ipt from the Parts\Chapter 7 folder, making certain that the 2012 Essentials project file is active.

2. Set your view to look at the front of the ViewCube.

Revolve

3. Start the Revolve tool from the Create panel on the Model tab.

4. Click the open profile that is in the sketch and move the mouse toward the solid until it shows a preview of the area the sketch that will be projected toward the body of the part. See Figure 7.22.

FIGURE 7.22 Previewing a projected profile

5. Click to use this option.

6. Click the y-axis in the Browser for the axis or the centerline in the sketch.

7. Once selected, the preview will change color. Click OK to create the complete feature. Figure 7.23 shows your finished part.

Open profiles work well for dealing with parts that include draft on faces. It is difficult to align a close profile with these faces.

FIGURE 7.23 The finished part
showing the revolved lip

THE ESSENTIALS AND BEYOND

The advanced filleting tools in conjunction with lofting and sweeping tools open many
doors for exploration in part modeling. Patterns and mirrored parts and features are great
ways of simplifying and speeding up the creation of parts. Used in combination, these
tools make the possibilities endless.

ADDITIONAL EXERCISES

▶ Look at some of your current designs for opportunities to use mirroring and
patterning.

▶ Try using fillets instead of sketched curves.

▶ Shell features can be used to create thin parts by removing all but a few faces. Consider
whether you have parts on which you could use this technique, and give it a try.

▶ Using work features is a critical skill to master. Practice using them and combining them.

Advanced Assembly and Engineering Tools

Most of the tools needed for the day-to-day work of building assemblies were covered in Chapter 4, "Putting Things in Place with Assemblies." In this chapter, you will use a few more tools to build your assembly.

Being able to navigate in the assembly and maintain your system's performance is also important, and large assemblies can put you at risk of losing data if your system runs out of memory. Autodesk Inventor 2012's representations can solve these problems, and you will see how to control your assembly with them.

Much of the focus of this chapter will be on tools that allow you to work more efficiently by creating geometry in the context of the assembly. These tools also offer a unique opportunity by incorporating engineering calculators into them. You will see how to create common machine components, but you will also see how to make sure that they will do the job.

▶ **Controlling the assembly environment**

▶ **Using design accelerators**

▶ **Working with additional assembly tools**

Controlling the Assembly Environment

An often-overlooked aspect of working with assemblies is controlling both the look-and-feel of the assembly's view representation and, most importantly, its system demands. Both of these elements are easy to control but are not automatic. There are three kinds of *representation* in Inventor that enable this enhanced level of control: view, level of detail, and positional. In this section, you'll try the first two.

Creating View Representations

 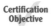

View representations allow the user to control the visibility and appearance of components in the assembly. Creating several view representations allows a user or multiple users to see the assembly in whatever way they want.

1. Open the c8–01.iam file from the Assemblies\Chapter 8 folder. Make certain that the 2012 Essentials project file is active.

2. Locate the Representations folder in the Browser. Expand the folder, and expand the View group.

3. Right-click the Default view representation, and select Copy from the context menu.

   This will create a new view representation named Default1 at the bottom of the list.

4. Click the new view representation twice slowly, and rename it **Natural Colors**.

5. Double-click the new view representation to activate it.

6. Right-click the Natural Colors representation, and select Remove Color Overrides from the context menu.

7. Select c8–01:1 in the Browser, right-click, and then uncheck Visibility in the context menu. Figure 8.1 shows the results.

8. Double-click the icon next to Default to set it as the active view representation, and then switch the view representation back.

The updates to the assembly affect only the visibility and colors of the components in the assembly. Another form of representation has a stronger effect.

FIGURE 8.1 View representations can save variations of color and visibility.

Creating Level-of-Detail Representations

Level-of-detail representations will not just remove a component from visibility; they will remove it from memory. If you need to work on large assemblies with limited system resources, the level-of-detail (LOD) representation is an invaluable tool.

1. Open c8-02.iam from the Assemblies\Chapter 8 folder, making certain that the 2012 Essentials project file is active.

2. Locate the Representations folder in the Browser. Expand the folder, and expand the Level of Detail group.

   On the right end of the status bar, two set of numbers report the number of components displayed in the Design window and the number of documents being accessed by Inventor.

3. Double-click the icon next to the Gears representation.

   This will reduce the number of displayed component occurrences and the number of open documents by removing all the components other than the shafts and gears that drive the mechanism.

4. Activate the All Content Center Suppressed representation and see the effect.

5. Right-click the All Content Center Suppressed LOD, and select Copy from the context menu.

6. Rename the new LOD **Primary Components**.

7. Double-click the Primary Components LOD to activate it.

8. In the Design window, click the wooden handle.

9. Right-click, expand the Selection options in the context menu, and select Component Size to be the selection filter for the assembly.

   This will open a dialog box showing the volume of the selected part.

 10. Change the selection value to 205, and click the check mark to select the components smaller than 205 cubic millimeters.

A substitute LOD can replace the assembly with a single part or a shrink-wrapped version to improve performance while maintaining a reference in the assembly. See Chapter 14.

11. Right-click and select Suppress from the context menu. The effects are shown in Figure 8.2.

FIGURE 8.2 LOD representations can remove components from memory.

You must save your work to preserve the changes made to an LOD representation before switching to another one.

POSITIONAL REPRESENTATIONS

Positional representations can override whether a constraint is enabled or suppressed. They can also use different offset values for a constraint. For example, a positional representation named Open can change the value of a mate constraint from 0mm to 10mm, which will cause a gap to appear between parts. These representations can be used to create overlays in a drawing to show an alternative position or used in an animation (see Chapter 13) to reduce the number of steps needed to create the animation.

Using Design Accelerators

Inventor has a number of specialized tools that build common machine components. Design accelerators come in two basic classes: calculators that work out what geometry you will need (such as weld sizes) and generators that can simply create components or use their built-in calculation tools to help you select the appropriate components such as bolts or the size of a shaft.

It helps to build something when learning advanced tools. In this chapter, you will be working on the design of a hand-driven metal grinder.

Using the Bearing Generator

Many bearing standards are global, so this tool will allow you to choose from a number of different components with the same basic geometry.

1. Open c8-03.iam from the Assemblies\Chapter 8 folder, making certain that the 2012 Essentials project file is active.

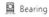 2. Click the Bearing tool in the Power Transmission panel of the Design tab.

   The Bearing Generator dialog has two tabs. The Design tab will select a bearing based on its size, and the Calculation tab allows you to verify that it will hold up to the demands of its job. All generators have at least these two tabs.

 3. Set the dimensional values for the dialog to be the same as Figure 8.3, and click the Update button to build a list of bearings that meet the physical specs.

FIGURE 8.3 The Bearing Generator dialog can quickly generate a list of bearings based on size.

4. Click the down arrow near the top of the dialog where it says *Angular Contact Ball Bearings* to open a selection dialog.

5. In the dialog, use the drop-down menu in the upper right to change the category of bearing to Cylindrical Roller Bearings, and then select the Cylindrical Roller Bearings (Figure 8.4) option in the upper left so that it creates a list of all of the bearings that fit.

FIGURE 8.4 You can change the category of bearing that you place in the assembly.

6. Scroll down the list, select the SKF NJ bearing, and click OK to create the geometry. You will have to hit OK in the File Naming dialog as well.

7. Click to place the bearing off to the side of the cover.

Using the Calculation tab, you can also test the bearing by checking how the bearing meets life span, loading, and speed ratings to be sure that it will hold up.

Using the Adaptivity Feature Within the Assembly

Certification Objective

 c8-10:1

Adaptivity is not a function of a design accelerator, but it is an advanced capability unique to Inventor. It allows part features to be modified by assembly constraints in certain conditions.

It is possible to identify an adaptive item in the Browser by locating the red-and-blue icon next to the part or feature or sketch.

1. Open the c8-04.iam from the Assemblies\Chapter 8 folder, making certain that the 2012 Essentials project file is active.

Distance

2. Switch the Ribbon to the Inspect tab, and start the Distance option of the Measure tool from the Measure panel, press the M key, or select Measure Distance from the marking menu.

3. Click the inside edge of the large hole in the tan part.

The hole in the part will measure 38mm. The bearing in the assembly has an outer diameter of 35mm. Adaptivity will allow the diameter of the hole to be changed to fit the bearing.

Constrain

4. Start the Constrain tool in the Position panel of the Assemble tab.

5. Hover over the exterior cylindrical face of the bearing.

6. When the axis of the bearing highlights, right-click and click Select Other from the context menu.

7. Click the first Face option from the list that highlights the outer diameter of the bearing, as shown in Figure 8.5.

Certification
Objective

F I G U R E 8 . 5 Use the Select Other option to click additional selection options for placing assembly constraints.

8. Select the large hole in the front cover, and click OK.

9. Click the front face on the ViewCube so you can see that the diameter of the hole is matched to the diameter of the bearing.

Adaptivity is a great tool for sizing one component based on another, but using it on too many features or parts can slow your performance. It is best used to establish a size, and then it can be disabled to lock that size in.

Using the Shaft Generator

It is a simple process to create a shaft by revolving a half section or creating a series of extrusions stacked end to end. The Shaft Generator design accelerator constructs the shaft through a dialog and lays out the segments of the shaft.

1. Open c8-05.iam from the Assemblies\Chapter 8 folder, making certain that the 2012 Essentials project file is active.

Shaft

2. Hold down your Ctrl key and click the Shaft tool in the Power Transmission panel of the Design tab.

    Holding the Ctrl key is necessary only if you want to start a design accelerator with the default options.

    When the dialog (Figure 8.6) opens, shaft sections will appear in the large window in the dialog. Each segment row will have columns for the left and right end treatments, the section shape, and any special additions. The size and shape will be listed to the right as well.

FIGURE 8.6 The Shaft Generator dialog showing the default shaft segments

3. Select the top segment. At the far right, click the Delete icon, and then click Yes in the dialog that appears.

4. Delete all but the segment listed as Cylinder 55 × 100.

5. Double-click the description of this segment.

6. Change the D (diameter) and L (length) values to **10mm** by clicking the current values in the Cylinder dialog that appears.

7. Click OK to update the size of the segment.

8. Locate and select the Insert Cylinder icon just above the updated section.

9. This will insert a duplicate segment below the original. Edit the size of the new segment to D = **12**, L = **3** and click OK.

10. Click the Insert Cylinder tool again, and create a new segment with D = **25** and L = **12** values.

11. Create another new cylinder, setting D = **12** and L = **16**.

12. Create the fifth segment to be the same as the first: D = **10** and L = **10**.

13. In the bottom segment, click the end treatment icon on the right, and click the Chamfer option in the drop-down.

14. When the small dialog appears, set the Distance value of the chamfer to .3, and click the OK check mark.

15. Add a .3 chamfer to the left end of the first shaft segment. Your dialog should look like Figure 8.7.

F I G U R E   8 . 7 Adding chamfers to the ends of the shaft

16. Click OK to generate the shaft and OK again to accept the names of the new files.

17. Place the new shaft into the assembly by clicking a location in the Design window.

▶

The Shaft Generator is great for hubs, too. A drop-down in the Sections group allows you to add internal geometry from either end.

At this point, you've developed the geometry that will fit in the assembly and that you think will handle the loads. Part of every generator in the Power Transmission tools can also calculate whether the geometry is up to the task at hand. Now, you should see whether this shaft will work.

Calculating and Graphing Shaft Characteristics

For this exercise, you will continue using the shaft you are in the middle of defining. The Shaft Component Generator's Calculation and Graph tabs have nothing to offer until you've defined geometry on the Design tab. In turn, the Graph tab cannot supply information until the calculation is done.

1. Right-click the shaft that you placed in the assembly, and select Edit Using Design Accelerator from the context menu.

2. Click the Calculation tab to open the options available. See Figure 8.8.

   The Calculation tab is where you can override and experiment with the material of the shaft and set up how it is supported and loaded.

FIGURE 8.8 The Calculation tab of the Shaft Component Generator

3. Click the check box next to the Material callout. This will open a Material Types dialog.

4. Select Steel, and click OK to make it the active material.

5. In the 2D Preview, click the Free support icon at the far left end of the preview, and drag it to the middle of the rightmost section. See Figure 8.9.

FIGURE 8.9 The 2D preview shows how the shaft is loaded and supported.

6. Click the Load icon, and the Loads & Supports area will change to show the type of load that is being used.

7. Double-click the Load icon to open the dialog box, showing the properties of the load.

8. Change the force to 200N, and click OK to close the dialog.

9. Click the Calculate button, and then click the Graphs tab.

10. The Shear Force graph is showing the results.

11. Click the Deflection graph in the Graph Selection area to see that the deflection of this shaft is .811 micron (Figure 8.10).

12. Click OK to close the dialog.

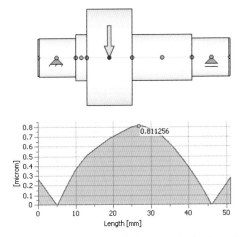

FIGURE 8.10 The Graphs tab displays the results of the calculations done on the shaft.

The Calculation tab varies based on the tool, but the information that you can enter or extract is precisely the information you would need in order to use engineering criteria to evaluate the components you're creating. You won't use the Calculation tools for all the tools I will review, but keep in mind that they are available.

Using the Spur Gear Generator

The Design tab of this dialog is broken down into three major sections. The top is the Common area where you specify the tooth characteristics of the gear. The middle is where you set the requirements for size of the gears that support the teeth, and the bottom is an information area that will offer feedback on the design and calculations.

1. Open the c8-06.iam from the Assemblies\Chapter 8 folder, making certain that the 2012 Essentials project file is active.

Spur
Gear

2. Hold the Ctrl key, and click the Spur Gear tool on the Power Transmission panel of the Design tab.

   The Spur Gears Component Generator dialog will open with its default values (Figure 8.11).

FIGURE 8.11 The default values for the Gear Generator

3. Beginning in the upper left, change Design Guide to Number of Teeth.

4. Set the Desired Gear Ratio value to 4.0000 ul from the drop-down.

5. Set the Module to .8mm and the Center Distance to 50.000mm.

   Now you need to make changes to the specifications for the individual gears.

6. Use the drop-down to change Gear1 and Gear2 from being a component to a feature. The Component option will build a new part in the assembly that can be fitted to the shaft. The Feature option will modify the shaft, and the No Model setting is used as a reference to develop the gear that mates to its values.

7. Set the Facewidth value for both gears to 13mm, and your dialog should now look like Figure 8.12.

FIGURE 8.12 The updated values in the dialog prior to selecting the geometry

8. Under Gear1, click the selection icon for the cylindrical face, and then select the cylindrical face on the largest-diameter segment of the gray shaft.

9. Click the selection icon for the start plane of Gear1, and click the flat face on the same shaft segment.

10. Start the Cylindrical Face selection for Gear2, and click the large, cylindrical face on the green shaft.

11. For the start plane of Gear2, click the large face on the same segment of the green gear.

12. Click the Calculate tool to update the geometry preview.

The lower section will indicate a design failure. You may have to select the double arrows to expand the dialog to see the error in the lower section.

13. Click OK to generate the gear features on the existing shafts, and click Accept to generate the gears (Figure 8.13) even with the incomplete information.

FIGURE 8.13 The updated shafts with the gear features added

Anyone who has created gears in 2D or 3D by developing a tooth profile and patterning it will appreciate the power of the Gear Generator. Along with spur gears, there are design accelerators for worm and bevel gears.

Using the Key Connection Generator

Keys are used to align components but typically need material removed from at least two parts to be able to place the key. In this case, a Gear component has been added to the assembly centered on the shaft.

1. Open the c8-07.iam from the Assemblies\Chapter 8 folder, making certain that the 2012 Essentials project file is active.

2. Double-click the large gear.

   The gear will be solid with no opening for the shaft or accommodation for reducing the weight of the gear. Since the part is a solid model, you can use any solid modeling tool to change it, but in this example, you will create the shaft accommodation using the Key Connection Generator.

3. Click the Return icon on the Ribbon or click Finish Edit in the marking menu to return to the assembly.

 Key 4. Switch the Ribbon to the Design tab, hold the Ctrl key, and click the Key Connection tool in the Power Transmission panel.

   The Parallel Key Connection Generator dialog (Figure 8.14) has some similarities to the Bearing Generator dialog. The process is straightforward. Select the type of key you want, and then tell it what kind of groove you want for the shaft and hub or if you want one.

FIGURE 8.14 The Parallel Key Connection Generator dialog default values

5. At the top of the dialog, the current key standard is displayed. Click the down arrow at the end of this space to open the selection dialog.

6. At the top of the dialog showing the available key types, click the Standard drop-down, and select ANSI to limit the options.

7. Click the Rectangular or Square Parallel Keys type.

8. Just below the key selection is the value of the shaft diameter. Change this from 20.000 to 12mm.

The next several steps will define where the key is positioned and what parts of the assembly will be changed. Selecting the correct geometry is critical. Figure 8.15 shows where to click to properly locate the key.

Face of gear to be cut

Curved edge to center feature on gear

Shaft segment for key placement

Shaft end to position key from

FIGURE 8.15 Select only the faces and edge (step 4) indicated.

9. Click the selection icon for Shaft Groove Reference 1, and then click the shaft segment between the gear and the smaller end segment.

10. Selection for Reference 2 will automatically activate. Click the end of the shaft.

11. Reference 1 for the hub groove is now active. Click the face on the large gear.

12. For Reference 2 of the hub groove, you need to select a curved edge. Carefully select the tip of one of the gear teeth. If you click a side edge, simply click the selection icon and try again. You can zoom in to make it easier.

> In the dialog box, you can choose whether to generate the hub groove, shaft groove, or key.

Once the fourth selection is made, a preview of the key and grooves will appear. You want to make one change to the shaft groove before we proceed.

 13. In the Shaft Groove group, click the groove with one Rounded End option.

14. There are two arrows on the ends of the preview of the key. Drag the left arrow roughly 11mm from the origin to the right.

15. Then drag the right until the key changes to its 11.113mm standard size, as shown in Figure 8.16.

FIGURE 8.16 The position and length of the new key can be changed by dragging icons in the preview.

16. Click OK to generate the geometry, and click OK again to approve the creation of the new files. See Figure 8.17 for the finished key component.

FIGURE 8.17 The finished key with the groove built into the shaft

Both the shaft and the hub will have new features added to them, and a new part will be created for the key. Editing the key's size will update all of the related features.

Working with Additional Assembly Tools

Constraints and design accelerators are great, but they're not the only capabilities Inventor provides for an assembly. Some of these tools are not even unique to the assembly environment, but they simplify the process of defining your products.

For the next exercises, you will use a gear housing that is machined from a casting. As you start, you have a casting for only one half of the part, and it may need reinforcement.

Mirroring Components

When modeling parts, taking advantage of symmetry or the ability to pattern a feature can save work and improve quality. The same is true when it comes to whole components that are opposites of one another. For these components, you can mirror the entire part. In the context of an assembly, you can mirror several parts at once and generate the new files for them.

1. Open c8-08.iam from the Assemblies\Chapter 8 folder, making certain that the 2012 Essentials project file is active.

🔲 Mirror 2. Start the Mirror Components tool from the Component panel of the Assemble tab.

3. The Mirror Components: Status dialog will be prepared to select components to be mirrored. Click the housing and the two bearings in the Design window.

4. Then click the selection icon for the mirror plane, and click the XY plane from the Origin folder of the assembly.

A preview of the mirrored components will appear, and they will be color-coded based on the action to be taken. Green components will create a new file that is a mirror image of the original. Yellow components are new instances of existing geometry. This is the default state for standard components such as bearings.

5. In the dialog, click the yellow icon next to the first bearing.

> The Ignore option in the Mirror Component dialog can be used to skip parts accidentally clicked with the window or crossing selection.

6. The icon turns gray, which indicates that the components will be ignored by the tool.

7. Your screen should look like Figure 8.18. Click Next.

FIGURE 8.18 A preview of the mirrored and instanced components

The Mirror Components: File Names dialog allows you to specify the filename and path for the components that are to be created. You can also apply a new naming scheme to all the new components by adding a prefix or suffix to them.

8. Click OK to create the new files and produce the new components in the assembly, as shown in Figure 8.19.

FIGURE 8.19 The mirrored housing in the assembly

Now that you have the mirrored part, you can make changes to the new part to make it uniquely different from the original if need be. It is important to use the side that is least likely to need uniquely different features as the basis for the mirrored component to keep from having to remove geometry not needed in the copy.

Deriving Components

The Derive Component tool is one of the most powerful in Inventor. It can be used for everything including linking the value of one parametric part into another, creating a mirror of a component, and, as in this exercise, using one part as the basis for another. The concept is to begin with the geometry, sketches, dimensions, or faces from one part and use them in another to ensure consistency.

1. From the Quick Access toolbar, start the New File tool, and create a new file using the Standard (mm).ipt template, making certain that the 2012 Essentials project file is active.

2. Click Finish Sketch in the Exit panel of the Sketch tab.

   Instead of sketching geometry, you will link to an existing part to begin your new part.

Derive

3. Switch the Ribbon to the Manage tab, and start the Derive Component tool in the Insert panel.

4. Use the Open dialog to select c8-12.ipt from the Parts\Chapter 8 folder.

5. Click Open to go to the next step.

   The Derived Part dialog (Figure 8.20) will allow you to choose what form your linked data will take. You can even choose to import only faces, sketches, or parameters. Once you've selected how you want to bring it in, you can change its scale or even mirror it around a plane.

FIGURE 8.20 The Derived Part dialog offers complete control over the reuse of existing data.

6. Leave the default options, and click OK to completely link the c8–12 part into the new part.

   You can now add features to the linked geometry to make a machining of this cast part. Now, let's open an existing machining and the original casting.

7. Open the c8–13.ipt file from the Parts\Chapter 8 folder.

   Take a moment to review the holes, extrusions, and other features that have removed material from the original casting.

8. Open c8–12.ipt from the Parts\Chapter 8 folder.

9. In the Browser, locate the end-of-part marker. Click and drag it to the bottom of the list of features.

   After the part updates, you will see that a rib feature has been added to the model.

10. Click the File tab below the Design window to display your new part. It will not show the change to the casting yet.

You can use Derive Component to create a single or multi-body part out of an assembly even as a mirrored or scaled geometry.

11. Click the local update icon in the Quick Access toolbar to bring the changes into your new part.

12. Switch your Design window to the c8-13.ipt file and update it. See Figure 8.21.

FIGURE 8.21 The updated part showing changes made to the casting file

If you use a single casting as the base for multiple components, the Derive Component tool will save you countless hours of updating machined parts. As mentioned in the introduction, this tool has many more uses and warrants exploration.

Constraining and Animating Assembly Motion

In Chapter 4, I covered the majority of Assembly constraint options that hold components in place. The Motion constraint can bind the movement of one component to another.

1. Open the c8-09.iam file from the Assemblies\Chapter 8 folder, making certain that the 2012 Essentials project file is active.

2. In the Position panel of the Assemble tab, click the Constrain tool.

Certification Objective

3. In the Place Constraint dialog, click the Motion tab.

4. Set the Ratio value to 4, and then set the Solution value to Reverse.

    This tool is click-sensitive. The ratio will be applied from the first selection to the second selection.

5. For the first selection, click a flat face or the end of the brass gear.

6. For the second selection, click the end of the gray shaft below it, as shown in Figure 8.22.

FIGURE 8.22 Selecting the components that will move together

7. Click OK to create the constraint.

8. Click and drag either the wheel or the wooden handle to see the mechanism work. Note that the last shaft turns at a final ratio of 16:1 over the handle.

9. Locate the Drive This Constraint item in the Browser under the New Shaft part.

   Even though this constraint is suppressed, it can still be used to animate the assembly.

10. Right-click the constraint, and select the Drive Constraint tool from the context menu.

11. In the Drive Constraint dialog, set the End value for the range of motion to 360.

12. Expand the dialog, and set the value for Repetitions to 3.

13. Click the Forward button to see how the mechanism works.

Applying motion constraints to an assembly will help you verify that your design is working the way that you need it to work. Being able to animate this action can help you show others what you intend the design to do.

You can save the animation of a Driven constraint to an AVI or WMV file by clicking the Record button in the dialog.

THE ESSENTIALS AND BEYOND

Representations can add control over how your assemblies look, but leveraging the level-of-detail (LOD) tools can improve the performance of your computer and save you time waiting for changes to update and money by keeping your hardware effective longer.

Design accelerators add a whole new dimension to CAD, adding engineering tools to common component tools. Integrating these calculations may help you improve the efficiency of your products.

ADDITIONAL EXERCISES

▶ Practice using LOD representations in your day-to-day work. These tools provide many different advantages, including speeding up the drawing view by using them as the basis for view creation.

▶ Try using the Cam, Spring, and other tools available on the expanded Power Transmission panel.

▶ Explore different shaft loads and loading options to see how the shaft reacts.

▶ Look at the Calculation tab on all the design accelerators as you try them to see what information you will need to supply to allow the calculators to work.

Creating Plastic Parts

A combination of specialized plastic part features and common solid modeling tools is needed to make any plastic part. Because certain types of geometry are common in plastic parts, automated tools were created to build this geometry quickly and easily. Taking features such as lips, bosses, and grills and building wizards around them can save you hours on even a simple part.

In this chapter, you will learn about many of these specialized tools in the context of a workflow that will show a different approach to building components. There are many options that I will not cover, but you will see that these tools are built to offer you all the options you need in a way that is nearly self-explanatory.

▶ **Developing the plastic shapes**

▶ **Creating and working with assemblies and their parts**

Developing the Plastic Shapes

Plastic part features are specialized tools that create geometry that you could create using traditional features, but it would take many features to create geometry that is common in these types of parts. Figure 9.1 illustrates the model you'll complete in this chapter's exercises. To create and refine its shapes, you'll use many of Autodesk Inventor 2012's most common sculpting tools.

FIGURE 9.1 The completed model from this chapter

Sculpting a Plastic Surface

In Chapter 7, you used the Replace Face tool to substitute a face with a contour for a flat one. The Sculpt tool could be considered an evolution of Replace Face, but it is far more powerful. It will help you combine a series of overlapping surfaces into a solid model. You'll use it to create the initial shape.

1. Open the c9-01.ipt file from the Parts\Chapter 9 folder. Make certain that the 2012 Essentials project file is active.

  Sculpt   2. Start the Sculpt tool from the Surface panel of the Model tab.

3. Select all the surfaces in the Design window, including the plane at the base of the part.

4. As the surfaces are selected, a preview of solid bodies will appear. Once all the surfaces are selected, click OK.

Selecting the direction arrows in the surfaces will allow you to bias the direction of the volume that will be solidified if there is any ambiguity.

The complete solid should look like Figure 9.2. For creating components with a series of complex surfaces, it can be beneficial to create the surfaces as surfaces and sculpt them together instead of trying to construct a loft or other features.

FIGURE 9.2 The solid formed by the surfaces

Stitching Surfaces Together

You can combine surfaces to form a new surface, and then that surface can be used for other things. In this example, you'll use stitching to define a surface to be removed.

1. Open c9-02.ipt from the Parts\Chapter 9 folder, making certain that the 2012 Essentials project file is active.

2. In the Browser, expand the Solid Bodies folder.

3. Right-click the icon next to Solid1, and uncheck Visibility to turn off the solid model.

Stitch 4. Start the Stitch tool from the Surface panel of the Model tab.

5. Click the extruded surface and the boundary patch; then click Apply to create the new surface.

6. Click Done to close the dialog.

7. Make the solid visible again.

8. Start the Sculpt tool, and select the new surface.

9. Switch to the Remove option, and the preview will show that part of the body will be removed.

   A preview will appear showing the portion to be removed in red (Figure 9.3).

FIGURE 9.3 The Sculpt tool can also remove a portion of the solid using a surface.

10. Click OK to finish editing the part.

If you have a series of surfaces that meet at their edges, you can stitch them together into a solid. It will work, but cleaning up the edges of the surfaces is more difficult than allowing them to overlap and using the Sculpt tool.

MULTIBODY MODELS

You can turn a single part into separate bodies representing and even defining the multiple parts of an assembly. By forming these various bodies using the same geometry, you can maintain the consistency of their shapes.

Splitting Bodies

You can generate almost any sketched feature as a new body by simply selecting the New solid option in the dialog used to create that feature (i.e. extrude, revolve, loft). You can also use a plane or sketch geometry to split a face, remove a portion of a body, or even separate a body into separated bodies. To use the Split tool in this model, you will use a plane that will define the boundary between the two bodies:

1. Open c9-03.ipt from the Parts\Chapter 9 folder, making certain that the 2012 Essentials project file is active.

  Split **2.** Start the Split tool from the Modify panel of the Model tab.

3. Click the Split Solid option in the dialog, and click the visible work plane on the part or the Splitting Plane 1 feature in the Browser.

4. Click OK to break the part into two bodies.

5. In the Browser, expand the Solid Bodies folder, and see the new solids that have been added.

6. Rename Solid2 to **Front** and Solid3 to **Back** by clicking the name twice slowly, as you would rename a file in Windows Explorer.

7. Click the solids individually from the Browser, and change their colors using the drop-down in the Quick Access toolbar. My choices are shown applied to the solid in Figure 9.4.

FIGURE 9.4 Once the solid is split into multiple bodies, you can treat them differently.

You can divide and subdivide a body as many times as needed to suit your needs. You can also use an extrusion to cut a part and then share the sketch to form a new body from the same sketch.

Adding a Lip

A lip allows the plastic parts to remain aligned so the form can remain consistent. You can use other sketched features such as the Sweep tool to make the geometry, but the Lip tool makes it easier to adjust things like draft and to recess edges.

1. Open c9-04.ipt from the Parts\Chapter 9 folder, making certain that the 2012 Essentials project file is active.

2. Rotate the front body so that you can see the back side of it.

3. Start the Lip tool. It is on the Model tab in the Plastic Part panel.

4. In the dialog, make sure the option on the left is set to Lip, and then select the Pull Direction check box. This will change the dialog and make the selection of the Pull Direction option what Inventor is looking for.

5. Click the flat face around the perimeter of the part for the Pull Direction option.

6. Once the direction is selected, click the inner edge of the perimeter for the path edges, as shown in Figure 9.5.

FIGURE 9.5 Selecting model edges to place a lip feature

7. Click the Lip tab in the dialog, and review the options.

8. Click OK to place the feature with the default options, as shown in Figure 9.6.

FIGURE 9.6 The lip added to the front body

You can also select the back part and place a lip using the Groove option. If a lip feature is placed in a part, its properties will be picked up by a groove in the same part.

Adding a Boss

Like the Lip tool, the Boss tool comes with opposite geometry sets. The head and thread sides of the boss are complex collections of geometry that would normally take several features to create.

The bosses you add in this exercise will allow you to assemble the halves of the back together using screws:

1. Open the c9-05.ipt from the Parts\Chapter 9 folder, making certain that the 2012 Essentials project file is active.

2. Start the Boss tool, which is in the Plastic Part panel on the Model tab.

3. Make sure the Head option is active. It is the button in the upper-left corner of the screen.

4. Switch the Boss dialog to the Head tab, and set the bottom two size options from 6.6 to 6 and from 7.54 to 7.

5. Expand the Draft Options section in the dialog.

6. Change the first two draft options from 2.5 to 2 degrees. Refer to Figure 9.7 for the dialog values.

You can also build ribs around the boss, and you can adjust their height, thickness, and angle.

FIGURE 9.7 The Boss dialog options can control many parametric values.

7. Click OK to generate the Head side bosses.

8. Expand the Solid Bodies folder, right-click the Back–Top body, and select Hide Others in the context menu.

   This will make a new body visible and turn off the others. Now, you can add features to this body.

9. Scroll down in the Browser, and expand the Boss1 features.

10. Click and drag the sketch just above the Boss1 so that it is now shared.

11. Right-click the sketch, and make it visible so that it can be used to create a new feature.

 12. Start the Boss tool, and switch it to the Thread option.

13. Set the value of the fillet to 3 (Figure 9.8), and click OK to place the new features.

FIGURE 9.8 A boss can automatically add a fillet at the base for the new boss.

You can add stiffening ribs as part of the feature. You can also allow the hole to pass all the way through the component.

Creating a Rest

A *rest* is like an extrude command that understands a wall thickness. It is meant to build a flat spot and can construct the internal and external faces at the same time.

1. Open c9-06.ipt from the Parts\Chapter 9 folder, making certain that the 2012 Essentials project file is active.

2. Find and start the Rest tool in the Plastic Part panel of the Model tab.

3. After the preview appears, click the direction button option in the dialog on the left to put the hollow of the rest to the inside of the part.

4. Set the thickness to 2, and then click the More tab.

5. Set the values for Landing Taper and Clearance Taper to 2, as shown in Figure 9.9, and click OK to create the rest.

You can also place a rest on a steep angle; in that case, it would simultaneously add and remove geometry in different directions.

FIGURE 9.9 The Rest tool will create a flat on the plastic part.

The Rule Fillet Tool

The Fillet tool used in Chapters 3 and 7 is powerful but can require a lot of input from the user. The Rule Fillet tool works based on relationships between the body of the part, its features, and its faces.

   You will use this tool to add fillets between the rest feature and the other features of the solid by specifying how the features will blend, not the edges on which you want a fillet placed.

1. Open c9-07.ipt from the Parts\Chapter 9 folder, making certain that the 2012 Essentials project file is active.

 Rule Fillet 2. Start the Rule Fillet tool from the Plastic Part panel of the Model tab.

   The primary options for the tool are selecting a feature or a face.

3. When the dialog comes up, click the rest feature, set Radius to 2, and leave the rule set to Against Part.

   The fillet preview will appear anywhere the selected feature makes contact with the rest of the part.

4. Click below the first rule where it says *Click to add* to create a new rule.

5. Click the rest again, leave the radius at 1mm, but change the rule to Free Edges. See Figure 9.10.

   This will apply the second rule to any edge that is not tangent with another face or already slated to be affected by another rule.

6. Click OK to place the fillets based on these rules.

After the edges are selected, you can click a face or edges to be excluded from the rule fillet.

FIGURE 9.10 Adding a rule fillet between a feature and the part

A rule fillet placed between features or between a feature and the body will not cause an error to appear if the conditions don't allow it to generate. Instead, it will lie dormant until the conditions are restored and it can appear again.

Adding a Grill

A grill is an opening in a part that has ribs over the opening. It can also include areas of solid obstruction called *islands*.

1. Open the c9-08.ipt from the Parts\Chapter 9 folder, making certain that the 2012 Essentials project file is active.

2. In the Design window, orbit the part so you can clearly see the sketch that is visible.

3. In the Plastic Part panel of the Model tab, start the Grill tool.

   The Grill dialog has five tabs where you select the sketch geometry you want to use for that subfeature.

4. The first tab is for the boundary; it is ready to click a profile. Click the circle in the sketch.

5. Click the Island tab, and for its profile, select the ellipse in the middle of the sketch. Set the thickness of the island to 1.

6. Select the Rib tab, and then click the six parallel lines in the sketch. Do not change any of the dialog options.

7. After setting the Spar tab to be active, click the three lines that are perpendicular to the last lines. Set Spar Thickness to 2 and Top Offset to .5.

8. Compare your model to Figure 9.11.

FIGURE 9.11 The grill feature replaces several other features.

 9. Expand the dialog, and it will update to show what the open sectional area of the grill is, for ventilation considerations.

10. Click OK to generate the grill.

The grill is the most flexible feature for plastic parts, with a wide selection of subfeatures so that you can pick and choose only the parts you want to place.

Embossing or Engraving

The rules for creating an embossed or engraved feature, such as the product logo for the example part, are the same as if you were going to extrude a solid feature. You can use a closed sketch or text.

1. Open c9-09.ipt from the Parts\Chapter 9 folder, making certain that the 2012 Essentials project file is active.

2. Position the model so you can see the text in the sketch above the grill feature.

Emboss **3.** Start the Emboss tool from the Create panel of the Model tab.

4. When the Emboss dialog opens, click the text.

The Emboss tool has three options. One will add geometry, one will remove, and the third will do both if the sketch plane intersects a face on the part.

5. Keep the Emboss From Face option active, and set the depth to .5.

6. Make sure the direction indicator is pointed toward the part (Figure 9.12). It may be necessary to change it. Then click OK to create the feature.

FIGURE 9.12 Adding text to the face of a part

The Emboss tool also has the ability to wrap a profile or text around a face so that the edges of the feature are normal to the surface they're wrapped on.

The Snap Fit Tool

The two options for the geometry for this tool are the hook and the loop. The features are created with a wizard so all that is needed is a work point or a sketch point.

1. Open c9-10.ipt from the Parts\Chapter 9 folder, making certain that the 2012 Essentials project file is active.

2. Orbit the model so that you can clearly see the open portion.

Snap Fit **3.** Start the Snap Fit tool from the Plastic Part panel on the Model tab.

4. A preview of two features will appear, because there are two points in the sketch.

5. The features are pointing the wrong direction, so click the Flip Beam Direction button on the Shape tab of the dialog.

6. There are green arrows protruding from the previews that indicate the direction of the hook. One of them points inward. Click the arrow until both hooks are pointing outward.

7. Switch to the Beam tab of the dialog.

8. Match your dialog values to those in Figure 9.13, and click OK to build the features.

FIGURE 9.13 The Snap Fit tool creates complex geometry easily.

The hook side of a snap fit is placed in the same way. In general, all the plastic features follow a common process that makes them easy to learn.

Adding Ribs

The Rib tool is not a specialized plastic part feature. Ribs are used in many types of parts and can be used as a rib or a web; you have the ability to control the width and a depth.

1. Open c9-11.ipt from the Parts\Chapter 9 folder, making certain that the 2012 Essentials project file is active.

2. Orbit the model so that you can clearly see the open portion.

   Sketched in the interior of the front part is a series of lines that will locate the ribs. Those lines do not extend to the edges of the part and do not need to do so. The rib feature is capable of extending itself to fill in the geometry.

3. Start the Rib tool from the Create panel of the Model tab.

4. Click the four lines that are partially obscured by the block in the middle of the part.

5. Set the thickness to 2. See Figure 9.14 for the preview of the feature.

FIGURE 9.14 Rib features can extend beyond the sketch.

6. Click the OK button to create the ribs.

7. Orbit the part to see that the ribs did not penetrate through the front face of the part.

On parts with draft, it is difficult to properly create a sketch that doesn't risk creating a gap as it is created. Being able to create a rib with a sketch that doesn't meet the faces helps avoid problems when these parts change.

Adding Decals

It is possible to include geometry, text, or images in a sketch. A *decal* is a feature made from one of these images. It can be applied to flat or curved surfaces.

1. Open c9-12.ipt from the Parts\Chapter 9 folder, making certain that the 2012 Essentials project file is active.

   2. Create a new sketch on the XY plane.

🖼 Image **3.** Click the Image option in the Insert panel of the Sketch tab.

   4. In the Open dialog, navigate to the `Parts\Chapter 9` folder, click the `c9-01.png` file, and then click Open.

   5. Click a place in the Design window, and click to place the image. Hit Esc to finish placing.

   The size of an image can be controlled by a parametric dimension as well.

   6. Place a dimension on the top of the image file, and set the value to 60. Hit the Esc key to finish the dimension tool.

   7. You may have to use Zoom All to find the image in the sketch.

   8. Drag the sketch so it is roughly centered on the recessed face of the part.

   9. Finish editing the sketch.

🗔 Decal **10.** On the Model tab, expand the Create panel by clicking the arrow next to the panel name, and select the Decal tool.

   11. Uncheck the Chain Faces option in the dialog, and then click the image and the flat face behind it. See Figure 9.15.

FIGURE 9.15 Selecting the face onto which to project the decal

   12. Click OK to place the feature.

This was a simple placement of a decal. The tool doesn't really shine until you start wrapping images around faces. The Decal tool is capable of that as well.

Creating and Working with Assemblies and Their Parts

The multibody part simulates an assembly. It can also be used to create an assembly. This assembly will be made up of components created from some or all of the bodies in the part. Any change to the bodies of the part will be reflected in the part created from it.

Converting Bodies to Components

Converting the bodies to parts requires the user to specify a new assembly, select the bodies, and name the new part files.

1. Open the c9-13.ipt from the Parts\Chapter 9 folder, making certain that the 2012 Essentials project file is active.

2. Switch the ribbon to the Manage tab, and start the Make Components tool from the Layout panel.

3. When the Make Components dialog opens, it will be in selection mode. Click the three components from the Design window or from the Solid Bodies folder of the Browser.

4. In the dialog, set the Target Assembly Name field to **New Assembly .iam** and the Target Assembly Location field to **C:\Inventor 2012 Essentials\Assemblies\Chapter 9**.

5. Compare your dialog box to Figure 9.16, and then click Next.

6. You don't need to change anything in the Make Components: Bodies dialog. Click OK.

FIGURE 9.16 Set the name of the assembly and its path.

This will create the new files and then open the new assembly with the related parts. These parts will be grounded into position, so applying assembly constraints isn't needed.

Draft Analysis

There are tools for several types of shape and geometry analysis in Inventor. You can analyze the curvature, the sections of the body, and even the continuity of the surfaces.

Draft analysis gives a basic understanding of how a part might separate from a mold. It gives you the opportunity to make changes early in the process.

Draft

1. Open c9-14.ipt from the Parts\Chapter 9 folder, making certain that the 2012 Essentials project file is active.

2. Switch the Ribbon to the Inspect tab, and click the Draft tool on the Analysis panel.

3. Expand the Origin folder in the Browser, and select the XY plane for the direction to which the pull would be normal.

4. Click OK to close the dialog and display the results of the analysis, as shown in Figure 9.17.

FIGURE 9.17 Use draft analysis to see whether your part can be released from an injection mold.

5. After inspecting the results on the part, find the Analysis folder in the Browser, right-click, and uncheck Analysis Visibility in the context menu.

This tool does not analyze the shrinkage of material or do any material flow analysis. Those tools are available in more advanced versions of Autodesk Inventor.

THE ESSENTIALS AND BEYOND

Working with the specialized plastic part features, you learned how a common feature can have its options and variables built into a simple dialog.

Multibody parts have many applications beyond plastics. They can be used any time more than one part needs to share a common shape.

ADDITIONAL EXERCISES

▶ Apply the groove side of the lip to the back body in c9-04.ipt.

▶ When you are going to apply edge fillets between features, try using rule fillets instead.

▶ Use the Rib tool to create ribbing at an angle or across openings by defining a depth.

▶ The Emboss tool can also cut material. Try doing the exercise for the Emboss tool using a cutting option instead.

Working with Sheet Metal Parts

Sheet metal fabrication has to follow rules. For bending operations, certain things are not allowed. For example, you can't fold material if you cannot cut the part in the flat pattern, and material comes in certain standard thicknesses.

It's entirely possible to construct sheet metal parts using solid modeling tools such as Extrude and Revolve, but working with specialized tools will eliminate steps, and because these tools work with styles, updating the style will update the part.

In this chapter, you will create different parts using Inventor's sheet metal tools. The operation of these tools is essentially similar to other solid modeling tools, so they should be easy to learn.

▶ **Defining sheet metal material styles**

▶ **Building sheet metal components**

▶ **Preparing the part for manufacture**

▶ **Documenting sheet metal parts**

Defining Sheet Metal Material Styles

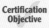
Certification
Objective

Like the styles you explored in Chapter 5, sheet metal defaults are styles used to establish consistency between components. You can create these styles within a part (with a scope limited to that part) or save them into a template to be available anywhere.

1. Open the file c10-01.ipt from the Parts/Chapter 10 folder. Make certain that the 2012 Essentials project file is active.

2. Click the Sheet Metal Defaults tool (Figure 10.1) on the Setup panel of the Sheet Metal tab, and click the edit icon next to the Sheet Metal Rule drop-down.

FIGURE 10.1 The Sheet Metal Defaults dialog controls whether you're basing your part on a predefined rule or what settings you use if you're not.

3. When the Styles and Standard Editor dialog opens, make sure the Default_mm style is active, and click the New icon at the top.

4. In the New Local Style dialog, enter the name **Aluminum 3 mm**, and click OK.

5. In the dialog, change the Material drop-down to Aluminum-6061.

6. Set Thickness to 3 and the Miter/Rip/Seam Gap value to **Thickness/2**.

7. Set Flat Pattern Punch Representation to Center Mark Only. See Figure 10.2.

8. Click the Bend tab, and change Relief Shape to Tear and Bend Radius to 2mm, as shown in Figure 10.3.

9. Click the Corner tab. Change the 2 Bend Intersection Relief Shape to Linear Weld.

FIGURE 10.2 On the Sheet tab of the Styles and Standard Editor, you define the thickness and material of the sheet.

FIGURE 10.3 Use the Bend tab to control the radius of the bend and how edges will intersect with the sheet.

10. Change the Relief Shape value for the 3 Bend Intersection to Full Round. See Figure 10.4.

FIGURE 10.4 The Corner tab regulates how material will be removed from the corner or left in.

11. Click Save, and then double-click the Aluminum 3 mm rule on the left to make it active.

By creating a series of sheet metal defaults and saving them as a template, you can use the styles in future parts made from the template.

Building Sheet Metal Components

Even though the Inventor sheet metal tools are limited to components that can be made with break press operations, the variety of components that can be made with this process is enormous. As a result, there are a large number of sheet metal tools to accommodate that variety.

Creating a Basic Face

The Face tool looks much like the Extrude tool, but with sheet metal features, there is no need to input a thickness from the material because that is determined by the sheet metal default style.

Certification Objective

1. Open c10-02.ipt from the Parts/Chapter 10 folder, making certain that the 2012 Essentials project file is active.

2. Start the Face tool from the Create panel of the Sheet Metal tab.

Face

3. The Face tool will begin, and because there is more than one closed profile, you will need to select the larger portion of the sketch, as shown in Figure 10.5.

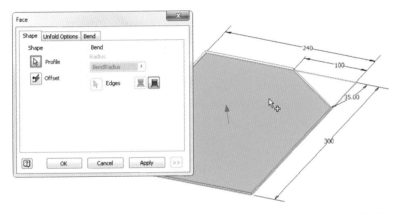

FIGURE 10.5 Select the portion of the sketch from which to create the face.

4. Click OK to create the face.

A face feature is frequently the base feature for sheet metal parts. You should try to use it to define the overall shape of your part.

Adding Sides to the Part

Flanges are typically features that are bent up from the base. In Inventor, these features can be created with the Flange tool, and they can be created using nearly every conceivable option.

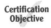
Certification Objective

1. Open c10-03.ipt from the Parts/Chapter 10 folder, making certain that the 2012 Essentials project file is active.

Flange

2. Locate and start the Flange tool in the Create panel of the Sheet Metal tab or the marking menu.

3. On the Shape tab, click the Loop Select mode, and click the front face of the part to highlight all edges and get a preview of the feature.

4. Set the Height Extents value to 40. If the flange preview is not in the same direction as Figure 10.6, hold the Shift key, deselect the lower edge, and then reselect.

FIGURE 10.6 Select the portion of the sketch from which to create the face.

When selecting edges for placing flanges, it's important to be aware of which edge you're selecting. The height is based on the edge you select.

5. Click Apply to create the new flanges.

6. Switch to Edge Select mode, and set Height Extents to 20.

7. Click the inside edges of the previously placed flanges, as shown in Figure 10.7.

8. Select the Corner Edit tool at the top-left corner of the part.

9. When the Corner Edit dialog opens, click the Corner Override check box, and select Reverse Overlap from the drop-down. See Figure 10.8.

FIGURE 10.7 Corners that would otherwise overlap are automatically mitered.

FIGURE 10.8 The automatic corner treatments can be overridden.

10. Click OK to accept the corner edit and then OK to place the flanges.

11. Start the Flange tool again, and click the front edge of the new flange on the angled face. (See Figure 10.8.)

12. Expand the dialog to see additional options, set Width Extents Type to Offset, and change the offset values to **10 mm**.

13. Change Flange Height to 15mm, as shown in Figure 10.9, and click OK to place the feature.

FIGURE 10.9 Adding a flange with the ends offset from the edge length

The angle of a new flange and how it is developed in the footprint of the existing parts are all important options worth experimenting with when using the Flange tool.

Building from the Middle

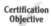
At times, you may need to build faces in space or from projections from other parts in the assembly. The faces can be created in space with no connection to the rest of the part, but eventually, you'll need to connect these faces to the rest of the part, and the Bend tool can help you do that using more than one workflow.

1. Open c10-04.ipt from the Parts/Chapter 10 folder, making certain that the 2012 Essentials project file is active.

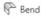 Bend   2. On the Sheet Metal tab, start the Bend tool from the Create panel.

3. Click one of the long edges of the red Face feature and then an edge on the nearest flange of the main body.

    The preview will show a feature that bridges the selected edges and cuts into the flange on the main part.

4. Click the Full Radius option in the Bend dialog, and see that the preview shows a feature that is tangent to both faces.

5. Return to the 90 Degree option, and click the Flip Fixed Edge option. Your screen should look like Figure 10.10.

FIGURE 10.10 The Bend tool builds geometry between features.

This will base the geometry on the selected edge of the main part.

6. Click OK to create the new feature.

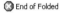 End of Folded

7. Move the end-of-folded marker to the bottom of the Browser to expose a sketch.

8. Start the Face tool from the Create panel, and the face will preview.

9. Click the Edges selection icon, and click the same edge on the main body as you did before.

10. After the dialog expands, click the 90 Degree Double bend, and click the Flip Fixed Edge option.

11. Click OK to generate the feature; Figure 10.11 shows the result.

FIGURE 10.11 The generated Bend feature

You can create these bend features from an existing feature or while creating a new one. The other bend options, such as limiting the bend to 45 degrees or using Flip Fixed Edge, can build geometry that could take several features to make without them.

Using an Open Profile

To create a long part with a consistent profile, you could build a series of flanges attached to one another, but using the Contour Flange tool is a much simpler way to go.

1. Open c10-05.ipt from the Parts/Chapter 10 folder, making certain that the 2012 Essentials project file is active.

Contour
Flange

2. Start the Contour Flange tool from the Create panel on the Sheet Metal tab.

3. Select the profile, and the preview will appear. Expand the dialog if need be, and set the Distance value to 300.

4. Change the Direction for the feature as shown in Figure 10.12.

FIGURE 10.12 The contour flange adds geometry from an open profile.

5. Click OK to create the feature.

Without this tool, creating the part you've just built would have taken a face and seven flanges. Contour Flange will add the band radii at the corners of the sketch. You can build curves into the sketch, and they will be maintained in the feature.

Adding Library Features Around Bends

A very challenging problem is dealing with features that transition across bends. Another challenge is working with features that you will use repeatedly. Punch tools are a common need in sheet metal, and you can define them and save them to a library for reuse.

Certification
Objective

1. Open c10-06.ipt from the Parts/Chapter 10 folder, making certain that the 2012 Essentials project file is active.

 Unfold   **2.** Start the Unfold tool from the Modify panel of the Sheet Metal tab.

3. When the Unfold dialog opens, click the top face of the part for the stationary reference.

4. Once the stationary reference is selected, the bends of the part will be highlighted. Click the bend shown in Figure 10.13, and then click OK.

FIGURE 10.13 Removing one of the folds in the part

An Inventor Punch Tool feature can be placed only on a flat surface. By unfolding a portion of the part, you've created a flat surface large enough on which to place the feature.

Punch
Tool   **5.** Click the Punch Tool icon in the Modify panel.

6. In the Punch Tool Directory dialog, find the Square Emboss.ide feature, and double-click it to start placing it on the part.

7. Because there was a pattern of hole centers in the sketch, four previews will appear for the Punch tool.

8. Switch to the Size tab of the PunchTool dialog, and set the Length value to **60 mm** and the Height value to **4 mm**, as shown in Figure 10.14. (The preview will not update.)

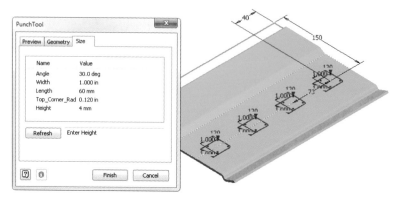

FIGURE 10.14 Placing the punch tools on the part

9. Click Finish to build the features.

Now, you need to restore the part to its original shape. This will require the punch tools to be bent with the other geometry.

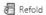 Refold **10.** Click the Refold tool in the Modify panel.

11. Once again, use the top face as the stationary reference, and click the only unfold feature that highlights.

12. Click OK to restore the shape of the part, as shown in Figure 10.15.

FIGURE 10.15 The part's bend restored

13. Move your end-of-folded marker to the bottom of the list to expose the cut sketch.

14. Edit the cut sketch by double-clicking it in the Browser.

 15. On the Format tab, click the Construction override.

Project
Flat Pattern

16. Expand the Project Geometry tool in the Draw panel of the Sketch tab, and click Project Flat Pattern.

17. Click the face that the rectangle of the sketch overhangs.

18. Add a 15mm dimension between the end of the rectangle and the end of the projection of the space between the punch tools, as shown in Figure 10.16.

FIGURE 10.16 Projecting the flat pattern makes it possible to dimension a position after it will be bent.

19. Finish the sketch.

Cut

20. From the marking menu or the Modify panel of the Sheet Metal tab, start the Cut tool.

21. In the Cut dialog, select the Cut Across Bend check box, and click OK to see the finished part in Figure 10.17.

FIGURE 10.17 The position of the cut can be controlled on multiple faces.

Measuring the distance between the new cut and the edge of the face on which it ends will show that the distance includes the transition across the two bends across which it transitions.

Exploring an Advanced Open Profile Tool

The Contour Flange tool uses an open profile to generate a complex shape normal to the sketch. You can use the Contour Roll tool to revolve a profile around an axis to develop a sheet metal part.

1. Open c10-07.ipt from the Parts/Chapter 10 folder, making certain that the 2012 Essentials project file is active.

 Contour Roll
2. Start the Contour Roll tool from the Create panel of the Sheet Metal tab.

3. It will detect the single sketch and select it, but still need you to select an axis.

4. Select the centerline to which the dimension of 200 is attached.

5. When the preview appears, change Rolled Angle to **30 deg**, as shown in Figure 10.18, and click OK to generate the feature.

FIGURE 10.18 Bending the open profile around an axis

The Contour Roll tool is interesting, and it can create components that would be difficult to calculate using other tools.

Building Transitions in Sheet Metal

There are many uses for sheet metal components that change from one shape to another. Defining these shapes for manufacturing has been a longtime challenge for designers.

1. Open c10-08.ipt from the Parts/Chapter 10 folder, making certain that the 2012 Essentials project file is active.

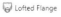 **2.** On the Sheet Metal tab, find the Lofted Flange tool in the Create panel, and start it.

3. Click the rectangle and the circle sketches in the Design window.

 4. After the preview appears, click the Die Formed option in the dialog to see how the part would look using that process.

 5. Return to the Press Brake option, and set the Chord Tolerance value to **3 mm**, as shown in Figure 10.19.

FIGURE 10.19 Being able to see how the transition will be fabricated can help guide decisions.

The model will update to show the number of facets that will need to be bent to create the part with this level of precision. Additional options for Facet Control include the angle between facets and the distance between points on the long edge.

6. Click OK to create the feature.

It will not be possible to create a flat pattern of the component as it is now. You will need to create a gap using the Rip feature to be able to unfold the part.

7. Start the Rip tool from the Modify panel.

8. In the dialog, use the Rip Type drop-down to set the value to Point To Point.

9. Set the model to the Home view, and select the large triangular face aligned with the bottom of the ViewCube as the rip face.

10. Make the start point the top tip of the face and the end point the middle of the bottom edge, as shown in Figure 10.20.

FIGURE 10.20 Making it possible to calculate the flat pattern

11. Click OK to create the rip in the part.

The exercise noted the eventual need to create a flat pattern. Later in this chapter, I will cover the tools for creating a flat pattern.

Working with Existing Designs

If you or your employer have a history of making sheet metal components, it is likely that you already have some flat patterns that work well for your designs. It is possible to use those existing .dwg or .dxf files to create the 3D part and even to add features to it.

1. Open c10-09.ipt from the Parts/Chapter 10 folder, making certain that the 2012 Essentials project file is active.

2. Edit Sketch 1 in the Browser.

ACAD   3. Click the Insert AutoCAD tool on the Insert panel of the Sketch tab.

4. Open c10-09.dwg from the Parts/Chapter 10 folder.

5. When the Import Destination Options dialog opens, make sure the Constrain End Points option is checked, and click Finish.

6. When the geometry appears in the sketch, finish the sketch.

7. Select Zoom All so you can see the entire sketch.

8. In the Create panel, click the Face tool, and click all four portions of the sketch.

9. Click the Offset tool to change the direction in which the face feature will be developed, and click OK to create the face.

10. In the Browser, expand the face feature, right-click the sketch, and click Share Sketch in the context menu.

Now the sketch is visible, and you can use the bend lines from the flat pattern to fold the material into a 3D form.

 Fold **11.** Start the Fold tool on the Create panel.

12. For the first Bend Line selection, click the red line beside the number 1.

This will display a glyph of a straight arrow showing which side of the bend will be folded and a curved arrow to show the direction of the fold.

13. Click Apply to fold a small portion of the part.

14. For the second edge, click the line next to the number 2, and select Apply.

15. Click the edge near the number 3, but the glyph will indicate that it will fold up the wrong portion of the part.

16. Click the Flip Side icon to make sure that the correct geometry (Figure 10.21) will be folded, and click OK.

FIGURE 10.21 Folding a flat portion of a face about a line

The component is now suitable to build new drawings from or develop new features. Changes to the sketch will modify the folded component as expected.

Adding the Finishing Touches

Creating the big portions of a sheet metal part has been covered so far, but the details are also important. Adding chamfers, fillets, and hems to the metal improve safety for the customer and add strength to the part.

1. Open c10-10.ipt from the Parts/Chapter 10 folder, making certain that the 2012 Essentials project file is active.

2. Zoom in on the top-left corner of the folded part.

◁ Corner Chamfer   3. Start the Corner Chamfer tool from the Modify panel.

   Once the dialog is open, you can select edges, but unlike the normal Chamfer, this tool will only select the edges created normal to the sheet so that the feature can be cut from the flat pattern.

4. Click the corner shown in Figure 10.22, set the value to **5 mm**, and click OK to place the chamfer.

FIGURE 10.22 Corner chamfers can be cut only in the flat pattern.

◻ Corner Round   5. Click the Corner Round tool on the Modify panel.

6. Select the edge shown in Figure 10.23, set the radius to **5 mm**, and click OK to place the fillet.

   Another useful option in the Corner Round tool is a feature selection option, which can find all the available edges with one click.

7. Find the Hem tool in the Create panel, and start it.

8. After the dialog has opened, click the long edge of the short face (Figure 10.24).

9. Use the Type drop-down to set the option to Teardrop.

10. Set the Radius value to **.8 mm**, as shown in Figure 10.24, and click OK to place the hem.

FIGURE 10.23 A corner round follows the same limitations as the corner chamfer.

FIGURE 10.24 Hems can be complex features but are added easily.

The Hem tool's four options should cover almost any requirement for fabrication. Now, you can focus on making your components suitable for the manufacturing process.

Preparing the Part for Manufacture

In some cases, you may choose to send data for the finished part to an external resource and allow them to calculate the material needed to create the part. Inventor has the capability to develop the flat pattern of the part. You can also edit this flat pattern to add material that isn't included in the folded part.

Building the Flat Pattern

Certification
Objective
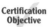

The flat pattern of the part will include calculations for the stretch of the material as it is formed. The type, thickness, or bend radius will affect this calculation. It is also common for companies to build in extra material to cause deformation, and this is done by modifying the flat pattern.

1. Open c10-11.ipt from the Parts/Chapter 10 folder, making certain that the 2012 Essentials project file is active.

Create
Flat Pattern

2. Start the Create Flat Pattern tool from the Sheet Metal tab's Flat Pattern panel. Figure 10.25 shows the resulting flat pattern.

FIGURE 10.25 The flat pattern of the part

Take a moment to look at the Browser. The flat pattern appears in the Design window, but the Browser is also updated to show the flat pattern state.

3. Start the Distance tool on the Measure panel of the Tools tab.

4. Click the far-left and far-right edges of the flat pattern, and make note of the measured distance.

5. Return to the Sheet Metal tab, and click Go To Folded Part in the marking menu or the Folded Part panel.

6. Start the Sheet Metal Defaults tool from the Setup panel or marking menu, and using the Sheet Metal Rule drop-down, switch to the Steel - 16ga style.

7. Click OK, and watch the part closely to see it change.

You should see that the material is thinner and the gaps between edges are smaller, and you may even see that the last flange added has a relief at either end.

8. Return to the flat pattern by double-clicking its icon in the Browser.

9. Make the same measurement, and see the difference in the size of the flat pattern.

10. Right-click the flat pattern in the Browser, and click Extents in the context menu. See Figure 10.26 for the results.

FIGURE 10.26 The Flat Pattern Extents dialog will report the material needs of the part.

11. Close the dialog, press the F6 key for a home view of the flat pattern, and then zoom in on the corner of the part that is near the bottom of the Design window.

12. Start the Fillet tool by pressing F (click OK to modify the flat pattern), and set it to a face fillet.

13. Click the two sides of the part shown in Figure 10.27, and set the radius to 5 mm.

14. Click OK to place the fillet in the flat pattern.

FIGURE 10.27 You can add features like fillets to the flat pattern.

The fillet that was added will appear on drawings of the flat pattern but will not propagate back to the 3D model. They are specifically for the use and benefit of the manufacturing process.

Documenting Sheet Metal Parts

The ability to create documentation in the drawing view that you've seen with other solid models works just as well for sheet metal components, but they need even more. For sheet metal, it's important to document not only the folded part, but also the flat part, and being able to communicate the process for forming it is a great benefit.

Establishing the Process

In the design phase, the flanges, bends, and faces of the part can be built in any particular order. That's not true for producing the part. Inventor has the ability to specify the order in which you want folds to be made in the solid model. The order you specify can then be accessed in the drawing.

1. Open c10-12.ipt from the Parts/Chapter 10 folder, making certain that the 2012 Essentials project file is active.

2. Activate the flat pattern in the model.

Bend Order
Annotation

3. Start the Bend Order Annotation tool from the marking menu or the Manage panel of the Flat Pattern tab.

   The flat pattern will display numbers that represent the order in which the part would be folded.

4. Click the balloon with the number 6, and the Bend Order Edit dialog will appear.

5. Select the Bend Number check box, and change the value to 1. Leave the Unique Number option selected, and click OK.

   This will change the number and the icon to identify it as an override.

6. Change the balloon for 9 to 3, and click OK, as shown in Figure 10.28.

FIGURE 10.28 Like BOM data in the assembly,
bend order information is kept in the part file.

Adding this information to the part makes it accessible by anyone who would
need to make drawings from your part.

Documenting the Process

Sheet metal parts often require two types of drawing. A drawing of the folded
part will help quality control and manufacturing verify that the part was built
properly. Drawings of the flat patterns can be used to cut the parts out of the
raw material.

Certification
Objective

1. Create a new drawing using ISO.idw from the Metric tab of the New
   File dialog, making certain that the 2012 Essentials project file is
   active.

2. Start the Base View tool from the marking menu or the Create panel
   of the Place Views tab.

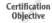 3. Click the Open An Existing File icon, and open the c10-13.ipt file
   from the Parts/Chapter 10 folder.

4. On the Component tab of the Drawing View dialog, click the flat pattern for the Sheet Metal view, and set the scale to 1:2.

5. Place the view in the middle of the page, right-click, and select Done
   from the context menu.

 6. Switch the Ribbon to the Annotate tab, and click Bend on the Feature
   Notes panel.

7. Click the bend line in the drawing closest to the top; when the note is placed, press the Esc key, or right-click and click Done in the context menu.

Clicking and dragging the insertion point of the bend note will place the note on a leader.

▦ General 8. Start the Table tool from the Table panel on the Annotate tab.

9. When the Table dialog opens, click the drawing view.

The dialog changes when the view is selected and lists the columns that will be shown in a bend table.

10. Click OK in the dialog, and then place the table on the drawing. See Figure 10.29.

FIGURE 10.29 The bend table and callouts on the drawing of the flat pattern

The numbers of the bends are added to the drawing views and correspond to any edits made to the bend order.

11. Press Ctrl+Tab or use the view tabs to switch to the c10-13.ipt tab.

12. Right-click the flat pattern in the Browser, and click Save Copy As in the context menu.

13. In the Save Copy As dialog, use the drop-down menu to change the file type to DXF, and then click Save.

14. In the Flat Pattern DXF Export Options dialog, set File Version to AutoCAD R12/LT 2 DXF.

15. Activate the Geometry tab, click the Merge Profiles Into Polyline check box, and click OK.

This will generate a new .DXF file, which is the most common file format for use with two-axis cutting equipment. You can also generate .SAT and .DWG files for solid export or direct use with AutoCAD.

THE ESSENTIALS AND BEYOND

Sheet metal tools keep the focus on creating the correct geometry as quickly and easily as possible. Inventor's use of styles to establish the material and its tools that use industry terms make using these tools more natural for anyone who commonly needs to create sheet metal parts. Tools like Contour Flange can simplify the process more by creating many features in one step. Manipulating the flat pattern is a necessity for manufacturing to make sure they can keep using processes that they've used in the past.

ADDITIONAL EXERCISES

▶ Set up templates using the material and sheet gauges you typically use.

▶ Use the Flat Pattern tools on the earlier exercises in the chapter.

▶ Experiment with other Bend options.

▶ Resize and reposition the profiles for the lofted flange and see the update.

Building with the Frame Generator

Inventor's specialized tools help you shortcut arduous and repetitive processes. The design accelerators and plastic part features you worked with in earlier chapters are great examples of this.

Another is the Frame Generator. The frames you create with this tool are constructed from dozens of metal shapes contained in the Content Center. Once they're placed, you can control how the frame members are joined together, and if the skeleton they're based on changes, the members will update as well.

▶ **Creating metal frames**

▶ **Editing metal frames**

Creating Metal Frames

To build a frame, you must have a sketch (2D or 3D) or a solid model to use as a skeleton. You place the frame members by selecting edges or by clicking a beginning point and an end point for the frame element. You can tell the frame member how to position itself along its direction based on nine control points around its section. You can also offset it a distance from that point or rotate the section.

Beginning the Frame

The techniques for building the skeleton of the frame are no different from any sketching or part modeling technique covered in previous chapters of this book. For that reason, I will shortcut the process by placing a finished skeleton part into an assembly.

1. Make sure that 2012 Essentials is the active project file, and create a new assembly file using the Standard (in).iam template from the English tab of the New File dialog.

Place

2. Use the Place tool on the Component panel of the Assemble tab to add the C11-01.ipt file from the Parts\Chapter 11 folder, as shown in Figure 11.1.

FIGURE 11.1 The frames skeleton is made up from a series of parametric sketches.

3. Press the Esc key to quit the Place Component tool.

4. Close the file without saving. For the next exercises, you will use an assembly with the frame already in place.

Whether you load a part file or create a new part in the assembly to use as the skeleton, this part will always be separate from the rest of the frame.

Inserting Members on Edges

The process of placing the members requires that you click the geometry on which you want to place them, select a standard of material, and then click the shape to use and the size. You can also select a color or material property for the member.

For this technique, you select a sketch element or model edge; then you can change its orientation along its path using the dialog and the various grip points and value options. With a skeleton in place, you can begin the process of building your frame.

1. Open c11-01.iam from the Assemblies\Chapter 11 folder, making certain that the 2012 Essentials project file is active.

Insert
Frame

2. Switch the Ribbon to the Design tab, and start the Insert Frame tool from the Frame panel.

3. In the Insert frame dialog, set Standard to ANSI, Family to ANSI AISC (Square) – Tube, and Size to $3 \times 3 \times \frac{3}{16}$, with the orientation in the center of the profile, as shown in Figure 11.2.

FIGURE 11.2 Setting the type of metal section

4. Make sure the Insert Members On Edges Placement option is active, and click all the black lines and only the black lines on the skeleton. Your results will look like Figure 11.3.

FIGURE 11.3 A preview of the steel components to be placed in the frame

5. Click OK to generate the frame members; then click OK again to approve the creation of the new files and a third time to approve the names of the new files.

   It is possible to change the names and paths of these new files to suit your needs.

It is a good idea to give unique names to the frame subassembly and skeleton when prompted. Filename prompting can also be disabled.

Inserting Members Between Points

Rather than creating a lot of extra lines or model edges, you can place the members by selecting a start point and an end point.

1. Open c11-02.iam from the Assemblies\Chapter 11 folder, making certain that the 2012 Essentials project file is active.

2. Switch the Ribbon to the Design tab, and start the Insert Frame tool from the Frame panel.

3. In the Insert frame dialog, set Standard to ANSI, Family to ANSI L (Equal angles) – Angle steel, and Size to L 1.5 × 1.5 × ³⁄₁₆, keeping the orientation in the center of the profile.

Selection points must be in a sketch. If there is a work point in the model you want to use, you will need to project it into a sketch first.

4. Make sure the Insert Members Between Points Placement option is active, and click the end point of the dashed, pink line and the line concealed in the upright of the frame, as shown in Figure 11.4.

5. Change the orientation to the bottom center, and rotate the profile to 270 degrees. Then set the offset values to -.2 and -.9, as shown in Figure 11.4.

FIGURE 11.4 Placing a frame member by clicking two points

6. Click OK to generate the frame members, and then click OK to approve the names of the new file.

The ability to realign the profile gives you flexibility with open metal shapes.

Inserting Members on Curves

Frame members can be placed on curved edges as well. Note that members placed on curved edges cannot be edited with the frame editing tools covered in the next section of the chapter. To edit curved frame members, use solid modeling tools like Extrude or Split to remove portions of these components.

1. Open c11-03.iam from the Assemblies\Chapter 11 folder, making certain that the 2012 Essentials project file is active.

2. Switch the Ribbon to the Design tab, and start the Insert Frame tool from the Frame panel.

3. In the Insert dialog, set Standard to ANSI, Family to ANSI AISC (Rectangular) – Flat Bar Steel, and Size to 2 ¼ × ⁵⁄₁₆. Keep the orientation in the center of the profile.

4. Make sure the Insert Members On Edges Placement option is active, and click all the yellow lines and arcs on the skeleton.

5. Change the orientation point to be the middle left, set the rotation angle of the section to 90 degrees, and select the Merge check box. Your results will look like Figure 11.5.

FIGURE 11.5 Building the metal shape across the straight and curved lines

   6. After the preview appears and is positioned correctly, click OK to create the new frame member, and click it again to approve the name for
   the part.

Placing the frame members always follows the same handful of steps. The
editing process is also direct. The tools are dialog-driven and typically require
only a couple of selections.

Editing Metal Frames

There are only a few editing tools for the Frame Generator, but they are more
than enough to make the type of changes typically needed in the process of
designing metal frames. Some of the tools allow for building in gaps for welding
operations.

   Any change in the skeleton will update the frame members as well as the edits
made to them.

Defining Joints with the Miter Tool

   A common joint for metal frames is an equal cut on both parts. A gap can
be included in the miter equally divided between both parts, or it can be taken
from one side or the other.

   1. Open c11-04.iam from the Assemblies\Chapter 11 folder, making
   certain that the 2012 Essentials project file is active.

⚑ Miter **2.** Switch the Ribbon to the Design tab, and start the Miter tool from
   the Frame panel.

   The Miter dialog will open. In the dialog, you will be prompted to
   click two frame members.

   3. Click the blue beam for the first option and the red one for the
   second.

   4. Set the gap to 0.130 in, as shown in Figure 11.6, and click OK to create the miter.

   Adding the miter will change the length of both frame members. Any end
treatment applied to a frame member can be removed.

FIGURE 11.6 Adding a miter to the frame

Changing an Edit and the Trim to Frame Tool

The Trim to Frame end treatment will take two members and set one to butt against the other and then limit the length of the first member to the width of the second.

The existing frame has a miter applied to two sections. You need to change it to a Trim to Frame joint.

1. Open c11-05.iam from the Assemblies\Chapter 11 folder, making certain that the 2012 Essentials project file is active.

2. Switch the Ribbon to the Design tab, and start the Trim to Frame tool from the Frame panel.

   The Trim to Frame dialog will open. In the dialog, you will be prompted to click two frame members. The first, represented in the dialog in blue, will overlap the second, represented in yellow.

3. Click the orange section for the first option and the nearly vertical section mitered to it as the second selection, as shown in Figure 11.7.

4. Select the Delete Existing End Treatment(s) check box, and click OK to update the model, as shown in Figure 11.8.

FIGURE 11.7 Modifying the miter to be an overlap

FIGURE 11.8 Trim to Frame will accommodate the sizes of both frame members for a clean overlap.

This will remove the miter end treatment and then set the orange member to overlap the green.

The Trim/Extend Tool

When frame members are placed on the skeleton, they're often overlapping or may fall short of other members they need to butt against. This end treatment allows you to select several members and terminate them at a selected face, whether it means trimming or extending them.

1. Open c11-06.iam from the Assemblies\Chapter 11 folder, making certain that the 2012 Essentials project file is active.

Trim/Extend 2. Switch the Ribbon to the Design tab, and start the Trim/Extend tool from the Frame panel.

3. When the dialog opens, click the two longest members at the base. Once they're selected, right-click and click Continue from the context menu to select the trimming face.

4. Click the face that the two selected segments intersect, as shown in Figure 11.9, and then click OK.

FIGURE 11.9 Select a face to which to match the frame members.

You must select model faces for the trimming surface. The model face can be a face on the skeleton if it is a solid model.

Creating Notches

For more complex joints between frame members, you can cut one member with the shape of another.

1. Open c11-07.iam from the Assemblies\Chapter 11 folder, making certain that the 2012 Essentials project file is active.

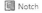 Notch

2. Switch the Ribbon to the Design tab, and start the Notch tool from the Frame panel.

With the Notch dialog, you select a frame member to cut first and then the member with which to cut it. These will be highlighted in blue and yellow as they are selected.

3. Click the red part first and then the green part for the cutting profile, as shown in Figure 11.10.

FIGURE 11.10 The notch will update with any changes to the geometry.

4. Click OK to create the feature.

5. Double-click the red part twice, first to edit the frame subassembly and then to activate the part. Figure 11.11 shows what happens to the part when the notch is applied.

FIGURE 11.11 A notch will remove an exact shape from the selected member.

 Return to Top   **6.** At the end of the Ribbon, expand the Return icon, and select Return To Top to put the assembly back to its top level in one step.

In cases where a pure notch creates too detailed a cut, it's advisable to do a traditional extruding cut or create a custom coping profile.

The Lengthen/Shorten Tool

The length of a placed frame member is based on the length of the selected edge or the distance between the selected points. The Trim/Extend tool is useful if you have a face to trim or to which to extend. This tool is for changing the length of a member in open space or when you don't want to use a face on another member without changing the skeleton itself.

1. Open `c11-08.iam` from the `Assemblies\Chapter 11` folder, making certain that the `2012 Essentials` project file is active.

Lengthen/Shorten 2. Switch the Ribbon to the Design tab, and start the Lengthen/Shorten tool from the Frame panel.

   The tool can add length to one end or equally on each end of the selected member.

3. In the Lengthen – Shorten Frame Member dialog, set the extension length to 4.5in, and leave the Extension Type set to Lengthen – Shorten Frame Member At One End.

4. For a single direction, the selection is click-sensitive. You need to click the end that will change. Click the end of the yellow piece that is in the open (Figure 11.12), and click OK.

FIGURE 11.12 Selecting the open end of the frame will add length to it.

If you need to add length to an end that has an existing end treatment, you will need to delete it first or select the Delete Existing End Treatment(s) option.

The Change Tool

Sometimes, you discover that a frame as originally designed needs to be changed. The frame members may need to be lighter or heavier or repositioned. The orientation, size, and family of any frame member can be changed. The Change tool will have you select a single or multiple members that are presently the same size and allow you to edit them with the same options used to place them.

1. Open c11-09.iam from the Assemblies\Chapter 11 folder, making certain that the 2012 Essentials project file is active.

↗ Change 2. Switch the Ribbon to the Design tab, and start the Change tool from the Frame panel.

3. When the Change dialog opens, click the green frame member in the base of the frame. After a short time, its properties will appear in the dialog.

4. Change the family of the part to ANSI AISC (Rectangular) – Tube and the size to $5 \times 3 \times \frac{3}{16}$ (Figure 11.13); then click OK to update the component.

FIGURE 11.13 Changing the family of a frame member

5. Click Yes in the dialog to approve the change to the family of the component, and click OK to create the new part.

6. Orbit the part to see the effect the change has in the assembly, as shown in Figure 11.14.

You can also change what standard the frame element is from the one that was originally placed.

FIGURE 11.14 Changing the family of a frame member

For all but radical changes to the family of a frame member, the end treatments should be maintained. This is also true for most cases when the skeleton of the frame is changed.

Changing the Frame Skeleton

The great advantage of using the Frame Generator over creating individual parts based on extruded profiles is the association between the frame members and the skeleton of the frame. A change to the skeleton will update the members of the frame rather than requiring you to edit individual parts one at a time.

1. Open c11-10.iam from the Assemblies\Chapter 11 folder, making certain that the 2012 Essentials project file is active.

2. Expand the c11-02:1 part in the Browser.

3. Right-click Sketch2, and turn on visibility in the context menu.

4. Locate the selection filter drop-down in the Quick Access toolbar, and set the priority to Select Sketch Features.

5. Double-click the 48.000 dimension to edit it. Change the value in the mini-dialog to 54, and click the check mark to update the dimension.

6. Then change Angle Dimension from 5 deg to 10 (Figure 11.15), and click the check mark to complete the edit.

FIGURE 11.15 Editing the parametric dimensions of the skeleton

 7. In the Quick Access toolbar, click the update icon to rebuild the assembly.

8. Turn off the visibility of Sketch 2, and inspect the completed frame assembly, shown in Figure 11.16.

The simplicity of the Frame Generator tools and the associativity of the generated frame with the skeleton make metal frames easy to create and maintain. If you have experience creating these types of frames, the tools should help you be more productive immediately.

FIGURE 11.16 The completed frame created with the Frame Generator

THE ESSENTIALS AND BEYOND

The Frame Generator tools open a new way of constructing the frames that are so common in machine design. Placing the frame members directly from the Content Center saves you the work of having to sketch the shapes and sizes of the parts. Using tools such as Trim/Extend, Trim to Frame, and Miter can save you hours of editing on a simple change. Using this workflow also bypasses the placement of the assembly constraints while maintaining the advantages of separate parts for detailing needs.

ADDITIONAL EXERCISES

▶ Make other changes to the skeleton model to see the effects.

▶ Try changing components to a non-ANSI standard shape.

▶ Change the material of the frame members to see how it affects the mass properties of the assembly.

▶ Experiment with changing closed profile members to ones with open profiles and see how the end treatments behave.

The Weldment Environment

A weldment is a specialized assembly. Like the sheet metal tools, the tools Inventor provides for working with weldments are built around the workflows and demands of a production environment. A weldment is an assembly that is regarded as a single, inseparable part.

Building the weldment as an assembly first makes it easy to understand how the components need to be positioned and what components are included in the weldment. The weldment environment also understands the ramifications weldments have on BOM structure and how to handle the weldment as a single component and document its members when needed.

Welds that are added to the weldment exist only in the environment and do not require you to maintain more files.

▶ **Converting an assembly**

▶ **Calculating a fillet weld**

▶ **Preparing to apply weld features**

▶ **Applying weld features**

▶ **Adding machined features to the weldment**

▶ **Documenting welds and weldments**

Converting an Assembly

There are a few special environments or shells within an assembly, and in order to access the weldment tools for Inventor, you must convert your assembly to a weldment.

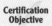
Certification Objective

1. Open c12-01.iam from the Assemblies\Chapter 12 folder. Make certain that the 2012 Essentials project file is active.

Convert to
Weldment

2. Click the Convert to Weldment tool on the Convert panel of the Assemble tab.

3. Answer Yes when prompted that you will not be able to revert this data to a basic assembly.

After you confirm the conversion, the Convert To Weldment dialog will appear for you to input specific information about the standards and structure of the weldment.

4. Set the Weld Bead Material to Welded Steel Mild from the drop-down.

5. Click OK to add the Weld tab to the Ribbon (Figure 12.1), and populate the Browser with a Preparations, Welds, and Machining group.

> Once converted, a weldment cannot be returned to a regular assembly.

FIGURE 12.1 The three additional states of a weldment

The assembly is still an assembly; it will just be treated differently in the BOM and have access to new tools.

Calculating a Fillet Weld

The design accelerators covered in Chapter 8 focused on tools that generated components. There is another class of tools associated with design accelerators; they are the calculators. Inventor can calculate several types of welds and solder joints.

1. Open c12-02.iam from the Assemblies\Chapter 12 folder, making certain that the 2012 Essentials project file is active.

Weld
Calculator

2. Expand the Weld Calculator tool in the Weld panel on the Weld tab.

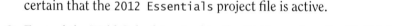

Fillet Weld Calculator (Plane)

3. Click the Fillet Weld Calculator (Plane) tool.

The goal is to keep the weld at the base of the blue arm under 7mm. The calculator will guide you to whether this is reasonable.

4. Set the weld form to an all-around rectangle.

5. Set the weld loads to be the bending force parallel with the neutral axis of the weld group.

6. Set the dialog options as follows:

> ► Bending Force Value = 12000N

> ► Force Arm length = 365mm

> ► Weld Height = 5mm

> ► Weld Group Height = 70

> ► Weld Group Width = 70

> ► Joint Material = Structural Steel SPT360

7. Click Calculate to get the results.

The calculator tells you that with the default safety factor of 2.5, you would need a weld bead of just over 5mm, but the stresses are too high.

8. Change the Weld height to **6 mm**, and click Calculate again to find a weld size that will work. Figure 12.2 shows the results.

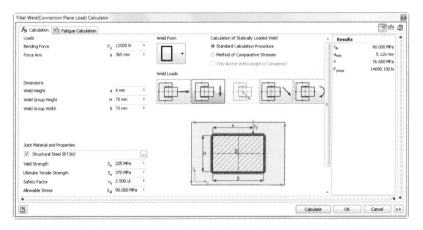

FIGURE 12.2 The properties for calculating the correct fillet weld size

Now that you've calculated the weld, you can apply it with confidence that it is sound. This and the other calculators can be used at any time and create the weld when you're ready or use it to guide your edit to a weld.

Preparing to Apply Weld Features

Preparations are features that are applied to a part after it has been cut but before the weld is applied. These features do not appear in the source part file, because a part may be placed in different assemblies and need different treatments for each.

A preparation can be an extrusion, revolved feature, hole, fillet chamfer, or sweep. The most common is the chamfer.

1. Continue using or open c12-02.iam from the Assemblies\Chapter 12 folder, making certain that the 2012 Essentials project file is active.

Preparation

2. To access the Preparation tools, click the Preparation tool in the marking menu or the Process panel of the Weld tab.

   This step will make tools available in the Ribbon and also change the Browser to show that these changes are added under the Preparations folder, not to the components in the assembly.

3. Click the Chamfer tool on the Weld tab in the Preparation and Machining panel.

4. Set the distance to 3 mm, and click the three edges highlighted in Figure 12.3.

FIGURE 12.3 Adding a chamfer to edges to prepare for the weld

5. Click OK to add the chamfers to the components.

6. Click Return from the Ribbon to leave the Preparation tools. Figure 12.4 shows the results.

FIGURE 12.4 The chamfers appear in the weldment but not the individual parts.

Now that you've added the preparation features you need, you can begin to add some welds to the assembly.

Applying Weld Features

Three types of weld are available in Inventor: fillet, groove, and cosmetic. In the next set of exercises, you will apply all of them and use a couple of options as well.

Adding a Fillet Weld and the End Fill Tool

Fillet welds are applied by selecting a minimum of two faces. There are two selection sets, but you can add as many faces to each set as you need to define the feature.

1. Open c12-03.iam from the Assemblies\Chapter 12 folder, making certain that the 2012 Essentials project file is active.

Welds

2. Access the weld tools by clicking the Welds icon from the Process panel on the Weld tab or the marking menu.

Fillet

3. When the tools appear in the Weld panel of the Weld tab marking menu, click the Fillet tool.

4. In the Fillet Weld dialog, click the Chain face selection check box, and then click the exterior surface of the blue tube.

5. Click the icon for selection set 2, and then select the face on the yellow plate against which the tube butts.

A preview of the fillet weld will appear at the default value of 10mm or the last size you used.

6. Set the first fillet value to **6 mm** per the weld calculation done previously in this chapter.

7. Click Apply to generate the fillet weld.

8. Deselect the Chain option.

9. For the first selection, click the face on the blue tube adjacent to the green gusset.

10. Switch to the second selection set, and click the triangular side and the chamfer surface shown in Figure 12.5.

FIGURE 12.5 A weld filling the gap left by a chamfer

11. Click OK to place the weld.

Because you selected the side and chamfer face on the gusset, the weld fills in all of the space. Selecting only the blue tube and the side of the gusset could still generate a weld, but it would leave a space.

One last touch is needed to make the weld look better.

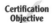 End Fill **12.** In the Weld panel of the Weld tab, find the End Fill tool, and start it.

The bare ends of the weld bead should highlight. If they do not, you can still click them.

13. Click one of the ends of the bead, and an image will be added to it, as shown in Figure 12.6.

FIGURE 12.6 Adding an end fill improves the appearance of the welds.

14. Press the Esc key to end the End Fill tool.

Now you've added fillet welds to the assembly. These welds do not require any new part files to maintain them in the assembly.

Adding a Groove Weld

Groove welds are used for filling gaps between parts. The direction of the gap to be closed is established in the dialog. There is another interesting option on which this exercise will focus—the radial gap.

Certification Objective

1. Open c12-04.iam from the Assemblies\Chapter 12 folder, making certain that the 2012 Essentials project file is active.

2. Access the weld tools by clicking Welds from the marking menu or from the Process panel on the Weld tab.

3. Click the Groove Weld tool from the Weld panel.

Groove

4. Click the exterior cylindrical face of the red part for Face Set 1.

5. Click the selection icon of Face Set 2, and then click the cylindrical face of the hole around in the blue part around the red part.

6. Select the Radial Fill check box in the Fill Direction group. This will present the preview shown in Figure 12.7 of a weld closing the gap between the parts.

Multiple faces can be selected for the groove weld to create an extended area.

FIGURE 12.7 The preview of the groove weld

7. Click OK to create the groove weld.

The groove weld could be left as is, or it could be added as part of a manufacturing process that would now add another weld to it.

Adding a Cosmetic Weld and Weld Symbols

The fillet and groove are the most common welds and therefore generate physical geometry to represent them, but there are many types of welds that need to be documented and considered in the weldment. The cosmetic weld will apply a weld to the assembly but will not build the geometry itself.

1. Open c12-05.iam from the Assemblies\Chapter 12 folder, making certain that the 2012 Essentials project file is active.

2. Access the Weld tools by clicking Welds from the marking menu or from the Process panel on the Weld tab.

Cosmetic

3. In the Weld panel of the Weld tab or from the marking menu, click the Cosmetic Weld tool.

4. In the cosmetic weld, set the Area value to **6 mm^2**.

5. Leave the Extents set to All, and select the Create Welding Symbol check box.

This will expand the dialog for selecting the specific type of weld that the cosmetic weld will represent. The default is a fillet weld for the opposite side.

6. Click the Swap Arrow/Other Symbols icon to make the fillet weld for the Arrow side.

7. Make sure the Bead selection icon is active, and click the edge shown in Figure 12.8.

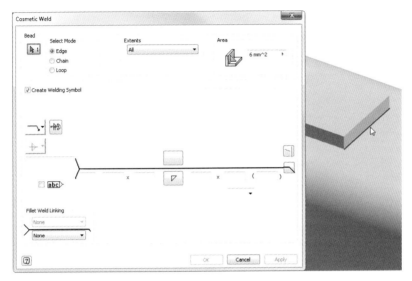

FIGURE 12.8 Select the edge for the cosmetic weld.

8. Click OK to place the weld, which is represented by a highlighted edge and the weld symbol shown in Figure 12.9.

FIGURE 12.9 A weld symbol can be added to any weld placed.

You can set the weld symbol inside the model. Move near the midpoint of the highlighted edge to show the concealed symbol, and use the grip points to relocate it.

Adding an Intermittent Fillet Weld

Sometimes referred to as a stitch weld, this feature creates fillet welds of a set length and distance apart, with the ability to specify a limited number.

1. Open c12-06.iam from the Assemblies\Chapter 12 folder, making certain that the 2012 Essentials project file is active.

2. Access the weld tools by clicking the Welds icon from the Process panel on the Weld tab or the marking menu.

3. When the tools appear in the Weld panel of the Weld tab, click the Fillet tool.

4. When the Fillet Weld dialog opens, set the first fillet size to 6 and the second to 4.

 5. Change the contour from Flat to Convex, and set the offset to 1.

6. Set the top Intermittency value to 9 and the one below it to 10.

7. Click the first bead selection on the side of the block and the second on the top face of the tube, as shown in Figure 12.10.

FIGURE 12.10 A preview of the intermittent fillet weld

8. Click OK to place the fillet welds.

Now you've added the final fillets to this weldment, and what was an assembly of parts can be produced as a single deliverable.

Adding Machined Features to the Weldment

Because of the distortion from welding components together and the need for some features to pass through several of the welded components, sometimes it is best to just machine features after components are welded together.

1. Open c12-07.iam from the Assemblies\Chapter 12 folder, making certain that the 2012 Essentials project file is active.

Machining

2. Access the machining tools by clicking the Machining icon on the Process panel of the Weld tab or the marking menu.

   There is already a sketch in the assembly; it was added in the machining process and appears in the Browser that way.

3. Click the Extrude tool from the Preparation and Machining panel.

4. Use the Extents drop-down in the Extrude dialog to set its value to To.

5. Click the interior surface of the red part for the termination. The preview will appear like Figure 12.11.

FIGURE 12.11 A preview of the intermittent fillet weld

6. Click OK to remove all material between the sketch plane and the selected face.

Like preparation features, the cuts made by the extrusion do not appear in the source files. They will remove the original component geometry and the geometry created by the welds themselves.

Documenting Welds and Weldments

Inventor keeps track of the physical properties of the welds as they're added. It also keeps track of the various states of the model so that the preparation, welds, and machining geometry can be documented as a workflow.

Extracting the Physical Properties of the Beads

To help estimate the materials needed to create a weldment, you have the BOM for the components, but you also need the volume and mass of the weld beads.

1. Open c12-08.iam from the Assemblies\Chapter 12 folder, making certain that the 2012 Essentials project file is active.

2. Expand the Welds category in the browser, and right-click the Beads folder.

3. Select iProperties from the context menu.

4. Switch to the Physical tab, and click Update to get the mass and volume information on the weld material for the assembly. See Figure 12.12.

FIGURE 12.12 The mass and volume of the welds is calculated even for the cosmetic welds.

You can also get the properties for individual beads by generating a bead report.

 Bead Report

5. Close the iProperties dialog, and click the Bead Report tool from the Weld panel on the Weld tab.

6. When the weld bead report is opened, click Next.

7. Choose a name and destination for the XLS file. Figure 12.13 shows an example.

Document	ID	Type	Length	UoM	Mass	UoM	Area	UoM	Volume	UoM
C:\Inventor 2012 Essentials\Assemblies\Chapter 12\c12-08.iam										
	Fillet Weld 1	Fillet	105.872	mm	0.011	kg	2.12E+03	mm^2	1.41E+03	mm^3
	Fillet Weld 2	Fillet	259.398	mm	0.038	kg	5.59E+03	mm^2	4.90E+03	mm^3
	Fillet Weld 3	Fillet	109.196	mm	0.011	kg	2.04E+03	mm^2	1.34E+03	mm^3
	Fillet Weld 4	Fillet	109.196	mm	0.011	kg	2.04E+03	mm^2	1.34E+03	mm^3
	Groove Weld 1	Groove	N/A		0.017	kg	2.12E+03	mm^2	2.19E+03	mm^3
	Cosmetic Weld 1	Cosmetic	30	mm	0.001	kg	6	mm^2	180	mm^3
	Fillet Weld 5	Fillet	28	mm	0.002	kg	383.879	mm^2	303.85	mm^3
	Fillet Weld 6	Fillet	28	mm	0.002	kg	383.879	mm^2	303.85	mm^3

FIGURE 12.13 The physical properties of each weld

Even though there is no physical geometry, the cosmetic weld is capable of contributing to the mass calculations if you apply an Area value in the dialog box.

Creating Weldment Drawings

The purpose of a weldment environment is to accommodate the needs of the production workflow. Documenting the steps is also important. Inventor can create drawing views of the stages of the weldment.

1. Create a new drawing using the ISO.idw template on the Metric tab of the New File dialog.

2. Create a base view from the marking menu or the Create panel of the Place Views tab.

Base

3. Click the Open Existing File button, browse to Assemblies\Chapter 12, and click the c12-08.iam file.

4. Set the orientation of the view to Iso Bottom Left and the scale to **1:3**.

5. Click the Shaded style.

6. Switch to the Display Options tab, and uncheck Tangent Edges.

7. Change to the Model State tab in the dialog.

8. In the Weldment group, set the type of view you want to place to Assembly, and then click a location on the drawing for the view, as shown in Figure 12.14.

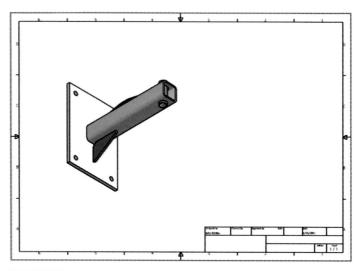

FIGURE 12.14 A drawing view of the Assembly state

9. Start the Base view tools again.

10. Repeat steps 3 through 7.

11. Set the view type for the weldment group to Machining, and place the view so that your drawing looks like Figure 12.15.

FIGURE 12.15 The drawing showing the beginning and end of the process

The intermediate steps of preparations can be shown in the drawing as well, and any type of drawing can be created from these states, just as you would any other file.

THE ESSENTIALS AND BEYOND

Working with tools whose approach is based on the production process builds efficiency into the design from the beginning and makes it easier to edit should production require that changes be made to the weldment.

The separate environments within a weldment make it easier to keep the focus on the steps of manufacturing a welded component and making sure that each step has all the information needed to complete the task.

By offering the flexibility of the cosmetic weld in addition to welds that add physical geometry to the weldment, like fillet and groove, Inventor ensures that you'll be able to document and plan for any type of welding that your design needs.

ADDITIONAL EXERCISES

▶ Try using a gap weld to connect the gusset to the tube instead of the fillet weld.

▶ See how different load types affect the results of the weld calculator.

▶ Add additional types of features to the machining state.

▶ Add welding symbols to the drawing from the Symbols panel of the Annotate tab.

Creating Images and Animation from Your Design Data

2D drawings have long been the standard in engineering communication, but increasingly they're seen as an incomplete means of communication. Building 3D geometry and using it only as a resource for 2D drawings is selling your work short. There is much more you can do with it.

Let's start with manufacturing and maintenance documentation. The exploded view is a great communication tool. In Chapter 6, you used an Autodesk Inventor 2012 presentation file to create an exploded view drawing. In this chapter, you will see how that presentation file was created.

Another valuable asset that you can create from the 3D work is a rendering or rendered animation. Marketing can then use these files to promote the products while the product is in engineering. You can also use this information to lobby inside the company for the opportunity to develop a concept.

▶ **Developing an exploded view**

▶ **Creating renderings and animations**

▶ **Building options to refine scenes**

▶ **Making a movie of the assembly**

Developing an Exploded View

The presentation file exists to enable the user to pull the assembly apart without really affecting the assembly. A presentation file is based on an assembly but does not change it. It will, however, reflect any changes made to the assembly just as a drawing view would. You'll use this behavior to create an exploded view of an assembly and then add simple animation.

Using the Automated Technique

When creating the exploded view in the presentation file, you will have two primary ways of placing the assembly. One automatically separates the parts based on the values of the assembly constraints, and the other simply places a representation of the intact assembly in the Design window for you to separate.

1. Open the c13-01.iam file from the Assemblies\Chapter 13 folder. Make certain that the 2012 Essentials project file is active.

2. Click the New tool on the Quick Access toolbar.

3. Double-click the Standard (mm).ipn template on the Metric tab to create a new presentation file.

Create View

4. Once the new file is loaded and the Ribbon updates with the new Presentation tab, click the Create View tool on the Create panel.

5. Set the Explosion Method option to Automatic, make the Distance value **60 mm**, and click OK.

6. Use the Orbit tool to see the results, as shown in Figure 13.1.

FIGURE 13.1 Creating an exploded view with trails

This assembly was constructed using Insert constraints to align the parts. Typically the Automatic explosion method does not produce such ideal results if the assembly isn't built this way.

Building One Step at a Time

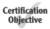
Certification
Objective

When you want complete control over the explosion separation and order, it is necessary to place the view intact and then move the components using the tools specific to the presentation file. In the following exercise, you will use the most commonly used tool in the presentation file, Tweak Components:

1. Open `c13-01.ipn` from the `Assemblies\Chapter 13` folder, making certain that the `2012 Essentials` project file is active.

2. Click the Create View tool in the marking menu.

3. In the Select Assembly dialog, use the Open Existing File tool to select the `c13-01.iam` file from the `Assemblies/Chapter 13` folder.

   This may seem a little strange, since there is already one exploded view of the same assembly already in the file, but like drawing files, presentation files can document as many assemblies as you like in one file.

4. Make sure the Explosion Method option is set to Manual, and click OK.

Tweak
Components

5. Click the Tweak Components tool in the Create panel of the Presentation tab or in the marking menu.

   From the number of icons with red arrows, you can tell this dialog wants a lot of user input.

6. Click the face of the blue part that the washer rests on for the direction.

7. For the components, click the bolt and the washer.

8. You can bypass setting a trail origin and just click in an empty portion of the Design window and drag to the right roughly 60mm, as shown in Figure 13.2.

   While you are creating a tweak or series of tweaks, you can add or remove components from your selection without having to reselect the direction.

FIGURE 13.2 Drag the components apart.

9. Click the blue part to add it to the selection, and drag the components to the right again by approximately 60mm.

10. In the value box in the Transformations group in the dialog, type in **65**, and click the green check mark to set the value of the last tweak to 65mm.

11. Now hold the Ctrl key and click the blue part and the washer to remove them from the selection.

12. Drag the bolt to the right approximately 50mm, and click the Clear button in the dialog.

    This clears your previous selections for Direction and Components but does not close the Tweak tool. This is a great way to change direction or focus without having to restart the tool.

13. If it's not already highlighted, click the selection icon for Direction, and then click the shaft of the bolt.

 14. Change the Transformation type from Linear to Rotational by clicking the Rotational radio button.

15. Select the bolt, change the Transformation value to **720**, and click the green check mark.

16. Click Close to finish adding tweaks to the exploded view, which will closely resemble Figure 13.1.

As it is, the current view would work well for showing someone how this assembly is built. But why limit yourself to a static view when you can easily build an animation from the work you've already done?

Controlling the Assembly Instructions

Certification Objective

Everything needed to create an animation is already done. Now, you need to be sure that this animation is done in the correct order and add controls for visualization and modify some of the values. These animations can show assembly or disassembly, and as you will see in the next exercise, you can control the order in which the parts are moved:

1. Open c13-02.ipn from the Assemblies\Chapter 13 folder, making certain that the 2012 Essentials project file is active.

Animate

2. Click the Animate tool in the marking menu or on the Create panel of the Presentation tab.

3. When the Animation dialog opens, click the Play Forward icon.

The tweaks you added in the previous exercise will animate in reverse order as the assembly comes back together.

4. Click Reset to restore the exploded view.

5. Expand the dialog to see the list of animation sequences shown in Figure 13.3.

FIGURE 13.3 The list of sequences making up the animation

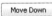

6. In the Animation Sequence list, click Sequence 1, and click the Move Down button until it is at the bottom of the list.

This sequence will now be labeled Sequence 4.

7. With Sequence 4 still highlighted, hold the Ctrl key, and click the two members of Sequence 3.

8. Click the Group icon to combine the three tweaks into a new Sequence 3, and click Apply.

9. Click the Auto Reverse button to see that the rotation of the bolt is now combined with the final step in the assembly process and to see the assembly expand again afterward.

You can change the Interval value to speed or slow the sequences, and you can set the number of repetitions for the animation. But there are options that can add additional control; you will use them next.

Adding the Details

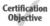

The order of the assembly is now correct, and the addition of the bolt turning gives the animation a little flair. To make the animation complete, you can have the sequences appear differently by changing the camera position and part visibility. You can also take this animation and export it as a video file for review by others.

1. Open c13-03.ipn from the Assemblies\Chapter 13 folder, making certain that the 2012 Essentials project file is active.

2. At the top of the Browser is the Browser Filters icon. Click it, and select Sequence View in the context menu.

   The Browser will update and show a series of tasks as well as the structure of the assembly that acts as a parent to the presentation file.

3. Expand the elements under Task1, and move your cursor over them to see that they highlight the components involved in the sequence.

> **There are also filters to view the assembly and a listing of each tweak.**

4. Expand Sequence 1 so you can see the Hidden folder.

5. At the bottom of the Browser is the assembly. Expand it, drag the c13-01 part under the Hidden folder of Sequence 1, and reposition the assembly to appear like Figure 13.4.

FIGURE 13.4 Each sequence can have a unique camera position to make the actions of the step easier to understand.

6. Double-click the Task1 icon.

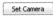

7. When the dialog opens, change the Interval value to 15, click the Set Camera button, and then click OK.

8. Use the Orbit tool to see the top, right, and back of the ViewCube.

9. Double-click the icon next to Sequence 2, choose Set Camera, and click OK.

10. Start the Animate tool again, and click the Record button in the Animation dialog.

11. The Save As dialog will open. Enter a filename, set the location to your computer desktop, and click Save.

12. Select Custom Profile from the drop-down. Change the Network Bandwidth value to BroadBand(250Kbps) and the Image Size value to 640×480 in the ASF Export Properties dialog, as shown in Figure 13.5; then click OK.

FIGURE 13.5 Select the options for creating the video of the animation.

13. This will return you to the Animation dialog. Click the Auto Reverse icon.

14. When the animation is finished, click the Record button again and then the Cancel button to finish the tool.

Go to your computer's desktop, and play the new video you created. Switching the file type to AVI in the Save As dialog will give you options to create a higher-quality video, but the steps are basically the same. A Completed c13-03 Assembly .wmv video is stored in the Assemblies\Chapter 13 folder.

Creating Renderings and Animations

The presentation file is a great way to quickly communicate with others how your product needs to be built. You can also use the engineering data to interest people in buying your product, but that requires a much higher-quality output. It's time to look at some of the tools of Inventor Studio. These tools will give you advanced rendering and animation capabilities and additional types of renderings.

Creating a Still Image

Certification
Objective

You can render any part or assembly file. The easiest way to do this is using the Realistic visualization mode on the View tab. To have more control, you need to enter the Inventor Studio environment.

1. Open the c13-02.iam from the Assemblies\Chapter 13 folder, making certain that the 2012 Essentials project file is active.

2. Make the Environments tab active.

Inventor
Studio

3. Click the Inventor Studio icon on the Begin tab to enter the Inventor Studio environment.

   Like the Sketch tab, the Render tab will be highlighted because it is a temporary environment, and you cannot do modeling tasks while in the environment.

Render
Image

4. Click the Render Image icon in the Render panel on the Render tab or in the marking menu, which will open the Render Image dialog.

5. Without changing any options, click the Render button. After the rendering is finished, it will appear like Figure 13.6.

FIGURE 13.6 The initial rendering

6. Close the Render Output window.

7. Change the Render Image dialog settings to the following:

Camera = Essentials 1

Lighting Style = Sample 1 Lighting

Scene Style = XZ Ground Plane

Render Type = Shaded

8. Click Render to create the image shown in Figure 13.7.

FIGURE 13.7 The rendering with more developed options

Pictorial images are not the only thing needed to show others; sometimes, you also need to create renderings for use in technical illustrations.

9. Close the Render Output window to prepare to make another rendering.

10. In the Render Image dialog, change the settings to the following:

Camera = Essentials 1

Lighting Style = (Current Lighting)

Scene Style = (Current Background)

Render Type = Illustration

11. Select the Output tab, and change the Antialiasing setting to High Antialiasing.

12. Click the Style tab, set Color Fill Source to No Color, and click Render to generate the image in Figure 13.8.

FIGURE 13.8 An illustration developed after a few settings changes

13. Close the Render Image dialog.

Even with basic changes to the options, the results are dramatically different. Next, you will see how to make changes that will help you create your own scenes and lighting to add more options.

Building Options to Refine Scenes

To add details and improve the appearance of renderings and animations, you need to expand upon the included library of surface, lighting, and scene styles as well as building cameras and local lights.

Customizing a Surface Texture

Some colors in Inventor include a surface texture. This texture is merely a visual effect. For any color, you can edit the color style to include a texture that, when rendered, will give the part's surface the appearance of a physical texture.

1. Open c13-02.iam from the Assemblies\Chapter 13 folder, making certain that the 2012 Essentials project file is active.

2. Click the red part in the Design window, and use the drop-down in the Quick Access toolbar to change the color to Blue Sea.

Changing the color of the part in the assembly does not change its color in the part file.

3. Click the Inventor Studio icon in the Begin panel of the Environments tab to open the Inventor Studio tools.

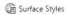 4. Click Surface Styles in the marking menu or in the Scene panel of the Render tab.

5. When the Surface Styles dialog opens, there will be a list of folders containing surface styles. Use the slider next to the list to find the Blue Sea style, and click it.

   Selecting the style from the list displays the color's properties in the tabs on the right side of the dialog.

6. Activate the Bump Map tab, and click the Use Bump Image check box.

7. When the Open dialog appears, select the AlloySand2_bump.bmp file; then click Open.

8. Drag the Scale slider to a value of 80, and click Save to get the results shown in Figure 13.9.

FIGURE 13.9 Creating a new surface style for the component

You can change the color values in the individual parts as well, and you can add bump maps to the color styles of Inventor. These bump map characteristics will appear in renderings and the Realistic visual style.

Changing the Scenery

A compelling visual effect is to place your design in an environment that looks like where it will be located or to create a scene that highlights the design by eliminating the background altogether.

1. Open c13-03.iam from the Assemblies\Chapter 13 folder, making certain that the 2012 Essentials project file is active.

2. Enter the Inventor Studio environment by clicking the Inventor Studio icon on the Environments tab.

3. Click the Scene Styles icon in the marking menu or the Scene panel to open the Scene Styles dialog.

4. Right-click the XZ Reflective GP style, and click New Scene Style in the context menu.

   This will create a new scene style named Default 1.

5. Right-click the new scene style, and select Rename Scene Style in the context menu.

6. When the Rename Scene Style dialog appears, give it the name **Essentials XZ**, and click OK to change the name.

7. Right-click the Essentials XZ style, and click Active in the context menu.

8. On the Background tab, click the Top Color icon in the Colors group, and set the color to black when the Color dialog appears.

9. Make the Environment tab active, use the slider to make the Show Reflections value 40, and uncheck the Show Shadows box.

10. Click Save and then Done to close the Scene Styles dialog.

11. Use the Render Image tool to generate an image like that shown in Figure 13.10.

Creating an array of scene styles will give you many options. You can also generate scene styles using images of the environment your designs will be in, including reflections of the lighting for the environment.

FIGURE 13.10 The
rendering with the modified scene

Applying Different Lighting

Changing the lighting in a rendering can make a huge difference in the quality of the images you create. Even small changes can have a dramatic effect. For this example, you will make a simple change to see what the total effect is.

1. Open c13-04.iam from the Assemblies\Chapter 13 folder, making certain that the 2012 Essentials project file is active.

2. Click the Inventor Studio icon on the Environments tab.

⌗ Lighting Styles 3. In the Scene panel, click the Lighting Styles tool, or select it from the marking menu.

4. Right-click the Sample 1 lighting style, and click Copy Lighting Style.

5. Give the new style the name **Essentials 1** in the Copy Lighting Style dialog, and click OK.

6. Right-click the new Essentials 1 style, and click Active in the context menu.

7. Expand the style, and click the Blue Fill element.

   The lighting type, placement, direction, intensity, and color can all be changed.

8. Click the Illumination tab; then click the Light Color icon, set the color to white, and click OK.

9. Use the slider to set the Intensity value to 80, and then click the Shadows tab.

 10. Select the Sharp Shadows option, and then activate the Directional tab.

11. Set the Longitude and Latitude values to 35, and then click Save and Done to finish the edit.

12. Click the Render Image tool on the Render panel to create a new rendering like Figure 13.11.

FIGURE 13.11 Updating the lighting has a huge effect on the rendering.

Additional shadows and highlights appear in the rendering thanks to the addition of shadows, the repositioning of the light, and the change in its color. Of the things that affect the scene, lighting is the aspect that will take the most practice and produce the most important results.

Adjusting the Camera Settings

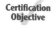
Certification Objective

The Essentials 1 camera that is used in the previous exercises was created by right-clicking in the Design window and selecting Create Camera From View in the context menu. Now you will modify it to give the renderings a little style:

1. Open c13-05.iam from the Assemblies\Chapter 13 folder, making certain that the 2012 Essentials project file is active.

2. Click the Inventor Studio icon on the Environments tab.

3. Expand the Cameras group in the Browser, right-click the Essentials 1 camera, and click Edit in the context menu.

4. In the Camera:Essentials 1 dialog, change the Zoom value to **36 deg**, and set the Roll Angle value to **-10**.

5. In the Depth Of Field group, click the Enabled check box, and set the Near value to **400 mm** and the Far value to **430 mm**. See Figure 13.12.

FIGURE 13.12 Editing the camera settings

These changes will rotate the view and zoom in a little closer. The focus limits will put the area between 400mm and 430mm in sharp focus, with parts of the model closer or farther from the camera becoming increasingly out of focus.

6. Click OK to make the changes to the camera.

7. Use the Render Image tool on the Render panel to generate the image in Figure 13.13.

FIGURE 13.13 Setting focus limits in the camera creates blur in portions of the rendering.

Creating cameras is easier done than said, but I still prefer to get a point of view in the Design window and initiate creating a new camera from there. Now, you can leverage all the changes you've made to create an animation of the assembly in action.

Making a Movie of the Assembly

It used to be that making an animation required another application besides the engineering tool. Translating the engineering data to the animation tool was difficult, and the animations often ended up being out-of-date because they couldn't be linked to the latest design changes. Inventor bridges that gap.

Creating the Timeline and Using the Camera

Certification
Objective

Camera changes in Inventor Studio can be as advanced as having the camera move along a path as it follows another path. But simple changes can add flair to an animation as well.

1. Open c13-06.iam from the Assemblies\Chapter 13 folder, making certain that the 2012 Essentials project file is active.

2. Open the Environments tab, and click the Inventor Studio icon in the Begin panel.

    Inventor can create multiple animations using different cameras, moving parts, and other variables. To keep track of it all, you have to create an animation within the file.

Animation
Timeline

3. Click the Animation Timeline tool in the Animate panel on the Render tab to create a new animation, and click OK to confirm that Inventor Studio will activate the new animation.

    The Animation Timeline (Figure 13.14) will appear across the bottom of the Design window. Toward the right will be a drop-down displaying the use of the current view for the animation.

FIGURE 13.14 The Animation Timeline is the main resource for editing animations.

4. Click this to make the Essentials 1 camera the active camera for the animation.

5. Just to the right of the drop-down is the Animation Options icon. Click it to open the Animation Options dialog.

6. In the dialog, set the Length value of the animation to 5 seconds, and leave the Default Velocity Profile value set to its defaults, as shown in Figure 13.15; then click OK.

FIGURE 13.15 The Animation Options dialog

7. The scale on the timeline has a slider that also displays the time. Click and drag it to read 4.0 (seconds).

8. Click the corner of the ViewCube to display the right, back, and top sides (Figure 13.16), and then click the Add Camera Action icon in the Animation Timeline.

FIGURE 13.16 The view that the animation will have at four seconds

Using Add Camera action repositions the active camera to that point of view at the selected point in time.

9. Drag the slider toward zero on the timeline to see how the camera motion is added to the animation.

▶ 10. Click the Play tool to see the changes you've made animated.

This is another example of how you can make an advanced tool easy to use. Defining a new path for the camera took only a handful of mouse clicks, and yet the result looks great.

Making the Components Move

Camera control isn't the only thing that has been dramatically simplified in Inventor Studio. The animation can use positional representations to define the beginning and ending conditions for mechanisms in the assembly.

1. Open c13-07.iam from the Assemblies\Chapter 13 folder, making certain that the 2012 Essentials project file is active.

2. Click the Inventor Studio tool in the Begin panel of the Environments tab.

Pos Reps 3. Click the Pos Reps tool in the Animate panel of the Render tab.

4. On the Animate tab of the Animate Positional Representation dialog, leave the Start position set to Master, but change the End position to Open using the drop-down menu.

5. In the Time group, click Specify As Measurement, and set the Start time at **0.2 s** and the End time to **1.5 s**, as shown in Figure 13.17.

FIGURE 13.17 Setting a transition time to move assembly components

6. Click OK to create the new animation element.

7. Now click the Expand Action Editor icon to see a full view of the timeline and activities on it.

In the timeline, you'll see blue bars that will show the duration of the actions on the rows to which they align.

8. Right-click the action on the slider bar with the PRAnim1 (Master<> Open) action, and click Mirror in the context menu, as shown in Figure 13.18.

FIGURE 13.18 Events in the timeline can be copied or mirrored rather than defining new ones.

9. A new bar will appear next to the old. Drag it all the way to the right so that the reverse action happens at the very end of the animation.

10. Click the Expand Action Editor icon again to reduce the Animation Timeline, and then click the Go To Start icon.

11. Use the Play Animation tool to see the combination of the camera transition and the moving positional representation.

The animation is now quickly taking shape, so you need to add only one more finishing touch to complete the work. The bolt needs to turn to open and close the vise.

Animating an Assembly Relationship

Assembly constraints reflect how components relate to each other in the real world. It makes sense that they would be used as the foundation of an animation to show how the assembly works.

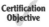

1. Open c13-08.iam from the Assemblies\Chapter 13 folder, making certain that the 2012 Essentials project file is active.

2. Click the Inventor Studio icon in the Begin panel of the Environments tab to open the Inventor Studio tools.

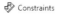 3. When the Render tab appears, click the Constraints tool in the Animate panel.

The Animate Constraints dialog will have a Select icon depressed and ready to click an assembly constraint from the Browser.

4. Expand the Browser view of the ISO 4017 M10 × 35:1 component, and click the Bolt Angle constraint.

5. In the dialog, set the End value to **360 deg**, click the Specify Time option, and start the action at **0.2 s** and end it at **1.5 s**, as shown in Figure 13.19.

FIGURE 13.19 Animating an assembly constraint

6. Click OK to create the new action.

7. Click the Expand Action Editor icon to see a full view of the timeline and activities on it.

8. Right-click and mirror the action for the Bolt Angle constraint.

9. Drag the new action to the end of the toolbar.

10. Play the animation in the Design window.

Now that you've created all the steps, you need to create the animation of the assembly. Next, you will render the animation to a video file.

Rendering the Animation

The camera moves, the vise opens and closes, and even the bolt turns out and then back in. Now, you need to share your work.

Certification
Objective

1. Open c13-09.iam from the Assemblies\Chapter 13 folder, making certain that the 2012 Essentials project file is active.

2. Switch the Ribbon to the Environments tab, and click the Inventor Studio tool in the Begin panel.

Render
Animation

3. Click the Render Animation tool in the marking menu or in the Render panel of the Render tab to open the Render Animation dialog.

4. Switch to the Output tab, and change the end of the time range to **5.0 s**.

5. If your computer has limited graphics, you can use the drop-down to set the frame rate to 10.

6. Click Render, and the Save dialog will open. Enter a filename, set the location to your computer Desktop, and click Save.

7. Change the Network Bandwidth value to BroadBand(250Kbps) and the Image Size value to 640 × 480 in the ASF Export Properties dialog, and click OK.

You can also create an animation as an illustration or as a series of still images.

The animation will be created by generating a rendering of each frame of the animation. The corners of squares will appear one for each processor in the computer. When it is complete, review the finished WMV file in the Completed c13-09.wmv file in the Assemblies/Chapter 13 folder.

THE ESSENTIALS AND BEYOND

Any reuse of the design data for marketing or production documentation, or even just for explaining an idea, multiplies the value of your work. Having drawings, presentation files, and animations all reflect any subsequent changes to that data is further reward for your efforts in creating the 3D geometry.

Creating renderings and animations is easy. Using assembly constraints and maintaining a focus on the function of the assembly will guide you to creating effective animations. When creating animations of presentation files, it is good practice to review the process with people who will produce the design to make sure it is valid.

(Continues)

THE ESSENTIALS AND BEYOND *(Continued)*

ADDITIONAL EXERCISES

▶ Consider creating an animation based on a presentation file for shop assembly instructions.

▶ Use the Save Copy As tool to make screen captures of exploded views.

▶ Change lighting types to see the differences and their effect on the rendering.

▶ Save a rendered animation as an AVI file to compare quality and file size.

Working with Non-Inventor Data

Autodesk Inventor 2012 is used in many industries to fulfill many different roles. A common role is to design tooling and do other manufacturing support, and this means working with data that may not be sourced from Inventor and may or may not be 3D. In turn, Inventor users may have to give data to users of other systems inside or outside the company.

Architects use the products of mechanical engineers and designers everywhere in the buildings they construct. Heating and cooling equipment, lighting fixtures, doors, windows, and curtain wall are all manufactured and ideal components to be designed in Inventor. Versions of Autodesk Revit can connect equipment that requires electricity, requires water, or does air handling with intelligence. If you're a building equipment manufacturer, you can use Inventor to share data with Revit users so they can include your products in their designs.

▶ **Exploring the data formats for Inventor Import and Export**

▶ **Working with AutoCAD data**

▶ **Exchanging 3D data**

▶ **Creating content for building information modeling (BIM)**

Exploring the Data Formats for Inventor Import and Export

It is important to understand what formats you can address with Inventor. By knowing the formats you can work with, you can better communicate with others about how you can most easily work with them.

Table 14.1 shows the file formats that Inventor can read or write primarily using Open ➤ Save Copy As. Some of these formats are read or written in less common tools such as when inserting an image into a sketch.

TABLE 14.1   External data formats Inventor can import or export

Certification
Objective

Import	Export	Format	Purpose
✔	✔	.idw	Inventor 2D drawing file format
✔	✔	.dwg	Inventor, Inventor Fusion, and AutoCAD drawing file format
✔	✔	.ipt	Inventor part file format
✔	✔	.iam	Inventor assembly file format
✔	✔	.ipn	Inventor presentation file
✔	✔	.ide	Inventor library feature format
✔	✔	.dwf, .dwfx	Autodesk Design Review Markup file
✔	✔	.dxf	Autodesk 2D exchange file format
✔	✔	.sat	ACIS kernel-based exchange format
✔	✔	.igs, .ige, iges	Product-neutral 3D surface file formats
✔	✔	.stp, .ste, .step	Product-neutral 3D solid file formats
✔	✔	.x_b, .x_t	Parasolid binary and text-based exchange formats
✔	✔	.prt, .asm	Creo Elements/Pro (formerly Pro/ENGINEER) part and assembly file formats
✔	✔	.g, .neu	Creo Elements/Pro (formerly Pro/ENGINEER) kernel-based exchange format
✔	✔	.prt, .sldprt, .asm, .sldasm	SolidWorks part and assembly formats
✔	✔	.prt	Seimens/PLM NX part and assembly formats
✔	✔	.jt	Compressed format file used by Siemens/PLM data management applications
✔	✔	.png	Adobe Portable Network Graphics file

Import	Export	Format	Purpose
✔	✔	.bmp	Windows raster file
✔	✔	.gif	Graphic information file
✔	✔	.jpg	Common graphic file (Joint Photographic Experts Group)
✔	✔	.tif, .tiff	Tagged image file
✔		.3dm	Rhino data format
✔		.model, .session, .exp, .dlv3	Dassault Catia V4 files
✔		.cgr, .CATPart, .CATProduct	Dassault Catia V5 files
✔		.wire	Autodesk Alias file
	✔	.adsk	Autodesk BIM exchange format
	✔	.CATPart	Dassault Catia V5 file
	✔	.pdf	Adobe Acrobat file
	✔	.stl	Stereolithography 3D-neutral format
	✔	.xgl, .zgl	Product-neutral 3D graphic viewing format

Working with AutoCAD Data

With millions of AutoCAD users, the chances are excellent that at some time, you will need to exchange data with an AutoCAD user. Working side by side with AutoCAD users, you can take advantage of Inventor's ability to create drawings in DWG format that AutoCAD users can open and to which they can even add data. In Chapter 10, you used AutoCAD data to develop a folded sheet-metal part from a flat pattern by placing the AutoCAD data into a sketch.

Opening AutoCAD Data

Often, you will only need to view the data to get information or create a print. Inventor is able to open a drawing file without modifying the source file.

1. Open the c14-01.dwg file from the Drawings\Chapter 14 folder. Make certain that the 2012 Essentials project file is active.

   The drawing will open and load a Review tab on the Ribbon (Figure 14.1) with tools to view, measure, and print the drawing.

FIGURE 14.1 The Review tab loads when you open an AutoCAD file.

2. Zoom in on the left view of the drawing.

Distance

3. Select the Distance tool in the Measure panel to verify the thickness of the material. This is 10mm thick but may be presented in inch units.

4. Zoom out to see the entire drawing, and then drag a selection window around the geometry of the front view.

5. Press Ctrl+C to copy the geometry to the Windows clipboard.

6. Create a new part file using the Standard.ipt template on the English tab and paste (Ctrl+V) the entities into the sketch by clicking in the Design window to place the data, as shown in Figure 14.2.

FIGURE 14.2 The dimension values from the AutoCAD data are updated in the new file.

Once the data is placed into a sketch, you can use it to create features using the geometry. You can also use Inventor's drawing tools to add drawing views to this drawing that can be seen by AutoCAD users who open the file.

Importing AutoCAD Data

At other times, you may want to import an AutoCAD drawing to be edited in the 2D environment of Inventor.

1. Start the Open file tool and select, but do not open the c14-01.dwg file from the Drawings\Chapter 14 folder. Make certain that the 2012 Essentials project file is active.

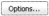 2. Click the Options icon, which will open the File Open Options dialog.

3. Change the option for dealing with a non-Inventor DWG file to Import, and click OK.

4. Now click Open to begin the translation steps.

5. When the DWG/DXF Wizard dialog appears, click Next.

6. In the next dialog, you will have the option of selecting what geometry will be imported. In this case, you want the entire drawing, so click Next.

7. In the Import Destination Options dialog (Figure 14.3), make sure the Constrain End Points option is selected and that the Destination For 2D Data value has New Drawing selected.

FIGURE 14.3 There are many options when converting AutoCAD data into Inventor.

8. In the Templates group, click the icon to browse for a drawing template.

9. Double-click the ISO.idw template on the Metric tab.

10. Click Finish when you return to the Import Destination Options dialog.

    This will open the drawing data in an Inventor drawing. This data is re-created with very good fidelity to the original data, as shown in Figure 14.4.

11. In the Browser, expand ImportedDraftView under Sheet:1 to see the sketches created from the AutoCAD layers.

Selecting Mapping Options in the dialog allows you to sort AutoCAD layers into separate Inventor sketches. You can also choose to put all geometry into one sketch.

FIGURE 14.4 The dimension values from the AutoCAD data are updated in the new file.

Because the geometry is in sketches, you can change it if you need to make a quick change to a drawing; however, most users want instead to take advantage of the AutoCAD Mechanical software that comes as part of Inventor.

Exchanging 3D Data

As you saw in Table 14.1, Inventor can import all of the most common 3D formats, both product-neutral and product-specific. Much of the time, this will allow you access to other people's design data with complete accuracy. The original features or parameters of the data are not accessible. Imported data is brought in a single entity referred to as a *base solid*.

Opening assemblies will import the individual components; although they will not be constrained together, they will be positioned as they were in the original data, so this imported data can be used without having to reconstruct the constraints.

Opening Neutral 3D Data

For opening neutral 3D data, you will work with a single part, but all the steps are the same for the largest data.

1. Launch the Open file dialog, and make certain that the 2012 Essentials project file is active.

2. Use the Files Of Type drop-down to click the STEP Files (*.stp, *.ste, *.step) format, and navigate to the Parts/Chapter 14 folder; then select the c14-01.stp file and open it, as shown in Figure 14.5.

FIGURE 14.5 The model after import into Inventor

Once the file is opened, it can be saved and used as a resource for creating drawings, assemblies, and any other data. The imported data can have parametric features added to it, but you cannot edit the features that are on the part.

Use the same process for importing data from other 3D CAD systems.

Editing Imported Data

To edit the base solid, you will use an application that installs with Inventor, called Inventor Fusion. Inventor Fusion offers many options for editing these solids.

Prior to Inventor Fusion, you could do basic solid editing using tools built into Inventor to edit base solids. This is still an option available through the application options.

1. Click the Open file tool, and if need be, switch the Files Of Type value back to Autodesk Inventor Files.

2. Open c14-01.ipt from the Parts\Chapter 14 folder, making certain that the 2012 Essentials project file is active.

 3. Locate the imported data icon, which includes the name of the imported file, in the Browser; then expand it, right-click the Base1 element, and select Edit Solid in the context menu.

4. A dialog will appear telling you how to return to Inventor from Inventor Fusion when you're done editing the solid. Click OK.

5. The Inventor session will be minimized, and Inventor Fusion will open with the model geometry in it.

   Inventor will make the changes you need, but it also has the ability to develop features on its own and can even be used as a stand-alone modeler. The changes you need to make will use a small fraction of what it can do, and you will finish the edits using Inventor.

6. Hold the Ctrl key and click the fillets on the existing part in the Fusion Design window. Use the ViewCube to make sure you can select all of them. See Figure 14.6.

FIGURE 14.6 Select all the fillets on the part.

 7. Once they're selected, right-click and click Delete in the marking menu. You can select the fillets in multiple steps if needed.

8. Once the fillets are gone, the model should have only sharp edges.

   Before you make the edits, let's change the unit of measurement.

When Inventor Fusion is used to edit an Inventor part, the changes can be saved to a DWG file, so an Inventor user can review the changes before adopting them.

9. In the lower-right corner, hover over the icon that shows the current units of cm, and click mm from the pullout menu (Figure 14.7).

FIGURE 14.7 Set the unit of measure to mm.

 10. Right-click in the Fusion Design window, and select Move in the marking menu.

11. Click the top of the handle, and an icon called a *triad* will appear as the face highlights. Drag the yellow arrow down 5mm to move the face, as shown in Figure 14.8.

Zooming in closer to the model will reduce the distance between snapping points if it tries to move more than 5mm.

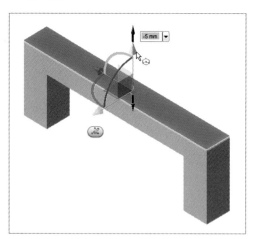

FIGURE 14.8 You can drag to edit the position of the face.

12. Right-click, and either click OK or drag to the right to complete the change.

Dragging the curved edges can change the angle of a face as well. Now that you've thinned the top of the part, you will add contour to the underside.

13. Click the Assign Symmetry icon in the Form Edit panel.

14. Three planes will appear through the center of the part. Click the long, vertical one shown in Figure 14.9, and then click OK to set the value.

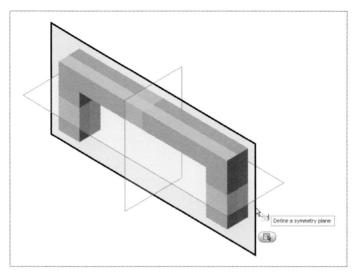

FIGURE 14.9 Clicking a symmetry plane will make edits appear on both sides of the plane.

Edit Edge

15. Start the Edit Edge tool from the Form Edit panel, and click the edge shown in Figure 14.10; then move your cursor near the middle edge, and click to place a grip point.

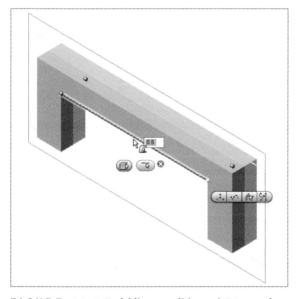

FIGURE 14.10 Adding an editing point to an edge

16. Click the front face on the ViewCube to rotate the view.

    Setting this view will isolate the movements of the point to be parallel to the view. This can be a very effective way to control the edits made to the model.

You can select a plane to isolate movement as well, or you can freely move a point in space.

17. Click the point in the middle of the edge and drag it downward, as shown in Figure 14.11. Release the mouse button, and click OK to finish the edit.

FIGURE 14.11 Dragging a point on an edge can reshape the part.

18. Click the Return To Inventor icon in the Inventor panel to update the model in Inventor with the changes made in Inventor Fusion.

Return to Inventor

You can use the Edit Edge tool to make very radical geometry changes to a model. These changes can be made to a parametric Inventor model as well, but it is best to make the changes before finishing touches such as fillets are added.

Exporting Data for Rapid Prototyping

Autodesk's philosophy of digital prototyping calls for the designer to develop and evaluate the function of a design in the digital world to reduce the number of physical prototypes needed. A tool that has been gaining popularity is the use of rapid prototyping equipment, which, for design reviews, provides the tactile feedback that can't be done in the digital domain. These systems will accept a large number of formats, but the one that was created specifically for this process is the stereolithography (STL) model.

1. Open c14-02.ipt from the Parts\Chapter 14 folder, making certain that the 2012 Essentials project file is active.

2. Open the Application menu, expand the Save As menu, and click the Save Copy As tool.

3. In the Save Copy As dialog, change the Save As Type value to STL Files (*.stl), and then click the Preview button.

The preview window will open, and the model will appear somewhat faceted. You can vary the amount of smoothness in order to judge whether a part that can be created more quickly will give you the level of quality needed.

4. Click the Options button at the top of the window.

5. When the STL File Save As Options dialog opens, as shown in Figure 14.12, set Surface Deviation to .01, and click OK.

Check the minimum resolution of your rapid prototyping equipment to avoid creating models whose surface quality cannot be met.

FIGURE 14.12 Editing STL file export options

6. Click the Show Facet Edges icon to display the edges of the model facets, as shown in Figure 14.13.

FIGURE 14.13 The edges of the model can be displayed to help you make better decisions about resolution.

7. Click Close to return to the Save Copy As dialog, set a path, and click Save to create the file.

Having the additional control over the model saves time and money and makes the rapid prototyping process more valuable.

Creating Content for Building Information Modeling

Building information modeling (BIM) is a philosophy in the architecture, construction, and engineering realm that is very similar to digital prototyping. Creating a database with as much detail about the elements and structure of the building as possible enables it to be built more efficiently, and the model can be used for maintenance in the future.

An add-on called Revit MEP is used to design the building's mechanical, electrical, and plumbing components. Much of the equipment used in these trades is created by people who can design it in Inventor. If these vendors can make it easy to put their equipment in a building design, they'll have a competitive advantage. Inventor enables these companies to generate this content for their potential customers.

Simplifying and Securing Your Design

Certification Objective

Sharing your design with potential customers is great as long as you don't put your intellectual property at risk. You can use the Shrinkwrap tool to create simplified models any time you like. It allows you to build substitution level-of-detail representations.

In this exercise, you'll build a simplified part to which to add BIM information:

1. Open c14-01.iam from the Assemblies\Chapter 14 folder, making certain that the 2012 Essentials project file is active.

BIM
Exchange

2. Click the BIM Exchange tool in the Begin panel of the Environments tab.

This will launch the BIM Exchange tab on the Ribbon.

Shrinkwrap
Substitute

3. Click the Shrinkwrap Substitute tool from the Component panel.

4. You can define filenames and paths in the New Derived Substitute Part dialog, but for this exercise, click OK to accept the defaults shown in Figure 14.14.

FIGURE 14.14 Set the filename and path information in the New Derived Substitute dialog.

5. In the Assembly Shrinkwrap Options that appear next, click the Range (Perimeter) radio button, and set Min to **5 mm** and Max to **1000 mm**.

6. For the Simplification mode, select Remove Geometry By Visibility, and leave the slider at 0 percent.

7. Set the style to Single Solid Body Merging Out Seams Between Planar Faces, and then click the Preview button. Figure 14.15 shows the results.

FIGURE 14.15 The Shrinkwrap model can be created as a single or multibody part.

8. Click OK to generate the file using the options.

9. The simplified model will become the active level of detail for the assembly.

   Note that the vent in the top of the housing and even the openings on the hose fittings are capped to remove geometry.

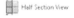 10. Switch your Ribbon to the View tab, and use the Section View drop-down menu to click the Half Section View tool.

11. Click top of the model, and drag the sectioning plane halfway into the part to see that the two internal components have been removed. Your model should match Figure 14.16.

FIGURE 14.16 Simplification can close gaps and remove components from the assembly.

12. Click the check mark in the dialog showing the distance of the cutting plane (Figure 14.17).

FIGURE 14.17 Click to accept the offset displayed.

   You can use the Section View tool to expose internal detail and continue to model with it switched on.

13. Using the Section View drop-down menu, click End Section View to restore the view of the assembly.

With the model simplified, it is now ready to have connection information added to it that will ensure your product will be properly connected in the BIM model.

Authoring MEP Content

In this exercise, you'll build a simplified part to which to add BIM information:

1. Open c14-02.iam from the Assemblies\Chapter 14 folder, making certain that the 2012 Essentials project file is active.

    This assembly will open with the substitute level of detail active.

2. Start the BIM Exchange tool in the Begin panel on the Environments tab.

Pipe
Connector

3. Click the Pipe Connector tool on the BIM Exchange tab's MEP Author panel.

4. When the Pipe Connector dialog opens, click the round face on the bottom fitting, and click the Make Direction icon so the flow is going outward, as shown in Figure 14.17.

5. The diameter will be filled in automatically. Set the Nominal_ Diameter value to 3/8 in.

6. Set the System Type drop-down to Domestic Hot Water, as shown in Figure 14.18.

FIGURE 14.18 Adding the hot water output to the heater

7. Click Apply to add the connector to the part.

   After you place the connector, the dialog will be ready to place another.

8. Click the round face of the upper fitting.

9. Set Nominal_Diameter to 3/8 in, but set System Type to Domestic Cold Water; then click OK.

10. Rotate the model to see the top, left, and front faces of the ViewCube.

Electrical
Connector

11. Start the Electrical Connector tool from the MEP Author panel.

12. Click the curved edge on the side of the model opposite the water pipe connectors.

13. Set System Type to Power Balanced, change Number Of Poles to 3 using the drop-down as shown in Figure 14.19, and click OK.

FIGURE 14.19 Adding the electrical connection to the product

Export Building
Components

14. Click the Export Building Components tool on the Manage panel.

15. Click the Browse button under the component type.

16. In the Classification dialog (Figure 14.20), navigate to the 23.65.35.11.14 Instantaneous Water Heater, and click OK.

FIGURE 14.20 Loading the appropriate product definition so Revit can use your data properly

In the Export Building Components dialog, you can add the information on your product including a URL for support or installation documentation. This gives the customer access to your data at any time in the life cycle of the building.

17. Click OK, define where to place the new file, and then click Save.

Communication with systems other than Inventor and providing rich data for people using your products give you flexibility to be more competitive and produce higher-quality designs. This is a great combination.

THE ESSENTIALS AND BEYOND

It is likely that you won't need to share data with people with systems other than Inventor. Inventor can import data from nearly any system and can export data in a number of formats accepted by other systems.

AutoCAD has millions of users (most likely including you), and you have several ways to edit imported data. Using Fusion can give old data created in other systems new life without having to start from scratch. Fusion can also be used as a conceptual modeler to quickly develop new ideas before using Inventor to prepare them for production.

The BIM content development is priceless if you make equipment that goes into buildings. Getting your equipment included in the design because you've made it convenient to be included can give you a huge advantage over competitors using systems other than Inventor.

(Continues)

THE ESSENTIALS AND BEYOND *(Continued)*

ADDITIONAL EXERCISES

▶ Ask a vendor or customer for a noncritical model to test the import and export capabilities of Inventor with them.

▶ Print an existing AutoCAD drawing to see whether the quality is comparable.

▶ Use Inventor Fusion to remove the holes in the bottom of the imported file.

▶ Create a model of an appliance in your home and categorize it using the MEP export tools.

Automating the Design Process and Table-Driven Design

No matter how quickly or easily you can build parts and assemblies, the repetition of building designs that are essentially similar is still a drain on resources. Certain parts or products can easily be defined by tables or dimensions of rules. Inventor works with these types of design on a few different levels.

Using iParts and iAssemblies, it's easy to create a family of parts using a table in the part or an external spreadsheet to manage the variations on the size and features of the components. Using iAssemblies, you can configure variations on an assembly in much the same way, and the process remains manageable.

The next level uses a technology called iLogic to establish rules that define what a valid part is and how parts are allowed to be combined. With the rules established, a request can be made to develop a unique part or assembly, and as long as it meets the criteria of the rules, it can be developed by the system with minimal input from the user.

▶ **Building a table-driven product**

▶ **Expanding the control options**

Building a Table-Driven Product

A familiarity with Inventor's ability to share parameters is important to working with configurations of parts and assemblies, but it's not as important as being familiar with your product. Knowing what does and doesn't change in your product will help you narrow down the number of variables that you must work with. It can also help you decide where the values will be stored. Like sharing a sketch that can define many features, setting up a part that contains many or all of the parameters can make building associations easier.

Creating a Named Parameter

Every dimension or feature value in Inventor is given a parameter name like d0, d1, or d13405, but they can be hard to keep track of. In Chapter 3, you learned that typing **Width=100** would rename the d0 dimension to Width while creating it. You can also edit these values after the fact using the Parameters table.

Later, when you create a tabled part, Inventor will search for dimensions to which you gave special names and automatically include them in the table.

1. Open the c15-01.ipt file from the Parts\Chapter 15 folder. Make certain that the 2012 Essentials project file is active.

2. Expand the Drawer Face feature in the Browser, and edit Sketch1, which was consumed by the drawer face.

3. Right-click in the Design window, expand Dimension Display in the context menu, and set the value to Expression.

   This will update the sketch dimension to display the name and current values, as shown in Figure 15.1. Note that the width is controlled by d0 and the height by d1.

FIGURE 15.1 Dimension Display can change the appearance of sketch dimensions.

4. Use Finish Sketch to go back to the solid model.

Parameters

5. Click the Parameters tool in the marking menu, the Quick Access toolbar, or the Parameters panel of the Manage tab.

   Parameter names are case-sensitive and cannot contain spaces or use some special characters.

6. In the Parameters dialog, click the cell under Model Parameters for d0.

7. Type **width** for the new parameter name; then click the cell in the Equation column that shows the current value of 18 in and change it to **12 in**.

8. Click the cell for d1, and enter **height** for its value; then change its Equation value to **3 in**, as shown in Figure 15.2.

FIGURE 15.2 Editing parameter names and values through the dialog instead of the sketch

9. Click Done to close the dialog and return to the part.

The model will update, showing the changes to the values of the dimensions on the part. Giving the parameter a meaningful name makes it easy to use the Parameters dialog to edit the part.

Linking Parameters to an External Source

A common technique is to use a Microsoft Excel spreadsheet to control the model parameters. Connecting to the parameters is easy, as you'll see in this exercise:

1. Open c15-02.ipt from the Parts\Chapter 15 folder, making certain that the 2012 Essentials project file is active.

2. Start the Parameters tool, and in the dialog, click the Link button.

3. In the Open dialog, click the c15-02.xls file in the Parts\Chapter 15 folder.

The parameters and their values from the spreadsheet will appear under the file path.

4. In the Equation value area for d0, right-click and click List Parameters in the context menu.

5. A small dialog will appear listing the two parameters. Click the Width parameter.

6. Type **height** for the value of d1, and click Done to update the model. See Figure 15.3.

Parameter Name	Unit/Typ	Equation	Nominal Valu	Tol.	Model Value	Key		Comment
▶ — Model Parameters								
d0	in	width	24.000000	○	24.000000	☐	☐	
d1	in	height	7.000000	○	7.000000	☐	☐	
d2	in	5/8"	0.625000	○	0.625000	☐	☐	
d3	deg	0.0 deg	0.000000	○	0.000000	☐	☐	
d4	in	0.177 in	0.177000	○	0.177000	☐	☐	
d6	in	3 in	3.000000	○	3.000000	☐	☐	
d12	in	0.177 in	0.177000	○	0.177000	☐	☐	
— User Parameters								
— C:\Inventor 2012...								
width	in	24 in	24.000000	○	24.000000	☐	☐	
height	in	7 in	7.000000	○	7.000000	☐	☐	

Add Numeric ▼   Update   Reset Tolerance   << Less

Link   ✓ Immediate Update   + ▲ ○ −   Done

FIGURE 15.3 Parameter values can be linked to cells of a spreadsheet.

7. Double-click the mouse wheel to zoom all to see the part.

8. Open the c15-02.xls file from the Parts\Chapter 15 folder in Excel, and change the value for Width to **12**. Close the spreadsheet, saving the change.

9. In Inventor, click the Local Update icon in the Quick Access toolbar to refresh the model.

Another technique that can save a lot of trouble is to link component parameters together. This avoids the need to edit two components to keep them fitting together or to use a spreadsheet to combine parameters.

1. Open c15-01.iam from the assemblies\Chapter 15 folder, making certain that the 2012 Essentials project file is active.

2. Click the Constrain tool in the Position panel of the Assemble tab or the marking menu.

Constrain

3. In the Place Constraint dialog, click the Constraint Set tab.

In the Design window (Figure 15.4), you can see two UCS triads. These can be placed apart from the body and be used to align parts rather than using constraints between faces and edges or traditional constraints.

FIGURE 15.4 UCS features can be placed in the components and used to assemble them.

4. Click the two UCS triads in the assembly to position the two components, and then click OK to complete the constraint.

   The components do not appear to be aligned correctly, because the position of the UCS in the part that makes up the back needs to be changed along with the height and width of that part. The parameters that will control this are embedded in the front of the drawer. Now, you will connect the back to the parameters of the front to make them consistent.

Object
Visibility

5. Change your Ribbon to the View tab, and click Object Visibility in the Visibility panel to extend its drop-down menu.

6. Uncheck UCS Triad and the other UCS elements to remove them from the Design window.

7. Double-click the c15-03 part in the Browser or in the Design window to activate it.

8. Open the Parameters dialog in the marking menu or the Quick Access toolbar.

9. Click the Link icon, and when the Open dialog comes up, change the Files Of Type drop-down to Inventor Files.

10. Double-click the Parts\Chapter 15\c15.04.ipt file.

 The Link Parameters dialog will open. In it are the user-named and special parameters in the part selected. Clicking the gray balloon will turn it yellow, and that parameter will be linked into your active part.

11. Deselect the Show All Parameters check box, and then click the drawer_depth, drawer_side_height, back_width, and bottom_thickness parameters (Figure 15.5). Click OK to close the dialog.

FIGURE 15.5 Selecting parameters to link into the active part

Some users create the shared parameters in the assembly itself or in a part file with no geometry.

12. Equate the named parameters in the part to the linked parameters as listed:

   ▶ width = back_width

   ▶ height = drawer_side_height

   ▶ thickness = bottom_thickness

   ▶ offset = drawer_depth

13. Click Done to update the part and then the Return icon on the Ribbon to go back to the assembly.

The back will move into place, sized based on the parameters of the front of the drawer, as shown in Figure 15.6. This relationship will remain until you change it and update all the parts that share those parameters. This is one way of building parts to connect, but the changes are limited to manual updating. iParts will provide a more powerful technique.

FIGURE 15.6 The drawer back repositioned by linking parameters

Building an iPart

You can think of an iPart as a part family—a part that includes a table so you can give different members of the part family different values to the same parameter or control whether a given feature appears in a family member.

In this exercise, you will build a second drawer front based on the one already in the file. You'll change its size and go from using a pull for opening to a knob.

Certification Objective

1. Open c15-05.ipt from the Parts\Chapter 15 folder, making certain that the 2012 Essentials project file is active.

Create iPart

2. Change the Ribbon to the Manage tab, and click Create iPart in the Author panel.

   When the iPart Author dialog opens (Figure 15.7), take a moment to click through some of the tabs that select which features will be controlled as part of the iPart. Notice that columns for the named parameter and a suppressed feature were automatically displayed and that -01 has been added to the current filename to define the first family member's part number.

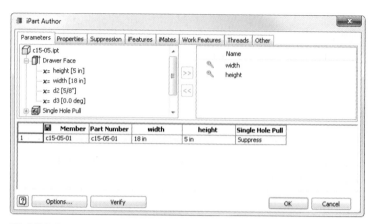

FIGURE 15.7 Beginning to create an iPart

3. Right-click the row of features for the current part, and click Insert Row in the context menu.

This new member is given a -02 extension and currently has the same values as the original.

You can specify part numbers for each member, or you can click Options to open a dialog where you can set the naming scheme.

4. Change the Width value for the new member to **20 in** and the Height value to **7 in.**

5. Click the Suppression tab, find the Double Hole Pull [Compute] feature, and double-click it to add it to the option columns in both parts.

6. In the c15-05-02 row, change the value for the Double Hole Pull to 0.

7. In the same row, change the value for Single Hole Pull to **Yes.**

Yes and No or 1 and 0 can be used as substitutes for Compute and Suppress in the iPart Authoring dialog.

8. Compare your dialog to Figure 15.8, and click OK to create the iPart.

FIGURE 15.8 Adding a new size, swapping a feature

9. A new node has been added to the Browser. Expand the table to see that there are now callouts for the -01 and -02 versions of the part.

10. Double-click the c15-05-02 part, and select Zoom All to see the part.

11. Activate the c15-05-01 version.

12. In the Author panel of the Manage tab, find the Edit Factory scope icon, and use the drop-down to change the mode to Edit Member scope.

13. Add .75 in fillets to the short edges of the drawer front, as shown in Figure 15.9.

FIGURE 15.9 Adding a fillet to one of the iPart members

14. Switch the part to the c15-02-02 version to see that the fillets were not applied.

15. Double-click the table to see the effect of adding a feature with Member Scope active (Figure 15.10).

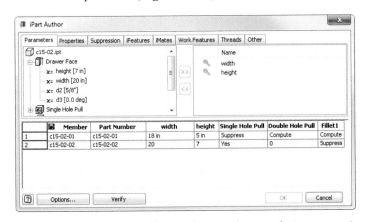

FIGURE 15.10 With Member Scope active, new features are not added to other members.

Perusing the tabs in the dialog will give you a sense of just how many variables these models can have. Think about the numbers of variables in your designs that are similar. It's easy for the number of variables between parts to get out of hand.

Working with an Assembly of iParts

To configure an assembly, you can use a combination of regular parts or iParts. In each version of the assembly, you can change out what components are being used and how they are assembled to one another.

The assembly you will convert was built using traditional assembly constraints. The -01 version of each of the iParts was used in the assembly.

1. Open c15-02.iam from the Assemblies\Chapter 15 folder, making certain that the 2012 Essentials project file is active.

2. Locate the c15-11-01 part in the Browser, and expand it so you can see the Table icon.

⬛ Table   3. Right-click the Table icon, and click Change Component in the context menu.

The Place Standard iPart dialog (Figure 15.11) appears, displaying the current version of the iPart you're using.

FIGURE 15.11 The Place Standard iPart dialog displays the current iPart information.

4. In the dialog, click the 2394-01 part number.

5. This will open a mini-dialog showing the available versions of the part. Click 2394-03, and click OK.

Because the holes for mounting the c15-16 part are suppressed in this version, there will be an error message concerning the failure of several assembly constraints.

6. Click Accept to continue working.

7. Locate the four failed constraints in the Browser under the c15-11 part.

8. Click one, and hold the Shift key to select the others. When they're all selected, right-click and click Suppress in the context menu.

9. Find the c15-17 part in the Browser and make it visible.

10. Create an insert constraint between the small hole in the drawer face and the bottom of the knob, as shown in Figure 15.12, clicking OK to place the constraint.

11. Expand the c15-17 part, and rename the insert constraint **Knob Insert constraint**.

FIGURE 15.12 Locating the knob for the optional drawer front

12. Orbit the assembly so you can see the back for the drawer front.

13. Add another insert constraint to the screw on the right and the hole in the drawer front, as shown in Figure 15.13.

FIGURE 15.13 Reusing a screw by applying another constraint

14. In the Browser, expand the first instance of the Cross Recessed Truss Head screw.

15. Rename the Insert constraint at the bottom of the list to **Knob Screw constraint**.

16. Unsuppress the four constraints you suppressed under part c15-11-03, and accept their failure in the warning dialog.

17. Use the Change Component tool to change the c15-11-03 part back to c15-11-01.

18. A warning dialog will appear, letting you know that two constraints have failed. Accept this.

Now the assembly is prepared for a conversion to an iAssembly. It is not absolutely necessary to create the constraints for the knob ahead of time. It is helpful to build several configurations in one step, but for your products, you may choose to create iAssemblies one member at a time, adding parts as you go.

Converting an Assembly to an iAssembly

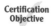 **Certification Objective**

All the pieces are in place and the assembly constraints are ready to be used. Naming the constraints has the same benefit as naming parameters in an iPart, but it makes them much easier to locate in the iAssembly Author dialog.

1. Open the c15-03.iam from the Assemblies\Chapter 15 folder, making certain that the 2012 Essentials project file is active.

Create
iAssembly

2. Click Create iAssembly in the Author panel of the Manage tab.

The iAssembly Author dialog (Figure 15.14) will be opened, and as you might expect, it will look a lot like the iPart Author dialog. The main focus of this dialog is to specify which iPart member to show in the assembly and whether any constraints need to change.

FIGURE 15.14 The initial appearance of the iAssembly Author dialog

3. On the Components tab, expand the c15-11 part.

4. Double-click Table Replace to add it to the pane on the right, and add it as a column for selection for the -01 version of the assembly.

5. Repeat the previous step for the c15-12, c15-13 (both instances), and c15-15 parts. See Figure 15.15.

6. Switch to the Exclusion tab, and expand the Components folder.

7. Double-click c15-16 and c15-17 to control whether they will be in the assembly.

8. In the column for c15-17, click the Include value, and use the drop-down to change it to Exclude.

A part usually has only three options for control—Include/ Exclude, Ground Status, and Adaptive Status—but with an iPart, you can control which version you use through the Table Replace control.

FIGURE 15.15 Control over the iPart version is added to the iAssembly member.

9. Add the last instance of the Cross Recessed Truss Head screw as well.

10. Now expand the Constraints folder on the Exclusion tab, and add the six named assembly constraints to the list.

11. Set the values for the two constraints for the knob to Exclude.

12. Right-click the iAssembly row, click Insert Row to add another member, and then add a third using Insert Row.

13. Change the iPart version of each iPart to match the member version of the assembly.

14. For iAssembly Member -03, exclude the c15-16 part and the Cross Head screw.

15. Then exclude the constraints that have *Wire Pull* in the name.

16. Set the c15-17 part and constraints that say *Knob to Include*.

17. Set the Part Number names to **24 inch** for -01, **20 inch** for -02, and **16 inch** for -03.

Since this iAssembly may be used in other assemblies, it's important to make it easy to click the version you want to use. Applying a key to the features or information that an end user might need makes it much easier for others to find the right iAssembly member.

18. Right-click in the Part number column, and hover over Key in the context menu until a list of numbers appears. Click 1 in the list to make the part number the first (and only, in this case) key for selecting a member of the iAssembly.

19. Compare all the settings in your dialog to Figure 15.16.

	Memb	Part Numb	c15-11:1: Table Replace	c15-12:1: Table Replace	c15-13:1: Table Replace	c15-13:2: Table Replace	c15-15:1: Table Replace	c15-16:1: ude/Excl	c15-17:1: lude/Exclu	Cross Recessed Truss Head Machine Screw - Type IA - Inch No. 8 - 36 - 7/8»2:	Wire Pull Insert 1: ude/Excl	Wire Pull Insert 2: ude/Excl	Wire Pull Screw constraint 1:	Wire Pull Screw constraint 2:	Knob Insert onstraint	Knob Screw onstrain
1	c15-03-01	24 inch	c15-11-01	c15-12-01	c15-13-01	c15-13-01	c15-15-01	Include	Exclude	Include	Include	Include	Include	Include	Exclude	Exclude
2	c15-03-02	20 inch	c15-11-02	c15-12-02	c15-13-02	c15-15-02	c15-15-02	Include	Exclude	Include	Include	Include	Include	Include	Exclude	Exclude
3	c15-03-03	16 inch	c15-11-03	c15-12-03	c15-13-03	c15-13-03	c15-15-03	Exclude	Include	Exclude	Exclude	Exclude	Exclude	Exclude	Include	Include

FIGURE 15.16 An example of how many options can be controlled in an iPart or iAssembly

20. Click OK to generate the iAssembly.

21. In the assembly, expand the Table folder near the top of the Browser.

22. Double-click the instances to see the versions of the assembly.

Compared with your products, this was probably a simple assembly. Managing the contents of an iAssembly can seem a bit daunting, but having the ability to access variations on a common assembly through a single assembly file is great for maintaining the design.

Using an iAssembly

The primary benefit of having an iAssembly is to have the option of placing different versions of an assembly family into the same primary assembly. The version inserted into the assembly can also be changed at any time.

1. Create a new assembly using the Standard (mm).iam template from the Metric tab, making certain that the 2012 Essentials project file is active.

2. Start the Place tool in the marking menu or the Component panel on the Assembly tab.

Place

3. In the Open dialog, double-click the c15-04.iam from the Assemblies\Chapter 15 folder.

Selecting an iAssembly will preview the component and display the Place iAssembly dialog. You can use this dialog to select which member of an iAssembly you want to place. The same type of dialog appears when you place an iPart into an assembly.

4. Click the screen to place the default version of the drawer.

5. After the screen shows the first instance, place two more drawers in the assembly, and then click Dismiss or hit the Esc key to close the dialog. See Figure 15.17.

FIGURE 15.17 Three instances of the same iAssembly placed in an assembly

6. In the Browser, expand the second instance of the assembly.

7. Right-click the Table icon, and click Change Component in the context menu.

8. Click the current 24 in value, and select 20 inch from the mini-dialog; then click OK.

   The assembly will update to the new version. In some cases, it may prompt you to save the new file; if so, just click OK.

9. Now use the Change Component tool for the third instance.

10. When the dialog opens, click the Tree tab to see a list of the size options.

11. Click the Table tab to see a view of the entire configuration table.

12. Click the bottom row; then click OK to update the assembly to that version.

Your screen will update to show the new version of the drawer (Figure 15.18), and now, you can see the differences between the configurations side by side. This is a common application for iAssemblies, where subassemblies are far more likely to have modules with options. Another feature is that in many cases, changing the family member doesn't require the reapplication of assembly constraints.

FIGURE 15.18 The three iAssemblies showing different states

Documenting an iPart and an iAssembly

Combining iParts and iAssemblies with Inventor's drawing associativity is a great way to simplify maintaining these documents. In this exercise, you will edit a drawing to include a table for an iPart and a specialized parts list that shows the mixture of parts used in an iAssembly.

1. Open c15-01.idw from the Drawings\Chapter 15 folder, making certain that the 2012 Essentials project file is active.

 General 2. Click the Table tool in the Table panel of the Annotate tab.

3. Click the drawing view of the drawer front.

   Once a view of an iPart is selected, the Table dialog will adjust to show a column for the Members.

4. Click the Column Chooser tool in the dialog to open another dialog, where you can select the properties of the iPart to include in the table.

5. In the Table Column Chooser dialog, add drawer_width, drawer_ height, and dbl_pull_width to the Selected Columns group on the right (Figure 15.19); then click OK.

FIGURE 15.19 Selecting items for the iPart table

6. Click OK again to begin placing the table in the drawing.

7. Place the table under the drawing view.

8. Double-click the table to open the editing dialog, right-click the drawer_width column, and click Format Column from the context menu.

9. In the Format Column dialog, uncheck Name From Data Source, and then change the Heading name to A, as shown in Figure 15.20.

FIGURE 15.20 Modifying the Column header

10. Repeat the process to change the heading of the drawer_height column to B and dbl_pull_width to C.

11. Click OK to close the dialog and update the table, as shown in Figure 15.21.

TABLE			
Member	A	B	C
c15-11-01	24 in	8 in	4 in
c15-11-02	20 in	6 in	4 in
c15-11-03	16 in	6 in	3 in

FIGURE 15.21 The completed table showing the values for the table dimensions

With the iPart table update, you can add a parts list for the iAssembly. The parts list for the assembly needs to be able to display quantities for any component that is a member of any of the various configurations. This is sometimes referred to as a *matrix parts list*. The Parts List tool has a special function to do this.

Parts List

12. Find the Parts List tool on the Annotate tab in the Table panel, and click it.

13. Click the drawing view of the assembly, and then click OK to place a standard parts list under the assembly view.

14. Double-click the parts list to open the editing dialog.

15. Click the Member Selection icon.

16. In the Select Member dialog, click all three versions of the iAssembly, and click OK.

17. Click the Column Chooser button, and remove the Description column from the Selected Properties list.

18. Click OK twice to update the parts list on the drawing.

As Figure 15.22 shows, the parts list contains the quantity of the parts in rows and the configuration of the assembly in columns.

PARTS LIST				
ITEM	QTY c15-04	QTY c15-04	QTY c15-04	PART NUMBER
1	1	0	0	5514-01
2	2	0	0	c15-22-01
3	1	0	0	c15-23-01
4	1	1	0	c15-18
5	0	0	1	c15-19
6	2	2	1	ANSI B18.6.3 - No. 8 - 36 - 7/8
7	1	0	0	2394-01
8	0	1	0	2394-02
9	0	0	1	2394-03
10	0	1	0	5514-02
11	0	0	1	5514-03
12	0	2	0	8650-02
13	0	0	2	8650-03
14	0	1	0	6705-02
15	0	0	1	6705-03

FIGURE 15.22 The parts list shows the quantities of parts for each iAssembly member.

For many years, "family parts" or configurations of an assembly could be included on 2D drawings only as tables. These tables could be very complex and include a lot of information, and if a change to a family member occurred, it was easy to miss it in the drawing.

Expanding the Control Options

Using iParts and iAssemblies will give a good level of control over well-defined components, but it is limited to members that were predefined. If you want something unique, you have to build a new member.

Certification
Objective

The iLogic tools work with many of the same parameters but offer a way to programmatically change these parameters based on the condition of other parameters. Using iLogic tools, you can also establish a range of sizes rather than strictly working with a predefined set.

In the next exercises, you will do the same type of functions as you did with iAssemblies and iParts, but you will use the iLogic interface to establish connections in a more meaningful way and create a dialog box that will make it easy for you to edit the product.

Many of these exercises transition from one to the next, so you will be asked to save your work and continue using the same data for several exercises.

Using a Parameter in Another Parameter

To make sure the solid part of the drawer is cut to the proper size, you need to allow for the thickness of the edge banding material. To do this, you can build an equation into the value of the parameter.

1. Open c15-18.ipt from the Parts\Chapter 15 folder, making certain that the 2012 Essentials project file is active.

2. In the Parameters panel of the Manage tab or in the marking menu, click the Parameters tool.

3. In the lower-left corner of the Parameters dialog, click the filter, and set the dialog to show only renamed parameters.

    At the top of the Model Parameters list is a parameter named drawer_core_width, whose current value is 20 in. This is the parameter whose value you will modify.

4. Click the cell in the Equation column, and type **drawer_width- (edge_band_thickness * 2 ul)**; press Enter to update the dialog. See Figure 15.23.

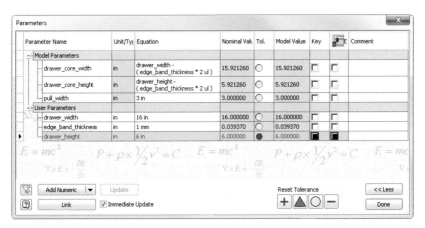

FIGURE 15.23 Parameters can be factored together to create a value for another parameter.

If you can see the part in the background, it will immediately change size. You can disable this for large models with the check box at the bottom of the dialog. The *ul* in the equation tells Inventor that the number is strictly a number and not a dimensional value.

5. Click Done to close the dialog.

6. Be sure to save your changes and close the part.

Now, your part will maintain the proper size when changes to the overall drawer width or thickness of the edge banding occur.

Creating a Multivalue Parameter

It's possible to set up any parameter local to a part to use a list of predefined values rather than typing in a value, but it's when you start working with the iLogic tools that the capability really shows its benefit.

1. Open c15-05.iam from the Assemblies\Chapter 15 folder, making certain that the 2012 Essentials project file is active.

2. In the marking menu or the Manage panel of the Assemble tab, start the Parameters tool.

3. Click the Add Numeric icon to add a new parameter to the model.

4. The new row will appear with the cursor ready to give it a name. Type edge_band_thickness, and press Enter.

5. In the Unit column, click the field next to the new parameter.

6. You can browse under the Length category in the Unit Type dialog, or you can just type **mm** for the Unit Specification and click OK.

7. Right-click the new parameter, and click Make Multi-Value in the context menu.

The Value List Editor will appear, showing the current value (1.0 in) listed in the bottom portion of the dialog.

8. Click this value, and then click the Delete button on the right to clear the list.

9. In the Add New Items field at the top of the dialog, type **1**, press the Enter key, and then add **3** to the list.

10. Click the Add button to put these values on the list shown in Figure 15.24.

FIGURE 15.24 Creating a defined list of possible parameter values

11. Click OK to close the dialog and go back to the Parameters dialog.

12. Click the drop-down in the Equation column, and set the value for the parameter to **1 mm**; then click Done to close the dialog.

13. Save the assembly, but do not close it.

You've now established a parameter in the assembly that will control the dimensions on two parts and modify the way a third part calculates a dimension. Furthermore, you've limited the sizes to standard materials.

Accessing the iLogic Tools

This assembly already has a couple of rules included to give you a head start. To see them, you need to turn on the iLogic Browser. If you did not do the previous exercise, the following steps will fail.

1. Continue using the c15-05.iam file from the previous exercise.

2. Switch to the Manage tab, and click the iLogic Browser tool in the iLogic panel.

The iLogic Browser (Figure 15.25) will appear and may be attached to your model Browser. On the Rules tab, you will see the two rules that were created in advance.

FIGURE 15.25 Clicking and dragging the header can make the iLogic Browser a floating window.

3. Right-click Edge Band Control, and select Unsuppress Rule from the context menu.

4. Right-click the rule again, and click Run Rule in the context menu.

5. The update icon will appear in the Quick Access toolbar as a result of parameters being updated. Look closely at the thickness of the edge band, and click Update.

6. Save the assembly.

The four bands will take on the value of the edge_band_thickness parameter. In a later exercise, you will change the thickness. Now, you need to build rules to make sure the edge banding is the proper length.

Creating a New Rule

Rules are simply ways to establish behavior or to create conditions in which an action will be taken if another action creates a condition. The rule you will create could be built as several rules; or, with good use of commenting, it can be handled in one rule.

1. Open c15-06.iam from the Assemblies\Chapter 15 folder, making certain that the 2012 Essentials project file is active.

2. Right-click in the iLogic Browser, and click New Rule in the context menu.

3. When the Rule Name dialog appears, type **Drawer Size Control**, and click OK.

   A large Edit Rule dialog will open. The first task in this new rule will be to limit the size of a drawer front.

f_x User Parameter **4.** Click the User Parameters icon under the assembly to display the user parameters in the assembly.

Setting a maximum and minimum size range is made easy thanks to a wizard included in iLogic.

Parameter Limits **5.** Click the Parameter Limits icon on the Wizard tab of the Edit Rule dialog.

6. In the iLogic Limits Wizard dialog, enter the parameter name of **drawer_width,** and set the Max. Value setting to 34 and the Min. Value setting to **10,** as shown in Figure 15.26.

FIGURE 15.26 Using the wizard to set a size range for the drawer front

You can add custom messages for violation of the minimum or maximum values in the dialog as well.

7. Click Apply to create the width control portion of the rule.

8. Change the parameter name to drawer_height, and set the Max. Height value to 12 and the Min. Height value to 4.

9. Click Apply and Close to see the rule up to this point in Figure 15.27.

Let's separate this part of the rule from the next part with a comment. To create a comment as a note or to remove a line temporarily from the rule, place an apostrophe at the beginning of the row.

FIGURE 15.27 Building rules to limit the size of a drawer face

10. Below the last line containing End If, press the Enter key a couple of times, and then type ' **This section is for linking assembly parameters to part parameters.**

This will make for a clean break and help you sort out what portion of the rule is controlling what functions or relationships in the rule.

11. Click OK. Save the assembly.

Now, you need to make the connections to the components of the assembly so that the size limitations can affect them.

Linking the Parameters Through Rules

In the first portion of this chapter, you learned how to link parameters between models by using a spreadsheet or by linking directly to another component. The next step does the same thing, but by using the lines of code, it can be set up very quickly.

1. Continue using the c15-06.iam file from the previous exercise.

2. In the iLogic Browser, right-click Drawer Size Control rule, and select Edit Rule.

3. Below the comment added in the previous section, type the following: **Parameter ("c15-21:1", "drawer_width") = drawer_width**.

   This statement simply says that the parameter named drawer_width in the first assembly instance of the model named c15-21 gets its value from the parameter named drawer_width in this assembly.

4. Highlight that line, copy it to the clipboard, and paste a copy directly below this one. It's a good idea to create a little space between lines.

5. In the new line, change the word **width** to **height** so that it reads Parameter ("c15-21:1", "drawer_height") = drawer_height.

   Now, you've linked the height value of the assembly to the part. Next, you need to leverage these values with the edge banding.

6. Paste the text into the window again and modify it to say Parameter ("c15-22:1", "length") = drawer_width.

   The last stage in the rule has an extra step because you need to subtract the thickness of the edge band, as you did when creating the equation in the Parameters table.

7. Create a new row of text to read Parameter ("c15-23:1", "length") = (drawer_height - (edge_band_thickness) *2).

8. Compare your rules to Figure 15.28, and click OK to save the rule you've created.

```
' This section is for linking assembly parameters to part parameters

Parameter ("c15-21:1", "drawer_width") = drawer_width

Parameter ("c15-21:1", "drawer_height") = drawer_height

Parameter ("c15-22:1", "length") = drawer_width

Parameter ("c15-23:1", "length") = (drawer_height - (edge_band_thickness) *2)
```

FIGURE 15.28 Rules can create connections between components.

9. To update the assembly, click the Update icon on the Quick Access toolbar.

10. After the assembly updates, save the file.

When the assembly updates, you will see that the edge band components are now the correct size. Once you become comfortable with the language iLogic speaks, you will see that you're just giving orders based on needs that already exist around your designs.

Controlling Features Through Rules

Now, you have your file parameters connected to each other, and the assembly is looking good. There is one last step before you test all the connections. There needs to be a rule that changes the number of holes when the drawer becomes narrow. Rather than continuing to test your typing skills, this exercise will leverage the ability to store rule content outside of the Inventor file:

1. Continue using the c15-06.iam file from the previous exercise.

2. Use Windows Explorer to open iLogic Feature Suppression.txt from the Assemblies\Chapter 15 folder.

3. When the text file opens, press Ctrl+A to select the entire contents, and then copy the selected text to the Clipboard by pressing Ctrl+C.

4. Switch back to Inventor.

5. Double-click the Pull Control rule in the iLogic Browser to open it in the editor.

6. Press the Enter key to create space beneath the existing contents in the rule, and paste the information you copied from the text file, as shown in Figure 15.29.

```
' ** This section switches the panel to one hole if 14 inches wide or less

If drawer_width < 14 in

' ***Single Hole Pull***
Feature.IsActive("c15-21:1", "Single Hole Pull") = True

' ***Double Hole Pull***
Feature.IsActive("c15-21:1", "Double Hole Pull") = False

ElseIf drawer_width = 21 in

' ***Single Hole Pull***
Feature.IsActive("c15-21:1", "Single Hole Pull") = True

' ***Double Hole Pull***
Feature.IsActive("c15-21:1", "Double Hole Pull") = False

ElseIf drawer_width > 14 in

' ***Single Hole Pull***
Feature.IsActive("c15-21:1", "Single Hole Pull") = False

' ***Double Hole Pull***
Feature.IsActive("c15-21:1", "Double Hole Pull") = True

End If
```

FIGURE 15.29 Features can be switched on and off by rules.

You'll notice that the actions and parameter names are automatically color-coded even if you didn't type the rule in the window. The rule says that if the value of drawer_width is equal to or less than 14 inches, then Inventor will suppress the Double Hole Pull feature and unsuppress the Single Hole Pull feature. If the drawer is larger than 14 inches, it will place two holes in the part.

7. Click OK to update the rule and close the dialog.

The Edge Band Control rule has a feature suppression function built in that suppresses a fillet on the edge band when the edge is 1mm thick and turns it on when it is 3mm.

As you continue to expand the application of iLogic for your designs, you'll also see that there is a tremendous amount of sample code available online and in the product. All you need to do is swap out file, feature, or parameter names as you've already done, and you're up and running.

Making the Rules Easy to Use

Any of the rules you create can be tested and used by changing a couple of parameters in the dialog, but that is still cumbersome for many users. Using a basic form to open and use with the tool is a great step forward in usability.

1. Open c15-07.iam from the Assemblies\Chapter 15 folder, making certain that the 2012 Essentials project file is active.

2. Open the iLogic Browser, and click the Forms tab.

3. Click the Drawer Front Size button.

The Drawer Front Size dialog opens in the Design window. You can test it on your assembly.

4. Set Drawer Width to 12in and Drawer Height to 3in, and click Apply.

An error dialog appears (Figure 15.30), warning that the height was below the minimum you specified in the parameter limits function of the Drawer Size Control rule.

FIGURE 15.30 An error dialog was built directly from the wizard used to set size limits.

5. Click OK so the assembly can adjust to the width entered and the minimum height.

   Note that there is only one hole in the part because it is less than 14 inches wide.

6. Change the width to 16 and the height to 7, click the Edge Band tab, click the radio button for 3 mm Edge Band Thickness, and click Apply.

   The fillet will develop on the thicker edge band. Now, you need to add to this form the option of using two different size pull spacings.

7. Right-click the button on the Forms tab, and click Edit in the context menu.

   In the Form Editor dialog, you can browse the parameters available in the file and elements for making a dialog. First, you should add a tab to place controls for the pull size.

🗀 Tab Group 8. Click and drag the tab group from the Toolbox group onto the Drawer Front Size text in the top-right window.

9. Change the name of the new tab group to **Pull Width**.

A Label 10. Drag a label under the Pull Width tab, and set it to read **Select Pull Width**.

11. Locate the pull_width parameter on the Parameters tab, and drag it under the label.

12. Click the new item, and the window below it will change to display the properties.

13. Click Edit Control Type, and change it from Combo Box to Radio Group using the drop-down, as shown in Figure 15.31.

14. If you don't see a preview on your screen, click the Preview button in the dialog, and click the new Pull Width tab.

FIGURE 15.31 Editing the form to add control over the size of the pulls

15. Click OK to update the form.

16. Click the Drawer Front Size button again to test the new tab.

The tools I've covered are just the essentials of iLogic, but learning how to do this much should encourage you to explore how it might help you by removing tedium and repetition from your daily work. There are some amazing examples of what users with little programming experience have done using iLogic and Inventor.

THE ESSENTIALS AND BEYOND

Automation of design tasks is why many people moved to CAD and 3D CAD tools such as Inventor in the first place. That's why it's amazing how many users are just beginning to notice and take advantage of tools such as iParts, iAssemblies, and iLogic. Look around for something simple that has a lot of size variation but relatively few changes in the number or type of parts, and it will make a great project for exploring the tools of this chapter.

(Continues)

THE ESSENTIALS AND BEYOND *(Continued)*

Any time you can reduce the number of files you need to maintain, you reduce the cost of searching for data and the risk of parts with mismatched feature sizes. Using tables to control and understand your data is an elevated approach to parametric modeling and assembly control. Further still in the evolution of computer-aided design is implementing the rules that safeguard the quality of your product to produce them.

ADDITIONAL EXERCISES

▶ Edit a part using the values in the tables rather than editing the sketch or features.

▶ Construct an iAssembly of parts that are similar, but are not iParts, and use the table to swap them for each other.

▶ Try using iLogic to build rules to change materials more rapidly than the Style and Standards Editor.

▶ Download Microsoft Visual Basic Express (which is free), and build executable files out of your iLogic rules.

Inventor Certification

Autodesk Certifications are industry-recognized credentials that can help you succeed in your design career—providing benefits to both you and your employer. Getting certified is a reliable validation of skills and knowledge, and it can lead to accelerated professional development, improved productivity, and enhanced credibility.

This Autodesk Official Training Guide can be an effective component of your exam preparation. Autodesk highly recommends (and we agree!) that you schedule regular time to prepare, review the most current exam preparation roadmap available at **www.autodesk.com/certification**, use Autodesk Official Training Guides, take a class at an Authorized Training Center (find ATCs near you here: **www.autodesk.com/atc**), take an Assessment test, and use a variety of resources to prepare for your certification—including plenty of actual hands-on experience.

To help you focus your studies on the skills you'll need for these exams, the following tables show the objective and in what chapter you can find information on that topic—and when you go to that chapter, you'll find certification icons like the one in the margin here. *Inventor Essentials* does not cover all of the options of every tool but does make an excellent reference for preparing for your exam.

Certification Objective

Table A.1 is for the Certified User Exam and lists the topic, exam objectives, and chapter where the information is found. Table A.2 is for the Autodesk Certified Associate Exam, and Table A.3 is for the Autodesk Certified Professional Exam. The Section and Exam Objectives listed in the table are from the Autodesk Certification Exam Guide.

These Autodesk exam objectives were accurate at press time; please refer to **www.autodesk.com/certification** for the most current exam roadmap and objectives. Good luck preparing for your certification!

TABLE A.1   Certified User Exam sections and objectives

Topic	Exam Objectives	*Inventor Essentials* Chapter
User Interface	Name the four primary environments.	2, 3, 4, 6, 7, 8, 15
	Name the key features of the user interface.	1
	Describe the listing in the Browser for an assembly file.	1
	Demonstrate how to add Redo to the Quick Access Toolbar.	1
	Describe the steps required to change the background color of the graphics window.	1
	Demonstrate how to turn on/off the 3D Indicator.	1
	Name the key elements of the ribbon.	1
File Management	Name the file extension of a project file.	14, 15
	List the types of project files that can be created.	1
	Define the term *Workspace*.	1
	List the types of files stored in a library.	1, 4, 8
	List the three categories in Folder Options.	1
	Describe how to set the active project.	1
Sketches	Name the file extension of a part file.	2, 3, 7, 14
	Describe the purpose of a template file in the sketch environment.	5
	Describe the function of the 3D Coordinate System icon.	1
	Define a sketch plane.	3
	Label the entries on the browser.	9
	Complete a 2D sketch using the appropriate draw tools.	3
	List the available geometric constraints.	3, 7

Topic	Exam Objectives	*Inventor Essentials* Chapter
	Describe parametric dimensions.	3, 7
	Describe how to control the visibility of constraints.	3
	Describe the degrees of freedom on a sketch and how they can be displayed.	3
	Demonstrate how to pattern a sketch.	3
	Demonstrate how to modify a sketch.	3
	Describe how to format sketch linetypes.	3
	Discuss over-constrained sketches.	3
	Examine a sketch for errors.	3
	Describe the function of a shared sketch.	3
	Describe how parameters define the size and shape of features.	3
Parts	Name the file extension of a part file.	2, 3, 7, 14
	Label the entries on the browser.	9
	Define a base feature.	3
	Define an unconsumed sketch.	3
	Complete a part using the appropriate sketched feature tools.	3, 7, 12
	Describe the termination options for a feature.	3, 7
	Complete a part using the appropriate placed feature tools.	3, 7, 9, 12, 14
	Describe the use of work features in the part creation work flow.	7
	Complete a part using the appropriate pattern feature tools.	7
	Describe part properties and how they are applied.	3

Topic	Exam Objectives	*Inventor Essentials* Chapter
Assemblies	Name the file extension of an assembly file.	4, 8, 11, 12, 14
	Label the entries on the browser.	9
	Name the six degrees of freedom on a component.	4
	Demonstrate how to place a part in an assembly.	4
	Discuss degrees of freedom and a grounded part.	4
	Demonstrate how to apply various assembly constraints.	4, 8
	Describe the various assembly environment techniques.	4, 8
	Demonstrate how to create a new part in the assembly environment.	8
	Demonstrate how to place a Content Center part in an assembly.	4, 8
	Label the entries on the browser.	9
	Demonstrate how to animate an assembly using drive constraints.	8
	Demonstrate how to make and use an adaptive part.	8
Presentations	Name the file extension of a presentation file.	13, 14
	Label the entries on the browser.	9
	Discuss the various uses of presentation files.	6, 13
	Demonstrate how to apply tweaks to a part.	13
	Demonstrate how to apply trails to a part.	13
	Demonstrate how to animate an assembly.	13
Drawings	Name the file extension of a drawing file.	2, 6, 14
	Describe the use of template files.	2, 5

Topic	Exam Objectives	*Inventor Essentials* Chapter
	Label the entries on the browser.	9
	Describe the content within Drawing Resources.	5
	Demonstrate how to create a part drawing.	2, 6
	Demonstrate how to create an assembly drawing.	6
	Describe the various annotation options.	2, 6
	Demonstrate how to add balloons to an assembly.	6
Sheet Metal	Name the file extension of a sheet metal part file.	10
	Label the entries on the browser.	9
	Demonstrate the use of sheet metal defaults.	10
	Complete a part using the appropriate sheet metal tools.	10
	Demonstrate how to modify a sketch.	3
	Demonstrate how to create a flat pattern.	10
	Demonstrate how to insert a flat pattern in a drawing.	10
	Demonstrate how to export a flat pattern.	10
Visualization	Describe the process to activate Inventor Studio.	13
	Demonstrate how to create a new camera.	13
	Demonstrate how to create a rendered image.	13
	Demonstrate how to create a new animation.	13
	Demonstrate how to create an animation by animating a camera.	13
	Demonstrate how to create an animation by animating a constraint.	13
	Demonstrate how to create an animation by animating a fade.	13

TABLE A.2 Certified Associate Exam sections and objectives

Topic	Exam Objectives	*Inventor Essentials* Chapter
Advanced Modeling	Create and constrain sketch blocks.	3
	Create an iPart.	15
	Emboss text and a profile.	9
	Use iLogic.	15
Assembly Modeling	Describe and use Shrinkwrap.	14
	Modify a bill of materials.	6
	Use assembly constraints.	4, 8, 15
	Find minimum distance between parts and components.	8, 10*
Drawing	Create and edit dimensions in a drawing.	2, 6
	Edit a section view.	6
	Modify a parts list.	6
	Edit a base and projected views.	6
Part Modeling	Create a pattern of features.	7
	Create a shell feature.	7
	Create extrude features.	3, 7, 12
	Create fillet features.	3, 7
	Create hole features.	3, 7
	Create revolve features.	3, 7
	Create work features.	7
	Use the Project Geometry and Project Cut Edges commands.	3, 7
Presentation Files	Animate a presentation file.	13

Topic	Exam Objectives	*Inventor Essentials* Chapter
Sheet Metal	Annotate a sheet metal part in a drawing.	10
	Create and edit a sheet metal flat pattern.	10
	Describe sheet metal flange types.	10
Sketching	Create dynamic input dimensions.	2
	Use sketch constraints.	2
User Interface	Identify how to use visual styles to control the appearance of a model.	1

T A B L E A . 3 Certified Professional Exam sections and objectives

Topic	Exam Objectives	*Inventor Essentials* Chapter
Advanced Modeling	Create a 3D path using the Intersection Curve and the Project to Surface commands.	7
	Create a loft feature.	7
	Create a multi-body part.	9
	Create a part using surfaces.	9
	Create a sweep feature.	3, 7
	Create an iPart.	15
	Use iLogic.	15
Assembly Modeling	Apply assembly constraints.	4, 8
	Create a level of detail.	8
	Create a part in the context of an assembly.	8
	Create a positional representation.	8
	Create and edit a frame using the Frame Generator command.	11
	Create components using the Design Accelerator commands.	4, 8, 12
	Use the frame generator command.	11
	Use surfaces in modeling.	7, 9

Topic	Exam Objectives	*Inventor Essentials* Chapter
Drawing	Edit a section view.	2, 6
	Modify a style in a drawing.	5
	Edit a hole table.	6
Part Modeling	Create extrude features.	3, 7
	Create hole features.	3, 7
Project Files	Control a project file.	1
Sheet Metal	Create flanges.	10
Weldments	Create a weldment.	12

INDEX

Note to the Reader: Throughout this index boldfaced page numbers indicate primary discussions of a topic. *Italicized* page numbers indicate illustrations.